THE
Arabian
Delights
COOKBOOK

*Mediterranean Cuisines from
Mecca to Marrakesh*

ANNE MARIE WEISS-ARMUSH

illustrations by Penny Williams-Yaqub

Lowell House - LOS ANGELES

Contemporary Books - CHICAGO

Also by Anne Marie Weiss-Armush:

Arabian Cuisine

Library of Congress Cataloging-in-Publication Data

Weiss-Armush, Anne Marie.
    The Arabian Delights Cookbook: Mediterranean Cuisines from Mecca to
    Marrakesh / Anne Marie Weiss-Armush.
        p. cm.
    Includes index.
    ISBN 1-56565-126-X
    1. Cookery, Arab. 2. Cookery, Mediterranean. I. Title.
TX725.A7W453 1993
641.5953—dc20   94-33659
                                                        CIP

Requests for such permission should be addressed to:
Lowell House
2029 Century Park East, Suite 3290
Los Angeles, CA 90067

Publisher: Jack Artenstein
Vice-President/Editor-in-Chief: Janice Gallagher
Director of Publishing Services: Mary D. Aarons
Text design: Nancy Freeborn

Illustrations on the cover and on pages iv, 89, 122, and 162, are through the courtesy of
Aramco World.

Illustration on page 89 is from *Amina and Muhammad's Special Visitor*, by Diane Turnage
Burgoyne and Penny Williams Yaqub.

Manufactured in the United States of America
10 9 8 7 6 5 4 3 2 1

It is He who produces gardens,

With trellises and without, and dates,

And tilled lands with their produce of all kinds,

And olives and pomegranates of many varieties.

Eat of their fruit in their season,

But render the thanks that are proper

On the day that the harvest is gathered.

And commit no excess nor no waste:

For Allah does not love those who are wasteful.

FROM THE QU'RAN (Sura vi, 141)

This book is dedicated to

Dalia Carmel Goldstein

a "cousin" born in Jerusalem
who exemplifies the Arab virtues of generosity and kinship

*"One's cousin is like a wing to a falcon.
Can falcons fly without wings?"*

Acknowledgments

I'd like to thank some of those who have generously helped with this project
and shared with me the intriguing cuisine of the Arab world:
Basna Ahmad, Ibtisam Al Dayel, Leila Al Mana, Dr. Abdul Aziz Al Sweel,
Jan Andary, Fatima and Hiyaam Armush, Alice and Robert Arndt,
Kay Hardy Campbell, Sophie Fanous, Paula Farkhojasteh,
Miriam Hashem, Mona Hariri, Fauzia Hasan,
Raghda Haykal, Joy May Hilden, Yusuf Yusaf Isaf,
Nevine Kamel, Rajaa Killough, Dolores Lehman,
Sharlene Maayeh, Lillie Matarwe, Miriam Muallem,
Rakia Muhammed, Julia Najjar, Wafa Own,
Marjan Parekh, Arafa Osman Muhammed Salih,
Eliana and Muna Shaheen, Nach Waxman,
Penny Williams-Yaqub, Paula Wolfert,
Safeeya Zatout, Susan Zilber,
and my family, Said, Maha, Leila,
and, Ma'Amun Armush.

Table of Contents

Oasis in the Sultanate of Oman

The Romance of Arabian Cuisine

F ood lovers have long raved over the seductive flavors of southern France, Italy, and Greece. But only recently have we come to understand that the traditional peasant diet of the Mediterranean world—high in vegetables and fruit and low in animal products—is also good for us.

Today, in an odyssey of rediscovery, culinary guides, symposiums, and restaurateurs continue to explore and promote these delicious and healthy dishes. I am delighted to find that the cuisines of Morocco and Turkey, both major producers and exporters of the olives and olive oil considered the heart and soul of the Mediterranean diet, are frequently included. But the remaining banks of what the Arabs know as the "White Sea in the Middle," those that sweep majestically along its southern and eastern shores, are too often overlooked, ignored, or restricted to the periphery of the "Mediterranean Club."

I can't help being surprised that the celebrated cuisine of Syria is neglected, when this Mediterranean country produces more than five times as much olive oil as France, a hefty 7% of the Mediterranean's total olive oil harvest. Favorite recipes like **Baby Okra in Olive Oil** and **Artichoke Melange**, scented with garlic and the fruitiness of fine olive oil, are as wonderfully light and cleansing as the famous foods of Provence.

Along with other Americans, I enjoy trying innovative risottos and paellas as I dream of simpler places where the food is affordable, fresher, and alluring. But I find the Arabian Gulf's delicate textured *biryani* and dazzling layered pilafs even more exciting than these Italian and Spanish rice dishes, and I love introducing them to my friends.

Libyan Shakshooka with Sun-Dried Meat in herbed tomato sauce is every bit as inviting as its carbonara cousins available in Sicily, just a few miles across the "White Sea" to the north. Also from Libya, **Grilled Fish with Cumin**, brushed with olive oil and red pepper, is a delightful, healthy treat. An outpost of both the ancient Greek and Roman Empires and early in this century an Italian colony, Libya boasts a splendid Mediterranean cuisine—one that is totally overlooked.

This book is a passport to those intriguing lands, an invitation to explore and savor the healthy cuisines of the "other" fascinating half of the Mediterranean.

My Introduction to the Arab Table

One dusky evening our taxi groaned up a hill to brake in the Syrian dust before a flaking adobe wall. As we arrived in my husband's mountain hamlet, the last plaintive strains of the call to prayer had just pierced the silence. I was carrying the excess baggage of my countrymen's cultural misconceptions, and the mysterious Middle East where I was to live for the next 11 years never seemed more foreboding.

The green metal gate embellished with arabesques creaked open ominously, but only to reveal Mother's twinkling eyes and exuberant *zaghareets*— the traditional Arab trills of joy and welcome. I stepped down into a rosy courtyard filled with pomegranate trees, where grape clusters dangled from a lush roof of vines. From the welcoming arms of Mother's embrace I was passed on to her daughters, who continued the ritual of hugs and kisses.

My husband soon vanished to the men's quarters, leaving me seated stiffly in the kitchen with his sympathetically smiling sisters, and no one to translate. But it didn't take a common language for me to determine that life in the Arab world revolves around the shared warmth of family and friends, the simple pleasures of hospitality and food.

Early each morning just after the dawn prayer, Mother set plates of ingredients for the day's feast on the immaculate kitchen floor and lowered herself onto a fluffy sheepskin beside them. Filled with the anticipation of pleasing the son who had finally returned home, she chopped onions, shelled walnuts, and stuffed *kibbeh* (ground meat and wheat croquettes) until midday, as neighbors and relatives dropped by to stare at the strange American bride. Dozens of times we prepared coffee for gray-bearded peasants dressed in baggy black *sirwal* trousers and checkered turbans. Stylish city cousins whose discreet head scarves fashionably matched their silky dresses dropped by to visit and sip tea, with a horde of irresistible dark-eyed children in attendance. My apprehensions faded in the face of a society that holds as its cultural ideal the generous, virtuous man who "makes coffee day and night" for his guests.

When my husband Ma'Amun asked if there was milk for his pregnant American wife, his sisters brought some in a plastic pail, warm and foaming from the neighbor's cow, and heated it up with a few spoonfuls of sugar. If I seemed to hesitate before the *kibbeh* in yoghurt sauce and rice-stuffed intestines, special treats that promised an expectant mother "heavier blood" and "plentiful nursing," they would offer me a scrambled egg, lavishly thick amber honey, and stuffed baby eggplants to make sure that I couldn't possibly be hungry.

A few days later we headed south to our new home in cosmopolitan Jeddah, the crossroads of the world poised on the Red Sea. Since the days of the prophet Muhammad this port city in mysterious Saudi Arabia has received pilgrims en route to Mecca, Mother of Towns. Throwing on my black abaya, I joined the eddy of veiled women in adventures I couldn't possibly have anticipated, dancing to haunting chants and bedouin drums, serving green cardamom coffee and burning fragrant sandalwood incense, dipping my right hand into trays overflowing with lamb and spiced rice. And I found that the woman behind the veil rules her house as well as her kitchen.

There and throughout the Middle East, I discovered a loyalty to custom and tradition: in flat-roofed adobe houses nestled under rustling palm trees, in the shadows of ancient Roman ruins, and among dramatic mountain crags, generations of Arab cooks have learned how to transform vegetables,

The Arab World

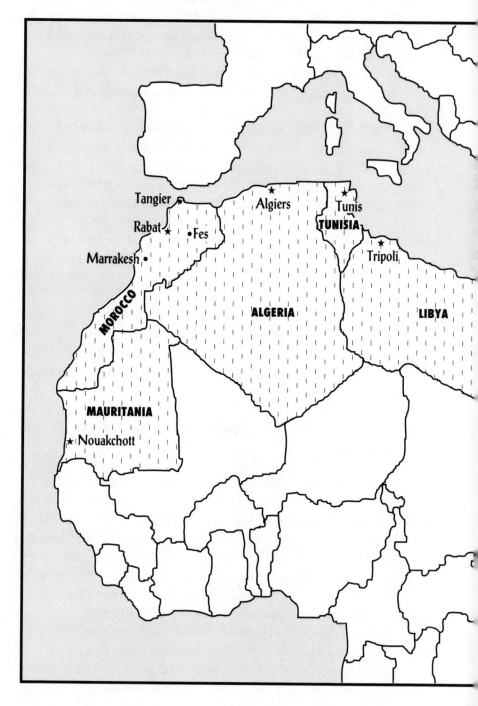

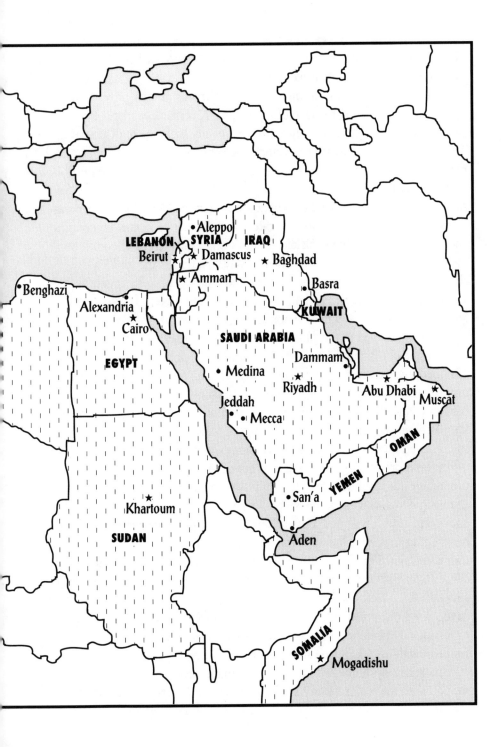

legumes, and grains, with only small amounts of meat, fish, and poultry, into spectacular meals. Daughters learn to cook at their mother's knee, and a daughter-in-law in the extended family home patiently follows Mother's example until she has mastered her husband's favorite dishes. Recipes are carried in the mind and guarded in the soul.

Like most Arabs, my mother-in-law frequently quotes proverbs that reflect the wisdom and heritage of the region. A veritable walking encyclopedia of cooking, she is patiently tolerant of my techniques of preparing Arab food, but like most village women she is not at all interested in acquiring any of my recipes or those belonging to her neighbors. "A mouthful from my house is better than a whole loaf from my neighbor," she says, standing guard over her kitchen whenever I am at the stove. Mother is paralyzed with distress when I incorporate into her favorite dishes procedures and ingredients that I have picked up from other talented Arab cooks. *Broil* the eggplant slices instead of fry them? "May Allah grant me Job's patience," she grumbles. Her daughters, however, are proud of their ingenuity in adding a bit more garlic or lemon juice to a family recipe, following the boundaries of tradition while demonstrating their own artistic skills.

When we moved to the Arab world in 1976, Mother still presented most meals in the old-fashioned style on a spotless white cloth spread on the floor. The food was served on large platters or arranged cleverly on several small oval serving dishes and carried in on a huge round tray. Later, as our numbers grew and the family's economic status improved, we moved to a small, intimately crowded table in the kitchen, with the large formal dining table still reserved for more ceremonious occasions such as wedding dinners.

In the more cosmopolitan cities of Lebanon and the Gulf, well-traveled urbanites dine in modern and elegantly appointed dining rooms. But in the Arabian peninsula these same Saudis and Kuwaitis, who offer sophisticated and beautifully presented buffets served on costly European china and hand-cut crystal, may still take their family meals on the floor in the traditional manner. I'm always surprised and enchanted to be invited to the *diwan* (family sitting room) for an informal meal, because it implies that I am considered a close relative, a great honor in that part of the world. "You have shared our bread and our salt," my friends said one Ramadan evening as we sat on the carpet bent over a sheet covered with a smorgasbord of Saudi specialties. "Thus, you have become our sister."

Unfortunately, home-style meals are virtually unavailable in restaurants, so visitors to the region often have little opportunity to enjoy these culinary highlights. Most of my expatriate friends who lived in Saudi Arabia tried the Lebanese foods served in restaurants, but left the Kingdom without tasting a single national dish. I hope these pages will open the kitchen door on the wonderful cuisines of the Arab world with a collection of recipes popular across the banks of the southern Mediterranean from Marrakesh in Morocco to Mecca and the states of the Arabian Gulf, from the Fertile Crescent's Tigris and Euphrates valleys to the modern countries that once composed the Ottoman Empire's province of Greater Syria.

The "Other" Mediterranean Table

Arabian cuisine, regardless of the country of origin, shares certain general characteristics. Rice and wheat dishes abound, along with stuffed vegetables, savory meat and cheese pies, and charcoal-grilled meats and fish. Many combinations are cooked slowly with fresh aromatic herbs, and a multitude of spices play a leading role in the delicate balance of flavors. Fruit, raisins, and pine nuts appear frequently, as does yoghurt. Perfumed rice puddings and syrupy multilayered pastries filled with nuts are favorites in every Arab nation.

An everyday meal in the Arab world is an economical affair, but splendidly flavored, and must include quantities of fresh bread. A filling pilaf of rice, *burghol* (processed wheat from the Levant), or couscous usually coordinates with a light stew of vegetables that may contain a bit of meat or poultry. On the rare occasions when the main dish does not include vegetables, they may appear as a side dish or as a marvelous salad. Some dishes are designed to layer all these ingredients and seasonings in one grand and glorious tray.

Arabic cooking is a mixture of elements that originated in many regions: the meat dishes of the bedouin and the lovely vegetarian creations of Egypt's Coptic Christians; sophisticated court cuisines of Baghdad, Damascus, and Andalusia; yoghurt and noodles from the Central Asian steppes; Turkish stuffed vegetables and puddings; Persia's love affair with rice; fascinating spice combinations originally Indian; and recent influences from French and Italian colonizers.

Of course, while the similarities in dishes are extensive, Arab food is not interchangeable across the states. Regional styles reflecting both historical influences and availability of ingredients developed when the transport of raw materials between relatively isolated areas was uncommon, or when natural products would not survive the trip.

For example, walnuts rather than dates typify dishes of Syrian and Palestinian origin. Leeks are a Saudi favorite but celery is standard only in Kurdish, Iraqi, and Gulf cooking. Yoghurt, which allowed camel's milk to be stored without refrigeration, is popular in countries with a nomadic tradition and in those colonized by the yoghurt-loving Turks. Couscous, which may be of Saharan origin, is the passion of North Africa.

Olive oil, the key element of this cuisine, holds a revered place in the region's cultural heritage. The romantic Mediterranean is actually a land of relatively poor soil and harsh, dry summers, but the thick, twisted trunks of olive trees, with their deep-boring roots, are drought-resistant and thrive without the benefit of regular rainfall. *Zeit hiloo*, Arab villagers affectionately call it—"Sweet Oil"—as they tend the gnarled old trees planted by their great-grandfathers and carefully pick a blessing of fruit from its silvery branches. The olives are carefully sorted by hand and a portion taken to the mill for stone pressing.

The wild olive may have appeared along the Nile delta, but it was first cultivated in Syria 6,000 years ago. Syria exported its high-quality oil to Greece, and Palestine supplied ancient Egypt, because neither of those countries produced enough of the golden liquid to satisfy demand. About 5,000 years ago, the Phoenicians (of today's Lebanon) taught the ancient Greeks to use oil as a source of light by burning it in terra-cotta lamps.

Olive trees also grew naturally in Carthage along the Tunisian coast, but it was the Romans, and later the Muslim caliphs, who spread them across North Africa, throughout the coasts of Libya and Algeria.

"This oil is from our own trees in the field up the hill," my mother-in-law Miriam proudly explained as she poured a small glass as a tonic for Father to quaff. "It protects his digestive system from blockage and lowers his blood pressure, too." (Arabs don't share our rather Victorian view of bodily functions, and Arab women of Mother's age are outspoken and direct.) Magical olive oil is rubbed into a newborn's skin as his first bath, while a caress of holy oil accompanies Christian rites. Young and old alike use olive oil as a beauty treatment, for cleansing the skin, and to fight dandruff. Its high nutritive value makes it a substitute for meat during the long months of Orthodox Advent and Lenten fasting, and it enriches a regional diet in which meat is used sparingly, more as a condiment than a main course.

So precious are the olive groves held by a family for generations that the denuding of vast areas of trees has even been used as a weapon of war by occupying forces in the region.

The Qur'an includes numerous lyrical references to the olive tree. The Lord gives emphasis to certain lines by swearing by four sacred items: "by the fig, and by the olive, and by Mount Sinai" (where Moses received the law), "and by the holy city of Mecca" (Sura xcv, 1). God's message is compared to the pure beauty and radiance of an olive oil lamp "lit from a blessed tree, an olive tree, neither of the East nor of the West, whose oil is exceptionally luminous" (Sura xxiv, 36).

The second major element shaping Mediterranean cuisine is wheat, usually the durum variety that ripens quickly in the temperate rains of spring and is harvested in early June before the intense summer sun bakes the land. Wheat was first cultivated in ancient Mesopotamia, the Fertile Crescent that is modern Iraq. Syria was the breadbasket of the Roman Empire, and today its fat-grained Hourani wheat, considered among the best in the world, is exported to Europe in exchange for hard currency. Even in the parched torrid plateaus of the Arabian peninsula, wheat flourished along the fertile oases, where whole kernels of the grain were steamed in broths and shaped into dumplings. Saudi Arabia is currently the sixth-largest exporter of wheat in the world.

Bread is God's greatest gift and throughout this part of the world is treated with utmost respect. If a scrap of bread falls on the floor, some villagers teach their children to kiss it or to touch it to their forehead as an apology to God. Bread is never thrown away, but is kept for a layered dish called *fetteh*, or for **Fettoosh Salad**. Dry bread is placed at the bottom of a bowl of brothy soup or fed to the animals. City dwellers keep a "recycling bag" of old bread, which a peasant picks up once a week.

In Yemen, a loaf of whole-wheat bread is the foundation of most meals, while in North Africa *harissa* (red chili paste) and a small quantity of lamb, chicken, or fish flavor a large mound of couscous made from durum wheat semolina. In the Gulf States, *kebsa* (a paella-like rice dish) and delicate basmati pilafs crowned with seafood and rich with spices conceal a treasure of healthy vegetables.

Everywhere, vegetables and legumes form the core of the traditional diet, to be followed by the usual dessert of fresh fruit—the figs, apricots, plums, melons, and grapes for which the region is famous.

When meat is served in the villages, one pound normally is sufficient for the entire family. Milk is served infrequently, and butter is even more uncommon, but yoghurt and yoghurt cheese appear on almost every table.

The International Conference on the Diets of the Mediterranean in 1993 formally confirmed much of the data already in circulation, noting that "the geography of the diet is closely tied to the traditional areas of olive cultivation in the Mediterranean region," and that variations on this diet exist in North Africa and parts of the Middle East. Based on comprehensive studies and historical data, a pyramid of healthy eating was formulated, a pyramid that defines the optimal traditional Mediterranean diet as one that includes:

1. fruits, vegetables, legumes, and grains as approximately two-thirds of total food consumption;

2. olive oil as the principal fat (noting that total fat can be as high as 35–40% of the diet if saturated fat is at or below 7–8%, polyunsaturated fat ranges from 3–8%, with the balance from monounsaturated olive oil);

3. lean red meat to be consumed only a few times per month or somewhat more often in very small portions;

4. low to moderate consumption of dairy products, fish, and poultry.

The conference's pyramid is no less than a classic description of the healthy Arabian cuisines. In many cases, only the spices added to these hearty dishes of vegetables seasoned with tomatoes, garlic, onion, and olive oil mark them as originating along the Arab coasts of the Mediterranean. Here, in the traditional lands of the spice caravans, cumin, allspice, and cardamom may replace the classic oregano and basil of the northern shores in an untapped treasury of splendid dishes.

One fascinating piece of recent dietary investigation adds significance to the pyramid. In 1949 during a period of three months most of the Jewish population of Yemen was flown northward to the new state of Israel. Even today, Yemen is one of the Arab countries least touched by Westernization; for centuries the Yemenites had eaten an Arab Mediterranean diet heavy in grains, legumes, and breads that were dipped into dips of crushed herbs and spices known as *zhug* or *hilba*. On every stove a pot of fiery *salta* simmered— a brothy stew made from a few bones with larger quantities of rice, wholewheat kernels, potatoes, beans, along with bit of tomato paste and an extravagance of fresh herbs and spices. Half a pound of meat stretched to serve 10 or 15 people when added to a hearty rice or *burghol* stuffing for onions, potatoes, or beets. A yoghurt-like soured milk was the only dairy food, olive oil added body to meatless dishes, and fish was popular among those who lived

Optimal Traditional Mediterranean Diet

PRELIMINARY CONCEPT

This preliminary concept for a pyramid to represent the Optimal Traditional Mediterranean Diet is based on the dietary traditions of Crete circa 1960, structured in light of 1993 nutrition research. Variations of this optimal diet have traditionally existed in other parts of Greece, parts of the Balkan region, parts of Italy, Spain and Portugal, Southern France, North Africa (esp. Morocco and Tunisia), Turkey, as well as parts of the Middle East (esp. Lebanon and Syria). The geography of the diet is closely tied to the traditional areas of olive cultivation in the Mediterranean region. This is intended for discussion purposes only, and is subject to modification.

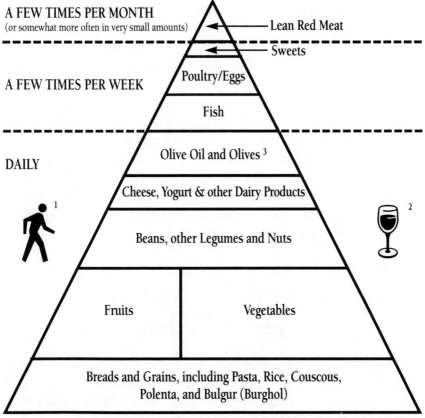

A FEW TIMES PER MONTH
(or somewhat more often in very small amounts) — Lean Red Meat

Sweets

A FEW TIMES PER WEEK — Poultry/Eggs

Fish

DAILY — Olive Oil and Olives [3]

Cheese, Yogurt & other Dairy Products

Beans, other Legumes and Nuts

Fruits — Vegetables

Breads and Grains, including Pasta, Rice, Couscous, Polenta, and Bulgur (Burghol)

SOURCE: 1993 INTERNATIONAL CONFERENCE ON THE DIETS OF THE MEDITERRANEAN

[1] Indicates the importance of regular physical activity.

[2] Following Mediterranean tradition, wine can be enjoyed in moderation (1-2 glasses /day) primarily with meals; it should be considered optional and avoided whenever consumption would put the individual or others at risk.

[3] Olive oil, high in monounsaturated fat and rich in antioxidants, is the region's principal fat. In the optimal, traditional Mediterranean diet, total fat can be as high as 35-40% of calories, if saturated fat is at or below 7-8% and polyunsaturated fat ranges from 3-8% with the balance coming from monounsaturated fat (in the form of olive oil). Variations of this diet where total fat (again, principally olive oil) is at or below 30%—such as is found in the traditional diet of Southern Italy—may be equally optimal.

along the sea. On rare occasions when a lamb or cow was slaughtered, every edible portion was roasted, stuffed, or preserved.

Israel's many ethnic groups make the country an ideal field for comparative medical studies, and it was immediately noticed that the surprisingly slender Yemenites demonstrated unusually long life spans. They had remarkably low cholesterol and blood pressure, and were freer than Jews of Western origins of such plagues of modern society as heart disease, diabetes, and lung cancer.

By the end of a 10-year study, researchers discovered that those Yemenite immigrants who adopted the rich Western-style Israeli diet heavy in dairy and meat products showed rates of disease equal to that of the general Israeli population. Individuals who continued to follow their original Yemenite cuisine remained as robustly healthy as noted when they arrived in the country.

Unlike the affluent nation of Israel and the prosperous countries of the northern Mediterranean coast, the Arab lands of the eastern and southern shores still offer few of the unhealthy foods found in the Western diet of excess. Most villagers have never seen whipped cream, steak, hot dogs, or other processed and artificial foods. Food imports are restricted in most countries, and economical meals are planned around the bounty provided by Allah and the land. The healthy traditional diet, a simple earthy menu born from poverty, remains virtually unchanged.

Hospitality and the Arab Table

It wasn't long before I became aware that in the Middle Eastern environment it is unthinkable to prepare just enough food for the immediate number of people in the house. Whoever happens to be present at the meal hour will be graciously invited to the table with sincere courtesy. This may include the imam or sheikh, the plumber and the barber (who sometimes offers his services in the client's home), several miscellaneous cousins from the city who stopped by to deliver a letter or fresh bread or a bundle of smuggled bananas, and an adult son or daughter with his children who were just passing by or are living nearby.

During our summer visits to my husband's village in Syria, the norm is to enjoy the company of 20 or 25 people at mealtime, as we sit around the tables under the shade of Father's sprawling grape arbor. More than once I have seen my Libyan or Saudi friends, after spending most of the day preparing a gigantic couscous or *kebsa*, return to the kitchen with a smile to start on yet another tray for last-minute invitees.

It is almost unheard of for an Arab to chat with a friend without mentioning that far too long has passed since his last visit. "Why haven't we been seeing you?" is quickly followed by an invitation. In fact, one should endeavor to be the first to make the gesture: "Invite him for lunch before he invites you for supper."

A formal dinner for important guests, whether they be family or new acquaintances, is quite different from a domestic affair, even if the latter includes several households. A proper meal for *dyoof* (visitors) must include at least seven principal dishes, and I guarantee that august and venerable matrons like my mother-in-law do count the platters. The key here is that the food be abundant and lavishly bounteous as well as memorably delicious.

Invariably, as a visitor in Arab households I was overwhelmed with my hosts' infinite thoughtfulness and generosity. Having prepared my favorite dishes or some especially time-consuming delicacy, they selected the tastiest morsels for me and repeatedly refilled my plate. "Eat more, to prove that you love us," they kept urging. In some bedouin tribes, the limits of thoughtfulness are stretched even further: the chiefs eat after their visitors, so they can properly supervise the serving of the guests' meal.

Journalist and author Paul Theroux, after an extensive visit to Syria, which he calls "an oasis of charm"—commented that he had never seen politer people than the Syrians. After traveling for 10 days, Theroux suddenly realized that he had yet to pay for a single meal. "We Arabs have a concept called *hospitality*," a young student encountered in a bookstore told the American by means of introduction, and then spent several days guiding him around Aleppo and its environs. As yet another proverb explains, it is difficult to resist such graciousness: "If you are generous and kind toward a virtuous person, you will have possessed his soul."

So, my soul hostage, I learned to return the courtesy, if perhaps not to the same genteel degree. Each dinner party I gave, whether for 8 guests or 50, required a minimum of three full days of cooking. For a proper party (across the Middle East the word "party" is synonymous with "food"), one must prepare *kibbeh* and grape leaves as well as one or two dishes of meat or perhaps a whole 10-pound fish, plus a huge tray of spiced pilaf with nuts and raisins and several delicately flavored vegetables or salads—not to mention a minimum of two sumptuous desserts to present dramatically with the fruit and tea. No wonder the saying recalls that "the woman killed herself with work, yet the feast lasted only one day."

The complex ethics associated with sharing food are probably of bedouin origin and are extremely important as a method of establishing mutual trust and assistance in interpersonal relations. In the harsh desert environment, stinginess or refusal to share food with a solitary wanderer could result in his death. Consequently, the bedouin ideal in generosity is renowned. Only after a stranger is offered tea and food will he be asked his business and where he is from. Even if he is an enemy, he becomes the tribe's guest for three days, and they are honor-bound to defend him even with their lives.

The prophet Muhammad, considered to be the perfect example of proper behavior, reinforced the traditional bedouin customs of hospitality, saying: "He who believes in God and the afterlife must respect and honor his guest," and "He who eats his fill and leaves his neighbors hungry is not a good Muslim."

It's clear that the American courtesy of "Just feel like one of the family and help yourself to whatever's in the fridge" does not hold for the Arab world. Nor should the cook congratulate herself if all the food has disappeared by the time she clears the table.

I remember when an Arab-American neighbor in Jeddah had a local Lebanese restaurant cater her first dinner party. The hostess was certain that her affair had been a great success because there were no leftovers. I didn't have the heart to mention that if grades were to be given, she would have failed the test on two counts. First, there was no excuse for her not to honor her guests by cooking at least some dishes for them herself. Second, if all the food was consumed, it was possible that some of the guests were still hungry when they left her house.

A Mediterranean meal is a source of sensual pleasure, a natural relaxing break in the day's routine. In the Arab world it is a time to enjoy people rather than places, an entertaining interval for the extended family and its multitudinous friends and relatives.

It is also an element in an evocatively different lifestyle that can never be reproduced in the West. I have no sisters, cousins, or aunts in my Texas neighborhood with whom to chatter away the morning while we turn a tower of juicy ripe tomatoes into sufficient crimson paste to last the winter. There is no time in our hectic days to stretch out for a siesta after a large midday meal. And spending three days cooking to ready a spectacular feast is impossible for those of us who are employed.

Nevertheless, these lovely provincial dishes that embrace a world of sun and color are not hard to fit into the practical realities of contemporary Western life. As many traditional dishes are quite labor-intensive, I have adapted them to American kitchen technology. It takes only 10 minutes to prepare a single recipe of seductive **Tabbooleh** using the food processor. Even stuffed grape leaves, when I'm not cooking for the whole Arab clan, require only half an hour to complete.

My family has chosen to reduce their consumption of meat, and we enjoy frequent meatless meals overflowing with the goodness of fresh vegetables, olive oil, onions, and garlic. I rarely miss an opportunity to prepare a tempting principal dish or side plate of pasta, rice, or *burghol*. For variation, especially on chilly winter evenings, the children love one of the hearty soups from the Arab Mediterranean, with lots of fresh bread and a couple of *mezzeh* to accompany it.

During my years in Saudi Arabia I played the dual roles of the wife of a traditional Muslim Arab and an activist in the expatriate community. Each day I entered the stage of a centuries-old drama and tried to imitate the examples of proper behavior and unlimited generosity that surrounded me.

The best models were close at hand and near to the heart: my father-in-law never fails to wipe up the last drop of his meal's tasty sauce with a torn piece of flat bread. He savors the final bite, and lays his spoon in his empty plate. Bowing his white-capped head for a moment, Father respectfully whispers, "*Al hamdu lillah.*"

Thanks be to God.

All Brothers at the Table

Although composed of 21 countries spread over two continents and four distinct subregions (Greater Syria, the Nile valley, the Arabian peninsula, and North Africa), the Arab world is no more diverse culturally and socially than the United States.

One single astonishing historical event that united Berbers and Aramaeans, Phoenicians and Mesopotamians, and created the Arab identity. Within one generation from the death of the prophet Muhammad in 632, the Muslim conquests had extended the great Arab-Islamic empire to include a vast area extending from Spain to Samarkand in Central Asia.

Within that empire, a new civilization was formed with Arabic the medium of culture and science and Islam the religion of a vigorous and growing cosmopolitan society. As the nation expanded, the triumphant Arabs brought to each new locality their own culinary tastes and techniques as well as those assimilated from other cultures. Muhammad's nomadic tribesmen from the harsh desert added Mongol yoghurt to their limited diets. Oranges, rice, and spices from India and beyond became pillars of Arab regional cooking.

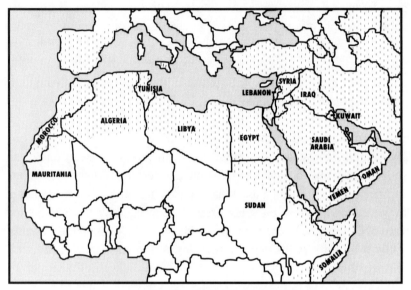

ARAB-ISLAMIC EMPIRE (CIRCA 1250)

Even as political fragmentation and disunity later broke up the empire, a common cultural heritage continued to guide the peoples of the region. In Cairo, Fez, and Damascus, merchants, scholars, and artisans preserved and continued to contribute to classical Islamic life and traditions, while maintaining links and exchanges with the other cities.

In medieval Baghdad, capital of "the navel of the universe" Iraq, Abassid chefs developed a renowned *nouvelle cuisine* there in the 8th century. Prince Ibrahim, half-brother of Caliph Harun al-Rashid, created the first Arabic cookbook *Kitab al-Tabikh*. Memorable dishes of the day included one hundred and fifty fish tongues molded into a fish shape and lamb simmered in sumac juice. The creative core of the cuisine was the intuitive and balanced use of herbs and spices.

The magnificent culinary arts lavishly formalized by great Baghdadi chefs soon reached the lovely kingdoms of Cordoba and Marrakesh on the north-western shores of the Mediterranean. Under the patronage of the Andalusian ruler Abd al-Rahman II (of Damascan Umayyad origin), the Baghdadi musician and singer Ziryab was invited to Spain, where he introduced from the eastern courts such revolutionary concepts as the use of knives and forks. Ziryab also laid down the sequence of courses of a meal that we continue to use today.

For 800 years the Arabs maintained a bastion of culture and civilization while the rest of Europe floundered in ignorance. In the 15th century, while English noblemen ate their meals off thick slices of dark bread called trenchers that were given to the poor after the meal, the Arabs (as reported by Saladin's great-great-nephew) lavishly cooked with imported ingredients, fruits and nuts, and rare spices and enjoyed a large variety of exotic fruits and vegetables.

In the Arab kingdoms, hard-working cultivators built water wheels (na'ura) to channel water to the dry countrysides, transforming them into gardens that brought forth a cornucopia of riches. Sugarcane from the Nile valley swayed in Andalusia's gentle breezes, and Medina Sidonia (just above Cádiz on the Andaluz coast) became an exporter of beautiful and talented pastry cooks to the Muslim seraglios of Asia and Africa. North African vine-yards produced fresh fruit and the sweet raisins essential to the cooking of both the Maghreb and the Fertile Crescent.

Arab kings and traders, famous for centuries of wealth and refinement, introduced many of these innovations into European cooking. Risotto rice was carried to Italy by these illustrious merchants. King Richard the Lionhearted's 14th-century cookbook includes many exotically rich recipes attributed to *out-remer*, the lands of Islam.

In 1492 the westward current became an eastward torrent as Muslims expelled by Queen Isabella joined those who had already fled from the Christian reconquest back across the Strait of Gibraltar, carrying their cuisine with them to the southern Mediterranean. Once again the foods of Andalusia and North Africa converged in an unexpected flow of population.

Shortly after the Mongol "Prince of Destruction" Tamerlane sacked and destroyed Damascus and Samarkand and erected 120 pyramids of skulls from 90,000 citizens of Baghdad, the Ottoman Empire began to extend southward through the Arab lands. From 1516 to 1918 much of the eastern Arab Mediterranean, including Palestine and coastal regions of Saudi Arabia, was united under Turkish rule.

"God's curses on the Turks!" protest those who recall the years of occupation by their non-Arab neighbor to the north. But cuisine has no political loyalties. This repressive period reinforced the solidarity of the Arab community while augmenting the richness of the cuisine. Turkey had been part of the great Arab-Islamic Empire: its sophisticated court dishes that grew out of an amalgam of traditions soon spread across the shores of North Africa,

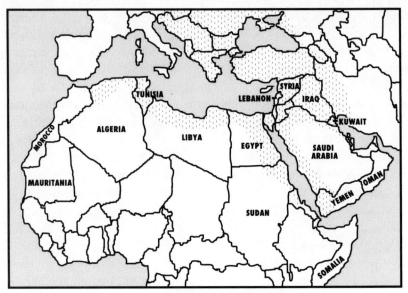

OTTOMAN EMPIRE (CIRCA 1550)

down the Nile valley and Red Sea coast to Yemen, and along the Tigris and Euphrates to the Arabian Gulf. Until individual independent nations like Iraq, Lebanon, and Egypt were born after World War II, they continued to share a common Arabic history, culture, and culinary heritage.

Cultural fluidity continues to shape the Arabs' self-image and spirit of brotherhood. Until recently, few people of the region traveled to the West, but exchanges within the Arab-speaking world were common. Even today Syrians and Lebanese export olive oil, vegetables, and textiles to the Arabian peninsula. Bahraini merchants, whose ancestors led camel caravans, still trade in spices, incense, and silk from the Indian subcontinent, which they send on to the Levant and the Maghreb. Libyans and Algerians travel to the Al Azhar mosque in Cairo to immerse themselves in Islamic studies. Gulf residents summer in Lebanon to escape the furious heat back home, and pass the fasting month of Ramadan along Egypt's temperate Alexandrian seacoast, while impoverished Egyptians and Palestinians still seek employment in Saudi Arabia and the rich Gulf States.

The annual Hajj, or pilgrimage to Mecca, continues today to be the ultimate expression of a common heritage, a great spiritual merging during which cultural (and culinary) trends are shared and exchanged in the traditional centuries-old pattern.

As Mother passionately repeated that first evening when we met in the village by the green gate, *"Ahlan. Ahlan. Ahlan wa sahlan!"*—Welcome. It's a fine level spot on which to pitch your tent, and you are among your relatives.

Special Ingredients, Spice Mixtures, and Cooking Techniques

Most of the ingredients required for the dishes introduced in this book are easily found today in your local supermarket. A few, however, may require a trip to a market specializing in imported foods. Natural food stores are a good choice for spices and many grains.

Luckily, today's multicultural America means that residents of my small Midwest hometown of Columbia, Missouri (population about 70,000), no longer must drive two hours to the Italian-American store in St. Louis to buy their *burghol* and *foul* beans. Arabic ingredients are available now in the grocery next door to the small but lovely mosque run by Sudanese students.

Within a 10-minute drive from my current home in Dallas I can shop at any one of three Iranian-owned ethnic markets, four of Indo-Pakistani character, and one incredibly exciting import supermarket stocking Italian, Hispanic, Greek, and Arabic foods. Two strictly Arab emporiums, a bakery, and innumerable other Middle Eastern establishments are slightly farther away. In other metropolitan areas you will find Armenian, Greek, and Israeli food stores. Or, order by mail from Dean and DeLuca (1-800-221-7714). All of these stock the special ingredients described below, and the proprietor is usually delighted to advise you on your purchase. He'll probably throw in one of his mother's most famous recipes at no extra cost.

amradeen—thin sheets of sun-dried pureed apricots, produced commercially and at home in Syria.

asfor—stamens of the safflower, which impart a yellow color to rice and flavor other Levantine dishes; an inexpensive substitute for saffron that can be used at a ratio of approximately 7 parts *asfor* for 1 part saffron.

basmati rice—Indian rice with small long grains and a distinctive flavor and aroma, usually soaked in water and subsequently prepared in a two-step cooking process.

burghol—nutritious wheat from the Levant with a nutty fresh flavor, parboiled and subsequently crushed and sorted into three or four sizes; sometimes called bulgar, or (incorrectly) cracked wheat.

bzar—the traditional Libyan spice mixture, which usually incorporates turmeric, black pepper, cinnamon, cloves, nutmeg, two roots from the ginger family, and sometimes cumin.

cardamom—aromatic pods from India used for flavoring a variety of Gulf dishes and in making green bedouin coffee; the generous use of this expensive spice is an honor to the guest.

cilantro—the fragrant, green leafy portion of the coriander plant.

couscous—semolina wheat traditionally rolled by hand into small grains that are subsequently steamed; also the national dish of Algeria, Morocco, and Tunisia, a brothy combination of meat, chicken, or seafood, plus a variety of vegetables that is served over the steamed semolina pilaf.

"Egyptian" rice—a short-grained, roundish rice that is somewhat glutinous and preferred for *dolmas* (stuffed vegetables) and puddings.

farina—slightly coarse flour made from a variety of wheat other than durum; cream of wheat, which is farina with added salt and preservatives, can be substituted.

fetteh—a layered dish built on dried bread, usually including broth and a bit of meat and topped with garlicky yoghurt.

filo—paper-thin pastry used for making baklava, similar desserts, and savory pastries; *filo* dough is available frozen.

foul—a mild-flavored Egyptian fava bean available dried or canned and in small and large sizes; fresh green beans, which are not interchangeable with the classic brown *foul* beans, are available frozen.

gadeed—thin slices of sun-dried meat from North Africa, also called *gargoosh*; you may substitute the type of beef jerky that is sold by the ounce in health food stores.

garam masala—Indian spice mixture, similar to a curry powder, occasionally used in Iraqi, Kurdish, and Kuwaiti dishes.

ghee—clarified butter, called *semneh* or *semn* in the Arab world, produced by removing the white foam from melted butter; *semneh* keeps for a long time without refrigeration and does not burn easily.

hamod—any sour flavoring, such as lemon juice, vinegar, or *hamod er rummaan*.

hamod er rummaan—syrup of the sour-sweet pomegranate used to flavor many dishes from the Levant countries; made by reducing the juice of ripe pomegranates.

harissa—North African red chili paste used to flavor couscous broths and other dishes, usually homemade but also available in a tube; in a pinch you can substitute a dash of Tabasco sauce or Chinese red-pepper paste.

'Japanese' eggplants—slender eggplants measuring 4–7 inches long, principally used for stuffing and pickles.

jareesh or **habhab** (Arabic), **dzedzadz** or **gorgod** (Armenian)—whole-wheat kernels, sometimes called wheat berries, popular in Saudi and Gulf cooking; available in yellow (with hulls) and off-white (hulled) grains.

kebab—roasted or grilled meat, either lamb, beef, chicken, fish, or ground meat.

kebsa spices—the traditional Saudi Arabian and Gulf spice mixture, consisting of cardamom, cinnamon, cumin, and red or black pepper.

kefta—mixtures of ground lamb or beef (or less frequently fish, wheat, or vegetables) with added spices and flavorings.

knafeh—soft strands of uncooked, threadlike pastry; available frozen in packages marked *konafa, kunafa,* or *kadaifa* dough.

koosa—a pale-green summer squash, similar to a fattish zucchini, that is a favorite for stuffing.

lebneh—Middle Eastern equivalent of sour cream, made by draining the whey from yoghurt, either in a strainer lined with a cheesecloth or by tying up the yoghurt in a cloth bag.

loomi—dried limes produced in Iraq and Oman that impart a pungent, sour bite to Gulf dishes; also called *leimoon Basra, leimoon aswad,* and *leimoon omani;* dried limes of Iranian origin are darker in color; can be used ground or whole (usually pierced).

Middle Eastern red pepper—fragrant seedless crushed flakes of spicy peppers that vary in hotness; a specialty of Armenian and Turkish cooking, found in great abundance in Turkey and northern Syria.

mlookheeyeh—a leafy green vegetable that forms the basis for one of Egypt's national dishes; available frozen or dried.

orange-blossom water—essence distilled from orange-blossom petals, used principally to perfume desserts.

pine nuts—tiny fruit of certain pine cones used in stuffings and as a garnish; rounder, shorter nuts of Chinese origin are less expensive than the richer-tasting *pignoli* from Portugal; to toast, heat a small quantity of oil to nearly smoking, toss in the pine nuts, immediately remove from the fire and stir.

preserved lemon—Moroccan lemons pickled with spices and used as a flavoring agent.

ras il hanoot—basic Moroccan spice mixture that includes cinnamon, cloves, ginger, cardamom, caraway, nutmeg, and other spices.

rice flour—ground rice used principally to thicken puddings; packaged Cream of Rice cereal is ground rice, usually with salt and preservatives added.

rosewater—essence distilled from rose petals, used principally to perfume desserts.

saffron—aromatic red or orange-red threads (the three stigmas of an autumn-flowering crocus) used to scent and color rice and other dishes; usually soaked in warm (not hot) or room-temperature water to release the color and aroma, but can also be ground or added in its original form to dishes; Iranian saffron is darker in color and sells for a fraction of the cost of the Spanish spice.

semolina—a protein-rich coarse yellow flour ground from the endosperm (branless inner kernels) of hard durum wheat, used principally in pastries.

shata—bottled hot sauce popular in the Gulf, usually Tabasco or a similar chili sauce.

sumac—dark red spice ground from the petals and berries of a shrub, used to add a lemony tang to Middle Eastern dishes.

tahini—thin paste made from ground sesame seeds, used primarily as a flavoring base.

tajeen—a braised or stewed meat dish from North Africa usually eaten with bread; also, the traditional clay pot with its cone-shaped cover in which the *tajeen* is simmered.

tamarind—a dried cinnamon-colored pod, the fruit of an Indian evergreen tree that imparts a pleasant sour flavor to Gulf dishes, available in the natural pod or in a commercially prepared paste; its Arabic name *tamer-hindee* translates as "Indian date."

turmeric—a ground Indian rhizome that lends golden color to rice and similar dishes, especially popular in the Arabian Gulf and North Africa, where it sometimes is a substitute for expensive saffron.

zatar—a Lebanese/Syrian mixture of four to six spices, including thyme, sesame seeds, and sumac.

Spices and Spice Mixtures

Spices are the palette of the kitchen artist, deepening sun-ripened colors, magnifying flavors, intensifying aromas. All regions of the Arab world share the basic Mediterranean seasoning pattern of olive oil with onion, garlic, and tomato. Often it is the particular spices flavoring a stew, soup, or dessert that identify the dish as Armenian, Moroccan, or Bahraini.

Each region in the Middle East boasts its own exclusive and distinct combination, lending credence to the saying, "If you add sufficient quantity of delectable spices, you can even let your enemy do the cooking" (meaning that he won't be able to ruin your dish). Another proverb suggests, "If low-quality spices find buyers" (a metaphor referring to unattractive daughters seeking husbands), "certainly saffron will."

For the sake of simplicity, we can subdivide the region's 21 countries into three broad overlapping brushstrokes of spices: North Africa or the Maghreb (Morocco, Algeria, Libya, Tunisia), Greater Syria or the Levant (Lebanon, Syria, Jordan, the Palestinians), and the Arabian Peninsula or the Gulf (Saudi Arabia, the United Arab Emirates, Bahrain, Kuwait, Oman, Qatar).

The following chart is intended to serve as a basic introduction to regional spice combinations and major flavoring ingredients. I've tried to list the items more or less in order of preference, with more outstanding spices toward the top of each list, and fresh herbs toward the bottom. Please don't consider it the final word on the subject, as there are no set rules when it comes to this sort of thing.

Egyptian cooking shows influences of both the Maghreb and the Levant, and most dishes are flavored with cumin.

Kurdish and Armenian recipes are related to the foods of Turkey and the Levant, but often include Middle Eastern red pepper.

Because Iraq is situated at the crossroads of three cultures, the Gulf, the Fertile Crescent, and Persia (modern-day Iran), its cuisine is electrifyingly diverse and alluring. Some of its dishes appear quite Syrian or Turkish in nature, while others call for spices and techniques with distinctive Gulf or Iranian influences.

An Arab cook always keeps a large quantity of her own preferred blend of spices on hand, ready to toss into a steaming pot of soup or vegetables. A few purchase a ready-mixed combination from the family's own spice merchant, who can be trusted to provide high-quality freshly ground spices, while others prefer to blend their own combination. In case you plan to do

The Maghreb	The Levant	The Gulf
saffron	allspice	cardamon
cinnamon	cinnamon	**loomi**
cumin	nutmeg	cinnamon
nutmeg	cloves	cumin
red pepper	**asfor**	saffron
ginger	red pepper	turmeric
cardamom	parsley	ginger
cloves	cilantro	rosewater
turmeric	garlic	orange-blossom water
dried rosebud		fresh green chilis
rosewater		cilantro
orange-blossom water		parsley
preserved lemon		garlic
cilantro		
parsley		
garlic		

a lot of Middle Eastern cooking and would like to keep a small quantity of each regional spice mixture on hand, each of the following recipes will produce about $1/4$ cup.

+ **Ras il hanoot** from Morocco: 1 tbsp. cinnamon, $1^1/2$ tsp. red pepper, 1 tsp. nutmeg, 1 tsp. cloves, 1 tsp. turmeric, 1 tsp. ground ginger, 1 tsp. allspice, 1 tsp. black pepper, 1 tsp. cardamom, 2 ground dried rosebuds.

+ For **Libyan Bzar**, omit the rosebuds and cardamom and add (optional) 2 tbsp. cumin.

+ **Bharaat** from Greater Syria: 2 tbsp. allspice, 1 tbsp. cinnamon, $1^1/2$ tsp. nutmeg, $1^1/2$ tsp. cloves.

+ **Kebsa** spices from Saudi Arabia and the Gulf States: 1 tbsp. red pepper, $1^1/2$ tsp. cumin, $1^1/2$ tsp. cinnamon, 1 tsp. cloves, 1 tsp. black pepper, 1 tsp. ground cardamom, 1 tsp. nutmeg, 1 tsp. ground coriander, 1 tsp. ground *loomi*.

On Culinary Variations

The shared cultural heritage of the Arab world makes it difficult to designate countries of origin for dishes that are common, with only moderate differences, to much of the region. Levantine specialties like *hummos* are popular not only in the Fertile Crescent countries that were part of the Ottoman Empire, but also in the Gulf States and Egypt. While *biryanis* are particular to countries close to India, such as Iraq and the Arabian Gulf states, the ground-meat recipes known as *kefta* are enjoyed by Arabs of all nationalities. Dishes like **Vegetable Soup a la Araby**, with its unlimited wondrous variations, defy categorization.

Ultimately, I decided to include certain recipes simply beause they are basic, prototype dishes of the region. Others are described because they are excitingly flavored combinations that, in my humble opinion, surpass the widespread tasty everyday versions. In every case, countries or subcultures of origin are noted, along with a phonetically written name for the dish in that particular local dialect.

However, I felt that it would be an oversight to ignore the wealth of delicious variations on most dishes. Cooks in Tunis, Tangiers, and Tripoli are all certain that their particular recipe for lentil soup is the most authentic and the most appetizing. Space does not allow for detailed instructions on all of these, but I've attempted to touch on many in the catalog of Variations following most recipes. I've also included Turkey, Andalusia, Kurdistan, and Armenia in these lists because their shared histories have bequeathed a wealth of related dishes. Similarly, the Palestinians treasure their national dishes although, like the Armenians, they are now dispersed throughout the Middle East and other parts of the world.

I encourage more experienced cooks to experiment with the diverse tastes and textures described in the Variations. Choose a regional combination that sounds good to you or one that excludes a certain ingredient you dislike. If you're unfamiliar with the cuisine, just relax and rely on common sense, adding spices incrementally until you are pleased with the intensity of flavor.

In this part of the world, each family prides itself on its own particular combination of flavors, and neighbors frequently disagree on the merits of allspice or red pepper in *kibbeh* or whether basmati rice should be soaked overnight or only a fraction of an hour. Should *Tabbooleh's* wheat be tenderized with the juice of its chopped tomatoes, with the lemony vinaigrette, or in water? It's often a question of personal taste, and until recently, Arabic cookbooks did not even specify quantities of minor ingredients nor details of preparation. Besides, if women in one village reach an agreement on a recipe, it is to be expected that those in the next valley will protest its inaccuracy. I hope you'll enjoy the challenge and excitement and dare to try some of these tempting regional adaptations.

General Cooking Tips

✦ All recipes will serve 4 Arabs generously, or perhaps 5 Americans. Many are main dishes requiring only a salad to be a complete meal.

✦ There really are no substitutes for the gorgeous flavors and textures of the authentic ingredients, which should always be fresh. Never substitute dried parsley, garlic powder, bottled lemon juice, or similar items for the real goodness of the fresh component. However, canned plum tomatoes are preferred for soups over our cardboard American fresh varieties. Arab cooks residing in the West or in the Gulf, where American-style supermarkets abound, generally prefer frozen peas and green beans. (If you've ever readied 2 or 3 kilos of green beans for the cooking pot, an amount required to serve the usual family gathering, you'll immediately understand why.)

✦ Quantities of meat, poultry, and fish listed may seem light by Western standards. These proportions are correct for the humble but delectable family meals of the Middle East. For guests or on special occasions, you may wish to increase the measurement of these items in your chosen recipes.

✦ When not otherwise specified, these recipes require average-sized American produce. When "2 carrots" appears on the ingredients list, select normal-sized ones—that is, unless you are especially fond of this nutritious vegetable. (In most cases, it won't unbalance the dish to add a bit more of certain items.) Similarly, cucumbers, tomatoes, onions, and the like should be of medium size. As most American potatoes tend to be large rather than medium-sized, you might wish to keep that in mind. American chickens are usually about $2^1/4$ to $2^3/4$ pounds in weight, but slightly smaller birds or more generously endowed ones are also fine, as long as they provide enough meat to serve the dinner party.

◆ In Middle Eastern cooking it normally doesn't matter if you chop the onions, cucumbers, or parsley coarsely or finely. The reality of this cuisine is that while some cooks prefer an ingredient diced, many will mince it, while others would cut it julienne-style. Enjoy the wonderful tastes, do your best but don't worry about producing precise sizes. After all, as Mother keeps reminding me, "Only Allah is perfect."

◆ There are no hard-and-fast rules to this cooking. Often, the ingredients and proportions can vary according to your personal taste and what you have on hand, so don't be afraid to improvise.

◆ Many Middle Eastern dishes, in particular the *mezzeh*, are served at room temperature, a pleasant custom in the warm Mediterranean climate. The usual Arab family is quite large, and on festive occasions the number of guests present may be beyond imagination. Add the complication of a kitchen that probably lacks a microwave and quite possibly— in a pastoral environment—an oven or even a refrigerator, and you'll understand why much of the cuisine tastes heavenly without being chilled or heated. Of course, soups, pilafs, and meat dishes are served steaming hot.

◆ Idaho potatoes, russets, reds, and other varieties will all work well in these recipes. Planning meals in the Arab world teaches tolerance and flexibility. One is usually quite pleased to find any sort of attractive potatoes and doesn't quibble over the type. This peasant cuisine is easily adaptable to whatever potatoes you have in the pantry. Besides, you can imagine the number of types available in 21 Arab countries, not to mention the fact that many different plants thrive in the region's distinct agricultural zones and throughout different growing seasons.

◆ Bouillon is a flavor intensifier and a handy emergency substitute for home-cooked broths, but it is wise to check the ingredients on the jar of beef or chicken bouillon before you buy it. Brands available in supermarkets usually list salt as their principal ingredient, and include numerous chemicals but no meat. Look for a label that specifies meat as the main ingredient or that at least lists natural elements. Health food stores stock a wide variety, but I use a marvelous paste by Tone's that I can find only at Sam's Warehouse. (Sam's is a division of Wal-Mart and can be contacted at 1-800-444-2582.)

✦ The red pepper called for in many recipes is neither cayenne nor paprika, but a fragrant seedless coarsely ground pepper from Turkey or northern Syria that varies from gently spicy to blistering. This is my secret ingredient, about which I feel quite passionate; it adds intensity to a wide selection of dishes, and when you inhale a whiff of its aromatic goodness, you'll understand why I have a weakness for it. Do ask for *filful ahmar halaby* or Aleppo pepper in Arab, Armenian, or Turkish markets, or mention it to Armenian friends or at Armenian restaurants (they'll be impressed and happy to help you out). Perhaps you know someone planning a trip to Istanbul who will bring back a bag of this magical flavoring. Don't substitute Mexican, Indian, or Ethiopian or other red peppers unless you've worn out all other possibilities. The latter are sharp and fiery but lack the subtle perfume of the Turkish pepper.

✦ Minced garlic is usually added to a dish when the sautéed onions have become transparent. When garlic is not cooked, as in a salad, it is crushed to a paste in a mortar, with the salt serving as a grinding agent. Garlic presses really do not do this job properly. Do not substitute minced or pressed garlic when the recipe suggests you crush it with the salt. Instead, I recommend that you purchase a functional apricot wood mortar and pestle of Syrian origin from your local import store. Rub it with olive oil and it will serve you until your daughter (or granddaughter) is married.

✦ Middle Eastern milk products usually come straight from the cow, goat, or sheep, but it's important to keep in mind that the total fat of the peasant diet is considerably less than in the West. Arabs living in the United States are happy to discover that low-fat dairy products do not affect the great flavor of their traditional dishes. If you prefer, or if you are on a restricted-fat diet, you may use nonfat dairy products in these dishes.

✦ All temperatures given are in degrees Fahrenheit.

Damascus: Souk El Hamideeyah

Mezzeh

Mezzeh, the fascinating array of small appetizers displayed on a multitude of miniature oval trays, undoubtedly form the most famous feature of the lavish Middle Eastern kitchen. Incredible in number and exciting in variety, the endless array of dips, marinated vegetable salads, glossy unblemished olives, perfect savory pastries, pickles, cheeses, stuffed vine leaves, and grilled meats delight and astonish me today as much as when I first encountered them. *Mezzeh* is so popular these days that a wide variety of American and continental restaurants in Washington, D.C., New York, and Los Angeles now list them among their regular hors d'oeuvres.

The word itself most likely originated in Italy and was borrowed from the Genoese spice merchants by Arab traders. *Mezza*, the Italian word for "half," reemerges as *mezedes* in Greece, *meze* in Turkey, and *mezzeh* in Arabic-speaking countries. Some food historians believe that the condiments (*kawamikh*) and cold dishes (*bawarid*) of the medieval Arab table might have grown into todays Mezzeh. Popularly considered a Lebanese creation, this form of appetizer is enjoyed across the region.

Even though the name suggests "half a dinner," most of us savor *mezzeh* as a meal in itself. As white-jacketed waiters in elegant Kuwaiti restaurants, or unpretentious village youths in humble Jordanian truck stops step up to cover the table with a bounty of tiny dishes, I usually know that I'll not progress beyond the first course of my meal. So the usual translation of *mezzeh* as "appetizers" is in fact incorrect: it is impossible to stop nibbling these wonderful specialties, and the appetite may be satiated rather than stimulated. A small assortment of these dishes will enchant a cocktail party crowd, while a wider variety will sustain the guests at an exciting buffet dinner.

Mezzeh is enjoyed as part of a business lunch in hotel restaurants as well as the highlight of a family's weekend outing in the crisp air of nearby mountains. On such occasions, the appetizers may or may not be followed by plates of roast meat or fish. *Mezzeh* is not, however, ordinary home fare, although occasionally one dish such as **Chilied Green Olives** or **Spinach Pies** may be served alongside the modest midday meal of couscous and stew or rice with seasonal vegetables in a tomato-based broth. An Arab housewife who has spent the entire morning rolling sufficient grape leaves to serve her extended family will understandably not want to prepare several more similarly spectacular delicacies, although for a special occasion she would do so with admirable devotion.

Many *mezzeh*, if prepared in large quantity, are equally excellent as main dishes or light lunches. **Stuffed Grape Leaves with Meat**, or **Potato Cakes with Meat Filling**, for example, might be presented as a family meal, accompanied only by yoghurt and salad.

The opposite is equally true: small quantities of main course recipes found elsewhere in this book may be added to the *mezzeh* table. Any finger food is ideal, as are salads, whose original purpose was to perk the appetite. Small pieces of roast meat are often included along with vegetable dishes intended to be presented at room temperature, like **Green Beans in Light Olive Oil Sauce**. Is **Lentil Dip with Cumin and Coriander** really an appetizer, or is it, as its name *Salatet Adas* would suggest, a salad? No firm lines are necessary here, so feel free to enjoy these marvelous dishes in authentic Arab fashion or as exotic and healthy additions to a Western meal.

Probably the *mezzeh* best known in this country is **Hummos**, a creamy dip prepared from chickpeas. Like *Baba Ghanooj*, an Arab puree made from roast eggplant, it is scooped up with torn pieces of flat pita bread. **Hummos** can quickly be prepared in the blender or food processor from chickpeas, tahini, fresh lemon juice, and garlic.

Only the availability of ingredients and the ability of the cook limit the number of dishes, and part of the fun is that one never knows exactly what delectable assortment to expect. Open-faced meat pies, crescent-shaped cheese pastries, and triangular tarts filled with spinach can be fashioned from a variety of commercial doughs. Some of these will be served hot from the oven, but because it is nearly impossible to ready 10 or 20 tiny warm dishes for presentation at the same time, most will have been prepared in quantity earlier in the day. Savory pies and pastries, in particular, are served at room temperature, because they are usually the specialties of ovens located some distance away from the home.

Fresh seasonal vegetables and greens are served at every Middle Eastern meal, so an assortment of vegetables always fills in the *mezzeh*. Overlapping slices of ripe red tomato, garnished with mint and crumbled feta or other white cheese, add dramatic color. Small dishes of green onions, tiny baby cucumbers, radishes, fresh herbs, and carrot sticks are popular. In winter, when these delicacies may not be available, pickled vegetables are served, but these are also popular throughout the year.

If you are completely overwhelmed and don't know where to start, an ideal *mezzeh* assortment would include one or two dips, little savory pastries filled with cheese or meat, **Tartare Style Kibbeh** or **Felafel**, and a vegetable or bean salad. *Mezzeh* need not be complicated, only substantial, so add some items that require little preparation time: olives from the nearest import food store, crudités to refresh the palate, commercially prepared Arab pickles, and an assortment of fresh vegetables. Set these out on the traditional miniature oval trays made of metal or on dessert-sized dishes, add a splendid rice dish and a main course, and you have a feast fit for an Arabian night.

Hummos

Hummos (ARAB STATES)

This silky protein-rich dip is the queen of the *mezzeh*, or at least the most famous of a profusion of splendid appetizers. Enjoyed as a light lunch by the shopkeeper in Damascus' ancient souk who scoops it from a cardboard platter, it also graces every fabulous hotel buffet—from Alexandria beside the Nile delta, to Sharjah on the rippling banks of the Arabian Gulf.

1³/₄ cups cooked chickpeas

¹/₄ cup low-fat yoghurt, water, or liquid in which the chickpeas were cooked

2 cloves garlic, crushed with salt

¹/₄ cup tahini

¹/₃ cup lemon juice

Garnish:
>   olive oil
>   paprika
>   cumin
>   black Middle Eastern olives
>   minced parsley

1. Puree the ingredients in a blender or food processor, reserving a few whole chickpeas for garnish.

2. Add additional tahini and/or lemon juice if necessary until you have achieved a flavor and consistency that suits your taste. This texture should be thinner than mashed potatoes but with enough body to hold an edge.

3. Spread in an earthenware dish or an oval serving platter, running the side of a spoon around the edge to create a slight rim. Drizzle with olive oil and garnish with the reserved chickpeas, paprika, cumin, and olives to add a bit of color. Serve with Arabic bread.

Eggplant Dip

Baba Ghannooj or *Mtebbal* (ARAB STATES)

A favorite of the *mezzeh* table, this luscious eggplant dip has an unforgettable bouquet. Its smoky flavor results from roasting the egglant over a gas or charcoal flame or toasting it directly under the broiler. Today, many upscale restaurants in the Arab world add a bit of yoghurt to their dip to brighten its translucent color and make the texture even more velvety.

Eggplant is frequently roasted before it is combined with other ingredients. This technique is also common in North African and Mexican cuisine, and over the years I have tried many different methods of charring the eggplant's skin. If your kitchen is equipped with a gas stove, you may try grilling it slowly over the flame, but I find it easier to control the process under the broiler element of my oven.

    1 large eggplant
    2 tbsp. low-fat yoghurt
    2 cloves garlic, crushed with salt
  1/4 cup lemon juice
    2 to 3 tbsp. tahini

Garnish:
> olive oil
> minced parsley
> black Middle Eastern olives
> chopped tomatoes
> pomegranate seeds

1. Grill the eggplant in the broiler, placing it about 2 inches from the heat. Turn every few minutes to blister and char evenly on all sides. (Many oven broilers perform more consistently with the door left ajar.) The eggplant is ready when the skin is black and the flesh has collapsed. If you feel that the outside is done while the inside is still too firm, turn the oven to about 350 degrees and bake the eggplant until it is quite wilted. Alternatively, if you do not like the smoky aroma that characterizes many eggplant dishes, cut the unpeeled eggplant in half lengthwise and brush with a small amount of olive oil. Bake at 400 degrees for 30–40 minutes, or until soft.

2. Scrape the inside of the skin gently with a spoon to remove all the pulp, and whirl it in a food processor. Alternatively, mash it with a pestle.

3. Add the yoghurt and garlic and salt. Process with half the lemon juice and half the tahini. Add the remaining lemon juice and tahini in increments, until you are pleased with the texture and flavor.

4. Spread in a shallow serving dish. Drizzle a bit of olive oil over the top and garnish attractively. Scoop up with pieces of Arabic bread.

Creamy Eggplant Guacamole

Salatet Beitinjan (SYRIA) ✦ *Patlijan Salataseh* (TURKEY)

During the 400 years of Ottoman occupation, Turkish influence on the existing Arab culture was extensive. This light summery dish, enjoyed throughout the Arab countries of the eastern Mediterranean, is undoubtedly a legacy of the Ottoman era. Although the olive oil and lemon dressing entices me to categorize it as a salad, it's more technically an appetizer with a fresh tantalizing flavor that goes well as an accompaniment to cocktails.

1 large eggplant

Dressing:

juice of 1 lemon

1/4 cup olive oil

1/4 tsp. red pepper (optional)

2 cloves garlic, crushed with
salt

Garnish:

black Middle Eastern olives

diced tomatoes

minced parsley

1. Prepare the eggplant as in the preceding recipe, step 1.

2. When the eggplant is cool enough to handle, scoop out the softened flesh with a spoon, scraping the inside of the skin to remove all the pulp. Mash the flesh in a bowl, using a pestle or a fork. Don't puree the eggplant because the flesh should remain creamy but with soft lumps.

3. Combine the dressing ingredients and pour over the eggplant, tossing to blend well.

4. Serve at room temperature or slightly chilled in a flat dish, garnished with olives, tomatoes, and parsley. As an appetizer with cocktails, serve with pieces of Arabic bread or fine crackers. Or offer it as a salad on individual plates, mounding the eggplant over shredded lettuce.

Variations

Tunisia: Season with ground coriander and garnish with roasted green peppers.

Morocco: Season with minced cilantro (1/3 cup), cumin, and red pepper, and garnish with roasted green peppers.

Armenia: Chop, sauté, and add 3 green onions, 1 small tomato, and 1 green pepper.

Lebanon: Add 3 minced green onions and 1 large chopped tomato.

Lentil Dip with Cumin and Coriander

Salatet Adas (SYRIA)

~~~~~~

Bored with *hummos* and *baba ghanooj*? This yummy lentil dip is a winter dish, served during the months when fresh vegetables are in short supply.

  1 onion, minced
 ¼ cup olive oil
  2 cloves garlic, minced
  4 cups water
 ¾ cup brown or green lentils
    salt
    black pepper
 ¼ tsp. cumin
 ¼ tsp. ground coriander
 ¼ tsp. cloves

1. Sauté the onion in the olive oil until slightly softened. Add the garlic and sauté for another minute.

2. Pour on the water and stir in the lentils, adding salt. Bring to a boil, cover, and reduce heat. As the water is absorbed, add only the minimum water necessary to keep the lentils from sticking. Simmer until tender, about 1½ hours, stirring frequently. If much water remains in the pan, discard it.

3. Puree in a food processor or using a pestle, incorporating the spices. Taste and adjust seasoning.

4. Serve with Arabic bread.

Variations

Syria: Add a generous squeeze of lemon juice and ⅓ cup minced parsley.

Gulf States: Add a bit of ground **loomi**.

Easy and Economical Homemade Yoghurt

Leban (ARAB STATES) ✦ *Zabady* (EGYPT)

More easily digested than milk, yoghurt supplants it in the Arab diet. Because yoghurt's beneficial bacteria colonize the intestinal tract and protect against infection, Arab doctors recommended yoghurt for sick babies and anyone suffering from intestinal abnormalities. It's also a great dairy choice for those who have trouble digesting the lactose in milk.

In the village, we send one of the family's young boys with an empty plastic bucket off to the yoghurt lady, a neighbor who owns a few cows and sheep. In the cities, yoghurt is also produced on a commercial scale.

When purchasing yoghurt to use as a starter for this recipe, look for a brand that contains *Lactobacillus acidophilus,* not just "live cultures." The trick to producing delicious yoghurt every time at home is to add the yoghurt culture when the milk has cooled to about 105 degrees. If the fermenting milk is left to incubate more than 4 or 5 hours, excess lactic acid may sour the taste slightly, producing a yoghurt that is better used in a cooked sauce. It is also helpful to use a ceramic pot or jar, which retains the warmth necessary for proper activation of the live bacteria.

1 to 2 quarts low-fat milk

½ small container plain yoghurt (without sugar, cornstarch, or additives)

1. Bring the milk to a boil. Pour into a crockery or ceramic bowl and cool to 100–110 degrees. If the milk is cooler than this, fermentation will not take place; if it is too hot, the yoghurt may sour or the bacteria will be killed.

2. Whisk in the purchased yoghurt, leaving the remainder of the container for your next batch of yoghurt. Cover and wrap in a thick wool or acrylic blanket. (A crocheted or knitted wool afghan works best because it holds in the heat.) Set aside for 4 hours. (Yoghurt that ferments for longer than 5 hours is usually slightly sour, and is best used in cooking.)

3. The yoghurt should be the consistency of a rich custard with a bit of whey floating on the top. Do not break the surface until it has chilled in the refrigerator for a few hours.

Yoghurt Dip with Garlic

Lebneh (ARMENIA)

~~~~~~

A concentrated source of protein, *lebneh* is a popular breakfast dish and is spread on bread as a "walking snack." It's no more than yoghurt (sometimes from sheep's or goat's milk) that has been strained to separate its whey component, usually by hanging the yoghurt in cloth bags. As the natural bacteria present in the yoghurt ferment, the flavor is slightly modified.

As a dip, *lebneh* is combined with garlic and dusted with red pepper and a few drops of olive oil. For a family breakfast or evening snack, the garlic is omitted and the *lebneh* is garnished with dried mint and olive oil.

4   cups low-fat yoghurt

2   to 3 cloves garlic, crushed with salt

Garnish:

olive oil

paprika

1. Line a colander with dampened cheesecloth and set it in or over a bowl.

2. Spoon the yoghurt into the colander and set aside at room temperature for 5–12 hours.

3. Beat the crushed garlic into the yoghurt.

4. Spread in a serving plate, drizzling with a bit of olive oil and sprinkling with paprika.

5. Serve with Arabic bread.

Variations

Syria: Omit the garlic, garnish with olive oil and crushed dried mint.

Lebanon: Add $1/2$ peeled chopped cucumber and mint.

Yoghurt Cheese Balls

Lebneh (LEBANON, ARAB STATES)

In the storage room of our village home, my mother-in-law always has two or three large glass jars of **Yoghurt Cheese Balls** stored alongside 50-kilo bags of sugar, huge bottles of pink turnip pickles, and cloth sacks of lentils and chickpeas. In Syria we buy *lebneh* and shape it ourselves into these pearly little balls stacked in amber olive oil. Usually families set them out for the morning and evening meals without bothering to roll them in spices.

In the United States, these tiny balls are available from import food stores, but it's a pity to pay the high price asked when they are so easy to make at home.

4 cups low-fat yoghurt

sweet paprika, red pepper, crumbled dried mint, or cumin

olive oil

1. Line a colander with dampened cheesecloth and set it in or over a bowl. Spoon the yoghurt into the colander and set aside for 24–36 hours. Alternatively, spoon the yoghurt into a dampened cloth bag or two layers of cheesecloth, then tie the ends together loosely. Hang from a spigot or showerhead for 24–36 hours.

2. Form the yoghurt cheese into small balls about ³/4 inch in diameter. Sprinkle generously with one of the spices. If you are serving these immediately, arrange on a plate and drizzle with olive oil. To store, transfer to a small jar, cover with olive oil to protect the cheese from drying out, and refrigerate. Or, they can be set aside to dry out several hours longer before refrigeration.

3. Serve with the olive oil in which the cheese is stored and with Arabic bread.

Harissa Red Chili Paste

Hareessa (TUNISIA, NORTH AFRICA)

North African housewives use this spicy paste as a flavoring agent in cous-cous broths and many other dishes, mixing up a new batch every few months. There are few foods in the Tunisian diet that do not include a bit of **harissa**.

Although not truly an appetizer, a few tablespoons of **harissa** can be spread in a tiny oval tray and offered as a dip. A tasty commercial product in an easy-to-use tube is available from imported food markets.

10 fresh or dried hot red chilis, seeds and veins removed
 2 tbsp. olive oil
 3 cloves garlic, crushed with
    salt
 1 to 2 sweet red peppers (optional)

1. If you are using dried chilis, soak them in warm water for 1–2 hours.

2. Combine all ingredients and whirl in a food processor or blender. (Traditionally, a brass mortar and pestle or meat grinder is used.) If the result is too fiery, 1 or 2 sweet red peppers may be ground into the mixture.

3. **Harissa** will keep for several months if stored in the refrigerator. Be sure to use a clean dry spoon to remove the chili paste as needed, or the mixture may become contaminated. Many cooks who prepare the seasoning in quantity cover its surface with a thin layer of olive oil to protect it from contact with the air.

Variation

Add cumin, caraway, and/or ground coriander.

Saudi Herbed Salsa

Salsa or *Dukoos* (SAUDI ARABIA, KUWAIT, GULF STATES)

The light, bracing combination of cilantro and aromatic green chilis is surprisingly similar to the salsa (sometimes labeled *pico de gallo* in the States) that sits on the table of nearly every Mexican restaurant. Some Saudis call it *dakoos* or *salata har* (spicy salad), but my Jeddah friends just refer to it as salsa. It's wonderful with every sort of food, but absolutely essential when fish or rice is served. The quantities given below are sufficient for a relish, but you'll want to prepare a double recipe if this salsa is to be served as a salad.

  2 large ripe tomatoes, chopped
  1 or 2 serrano chilis, seeded and minced
  5 green onions, chopped
$^{3}/_{4}$ cup minced cilantro
  2 tbsp. olive oil (optional)
  2 tbsp. lemon juice
     salt

1. Combine all ingredients.

Variation

Sauté the onions in the oil, stir in the remaining ingredients, and simmer for 5–10 minutes.

Preserved Baby Eggplants

Mhellal Beitinjan (LIBYA)

The traditional breakfast and supper spread in our village includes this dish's Syrian cousin: chubby baby eggplants, lustrous purple-black, stuffed with nuts from our walnut trees and spicy red peppers. In North Africa, where the Mediterranean climate is less supportive of nut production, fresh herbs are the preferred stuffing for these preserved eggplants, which are more of a mid-day salad. The eggplant originated in India but through the Gateway of Abbasid, Baghdad, was introduced into the Islamic world in the 8th century. If miniature eggplants (usually labeled "Japanese") are not available in your area, select the smallest ones you find.

    8 small fat Japanese eggplants, or:
 1⅓ pounds small normal eggplants
  ½ cup wine vinegar
  ½ cup olive oil
       salt

Stuffing:

    4 cloves garlic, crushed with
       salt
       black pepper
    1 or 2 serrano chilis, seeded and minced
    1 medium stalk celery with leaves, minced
  ½ cup minced parsley
  ½ cup minced cilantro
    2 tbsp. wine vinegar

1. Wash the eggplants and remove the stems. Drop them into a pot of boiling salted water and cook for 10 minutes (15 minutes for the larger ones), or until soft. Remove to a colander and drain.

2. Combine the stuffing ingredients.

3. Slit the tiny eggplants open lengthwise (cut the larger ones in 3 or 4 pieces lengthwise). Gently squeeze out the water, and stuff with the herbal mixture. Place the eggplants in a large plastic container with a tight-fitting lid.

4. Stir together the vinegar, olive oil, and salt to taste, and pour it over the eggplants, and refrigerate. It is not necessary to cover the vegetables completely with the liquid. Seal tightly and turn the container upside-down from time to time. This dish should be prepared a day or two in advance.

Potato Cakes with Meat Filling

Batata Chap (IRAQ, KURDISTAN)

~~~~~~

I was served this dish many years ago, and the rapturous response it evoked stayed in my mind for years. Fifteen years later, Chef Yusuf, a Kurdish refugee from Baghdad, taught me the secret of a very light and fluffy potato shell: when cooked white rice and day-old bread are ground and added to the mashed potatoes, the texture is sheer delight.

While most of the men in our local Kurdish community in Dallas list their former occupations as *peshmerga*—freedom fighters, fierce descendants of the great diplomat-warrior Salah-Al-Din (Saladin)—this astonishing recipe confirms Yusuf's tale that he spent his last years in Baghdad running a coffee shop, bakery, and catering service.

Potato shell:

- 1/4 cup white rice, any type except converted or instant
- 3 potatoes, peeled and cut into chunks
- 1 or 2 thick slices day-old sourdough, Afghani, or French bread
- salt
- black pepper

Meat filling:

- 1 small onion, minced
- 2 tbsp. olive oil
- 1/2 pound ground beef
- salt
- black pepper
- 1/2 tsp. **kebsa** spices, or:
- equal pinches of cinnamon, cumin, and curry powder
- 1/4 cup minced parsley
- oil for sautéing

1. Boil the rice in 4 cups or more of salted water until tender, about 20 minutes. Drain in a colander and set aside to cool.

2. Steam the potatoes in salted water until tender, about 15 minutes. Drain completely and use a potato masher to mash.

3. Tear the bread into pieces and whirl it in a food processor. You should have about 1 cup of crumbs.

4. Measure 1 cup of cooked rice, discarding any excess, and add to the food processor, processing again with the bread crumbs.

5. Add the potatoes to the rice-bread combination and knead the mixture until a relatively smooth dough is formed. Season with salt and black pepper to taste.

6. For the stuffing, gently sauté the onion in the oil until soft and transparent. Add the meat and the spices, stirring to break up all lumps as the meat cooks. When all traces of pink have disappeared, remove from the pan and drain well. Stir in the minced parsley.

7. To shape the potato cake, form a ball the size of a lime and insert your finger to hollow out the inside. Fill with a tsp. of the meat stuffing and close the potato mixture around the filling. Flatten slightly between your palms.

8. Lightly sauté in oil until pale golden brown and crisp. (I've tried baking these but the results were not memorable.) Serve hot or at room temperature.

Felafel

Felafel (ARAB STATES) ◆ Ta'amia (EGYPT)

The original Coptic Egyptian version of this recipe specified brown *foul* (fava) beans, but today the strong taste of the dark bean is most often replaced by the milder chickpea, or is mixed on a 50-50 basis. A major component of the *mezzeh* table, **Felafel** can also be a meal in itself. It's one of the few Arabic fast foods, eaten in a half loaf of flat bread with a dollop of tahini-based **Tarator Sauce**, a garlicky pickle, and a salad-like relish.

Felafel is surprisingly easy to prepare with a food processor. Muhammed from the Aziz restaurant showed me how to bake the traditional mixture so that the high-protein content of its beans can be enjoyed without the added fat of frying. (Traditionalists may also prepare the following recipe in the original manner.)

 1 cup chickpeas, soaked overnight and drained
 2 slices whole-wheat bread
 2 cloves garlic, minced
 4 green onions, minced
 1/4 cup minced cilantro
 1/4 cup minced parsley
   salt
   black pepper
 1 tsp. baking powder
 1/4 tsp. baking soda
 3/4 tsp. ground coriander
 1 tsp. cumin
 1/4 tsp. red pepper

Relish:

 1 ripe tomato, minced
 1/4 cup minced cucumber
 1/4 cup minced green pepper
 1/2 serrano chili, seeded and minced
 1 tbsp. minced parsley
 1 tbsp. minced cilantro
 (to taste) red pepper or Tabasco sauce
   generous squeeze lemon juice
   salt

Tarator Sauce:

 1/3 cup **tahini**
 1/3 cup lemon juice
 1/2 cup water
 2 tbsp. low-fat yoghurt
 2 cloves garlic, crushed with
   salt

1. Pass the chickpeas, bread, garlic, green onions, cilantro, and parsley through a meat grinder twice. Alternatively, process the chickpeas in a food processor, then add the bread, garlic, green onions, cilantro, and parsley. Whirl until the ingredients are tinted green and the texture of ground walnuts.

2. Transfer the ground mixture to your working surface and sprinkle with the remaining dry ingredients. Knead well for 3–4 minutes and set aside for $^1/_2$ hour.

3. Preheat the oven to 350 degrees.

4. Knead again and shape into balls the size of small limes. Flatten slightly between your palms and bake on an ungreased baking sheet for 8–10 minutes. Do not overbake or brown.

5. Combine the relish ingredients.

6. Combine the sauce ingredients in blender or food processor.

7. For a dinner party, arrange the cooked **Felafel** on a bed of parsley or shredded lettuce and garnish with slices of lemon. Offer the relish and **Tarator Sauce** in small bowls on the side, or place the bowls in the center of an oval tray, surrounded by the **Felafel**. **Felafel** is eaten in Arabic bread, along with a pickle spear and a generous spoonful of relish. Top with a dollop of **Tarator Sauce**.

Variation

Saudi Arabia: Add *kebsa* spices.

Sweet and Sour Green Olive Appetizer

Zeitoon bi Hamod er Rummaan (LEBANON)

The noble olive is entwined with the history of all the peoples of the Mediterranean. Tradition suggests that it was given as a gift by the goddess Athena to the people of Athens. Today, the vast range of olives available in the region offers an amazing array of flavors and colors. Each is unique, and villagers prefer their own region's product to the olives harvested by others.

This *mezzeh* dish was a specialty of the Yildizlar restaurant, a popular Lebanese establishment transferred to Jeddah's lovely seaside corniche in

1982. A Jordanian neighbor and I liked it so much that we were determined to unveil the unique combination of ingredients, and the following recipe is the result.

    1   cup green olives
  1/2   small onion, slivered
    3   tbsp. **hamod er rummaan** pomegranate syrup
    3   tbsp. water
    3   tbsp. olive oil
    2   tsp. brown sugar
        salt

1. Drain the olives of their brine.

2. Combine the remaining ingredients and pour over the olives. Cover and marinate in the refrigerator for at least 24 hours before serving.

Chilied Green Olives

Zeitoon al Had (SYRIA)

Olives are served at least twice a day in the Arab world, every morning and evening, and perhaps for a snack in between. The staff of life in the ancient world, the olive is still a basic element of Mediterranean cuisine, owing to its delicious flavor and high nutritional content. Poor villagers make a meal of a few olives, a cucumber or tomato, and a loaf of bread.

Although the meaty green, black, and purple fruits are ready to eat when scooped from the lustrous peaks heaped in the market, local customers like to add their own personal touch, a special dressing of fresh herbs and spice to season the olives.

Spicy hot and absolutely irresistible, these are perfect for the *mezzeh* table.

    1   rounded tbsp. minced onion
    3   tbsp. olive oil
  1/4   cup thinly sliced carrots, steamed for 5 minutes
  1/2   tsp. tomato paste
    1   tsp. minced lemon peel

1 small branch fresh thyme, or:
   pinch dried thyme

1/2 tsp. **Harissa Red Chili Paste** (p. 41)

1/2 cup brine from the olives

1 cup large green olives

1. Sauté the onion in the olive oil until soft and transparent. Add the steamed carrots, tomato paste, lemon peel, thyme, **harissa**, and half of the brine. Simmer for 5 minutes and remove from the fire.

2. Stir in the remaining brine and the olives. Cover and marinate in the refrigerator for at least 24 hours before serving.

Variation

Substitute pickled pearl onions for the sautéed onion in olive oil.

Cumin Peppered Mushrooms

Haraimi Fokaah (LIBYA, ANDALUSIA, ARAB STATES)

The modest subject of mushrooms evidences the vast physical and econopolitical diversity of the 21 Arab nations.

In Syria, a can of tiny Chinese mushrooms becomes a rare treat because it is available only through the services of a smuggler with government connections or one who has bribed the military officers guarding the border with Lebanon. In Saudi Arabia, however, not only are choice Chinese products available, and at one-third the stateside price, but French, Spanish, and American canned mushrooms crowd the supermarket shelves. And as if this bounty were insufficient, fresh mushrooms arrive twice a week by air from greenhouses located at one side of Amsterdam's Schiphol International Airport.

Libyan friends, on the other hand, tell me that mushrooms grow wild in their country, and they are an extraordinary treat in the early months of each new year. They also suggest that this recipe may be prepared using dried Oriental mushrooms.

8 ounces fresh mushrooms

2 tbsp. olive oil

4 cloves garlic, minced

1/2 tsp. cumin

1/8 tsp. red pepper

   salt

   black pepper

1. In a small frying pan, sauté the mushrooms in the olive oil for 5 minutes. Add the remaining ingredients and cook until the mushrooms are tender, about 3–5 minutes longer.

Variations

Lebanon and Andalusia: Substitute 2 tbsp. of minced parsley and lemon juice for the cumin.

Saudi Arabia: Add a minced tomato, 4 minced green onions, and *kebsa* spices.

Tartare Style Kibbeh

Kibbeh Neyeh (SYRIA, ARAB STATES)

Either you love this extraordinary appetizer or you don't. But if you prepare it, buy the freshest lean ground round, or have the butcher trim and grind a piece while you wait, and use equal amounts by weight of meat and dry *burghol*. As this dish is eaten without cooking, refrigerate and serve within a few hours.

1 cup medium or fine-grained **burghol**

1/2 small onion, minced

1/4 pound lean ground round of beef

   salt

   black pepper

   red pepper (optional), or:

   allspice (optional)

Garnish:

> sprigs parsley
> tomato wedges

1. Soak the *burghol* in water for 15 minutes. Drain and squeeze out the excess water. Set the moistened grain aside for 10 minutes.

2. Knead the *burghol* vigorously for 10 minutes, until it becomes doughy and cohesive. Incorporate the onion and continue to knead for 5 more minutes.

3. Knead in the meat until a smooth paste is formed, about 10 minutes. Add seasoning until the flavor is pleasing.

4. Shape into a flat cake that suits the dish in which the *kibbeh* will be served and garnish colorfully but modestly. (Leftovers can be baked or fried the following day.)

Variations

Kuwait, Saudi Arabia, Gulf States: Add cardamom and cinnamon.

Egypt: Add cumin.

Libyan Boorak with Two Cheeses

Boorak (LIBYA)

The texture of these crisp, fragile pastries is sheer enchantment. In Libya, the paper-thin dough for these cheese-filled triangles is usually purchased from a tiny specialty shop. In the United States, imported spring roll skins will produce the same delicate package. (The wonton and egg-roll doughs available in the produce section of most supermarkets are thick and heavy and therefore not recommended.)

This appetizer is almost as exciting when the filling is baked, Syrian style, on an open-faced yeast dough, as in the recipe for **Zatar Bread.**

1 package spring roll skins (approximately 8 inches square), defrosted

1 tbsp. flour

1 tbsp. water

oil for frying

Filling:

1 small egg, lightly beaten

1/4 pound feta cheese

2/3 cup low-fat ricotta or cottage cheese

1/3 cup minced parsley

1/2 tsp. cumin

1/2 tsp. thyme

1/4 tsp. oregano

1/4 tsp. **Harissa Red Chili Paste** (p. 41)

1. Combine the flour with the water. Combine the filling ingredients.

2. Cut each spring roll skin into 3 strips of equal width. (If the dough is not precisely square, use the slightly larger dimension for the length of the strip.) Lay out 3 or 4 strips on your work surface.

3. Place a rounded tsp. of the cheese mixture toward the bottom right-hand corner of each strip. Fold that corner diagonally over to the top left-hand corner, forming a triangle. As you fold, be certain that the side of the strip lines up perfectly with the folded portion. Continue as if folding a flag, alternately folding the bottom corners in a diagonal pattern. Seal the final flap with a bit of the flour paste.

4. Deep-fry and drain on absorbent paper.

5. Serve warm or at room temperature, with **Harissa Red Chili Paste**.

Variations

Libya: Omit the thyme and oregano.

Turkey: Use 3/4 pound feta cheese and 1/4 cup grated Kashkaval cheese, substituting 2 tbsp. fresh minced dill for the spices.

Lebanon: Use 1/2 pound feta cheese instead of two different cheeses, substituting 2 tbsp. fresh minced parsley for the spices.

Saudi Triangles with Meat Filling

Samboosak (SAUDI ARABIA)

From Saudi Arabia and the Gulf across to the Indian subcontinent, these flaky meat pies are eaten to break the Muslim fast every evening during the month of Ramadan. To the traditional meat stuffing of the northern Arab states are added leeks, boiled eggs, and regional spices.

- 1 package spring roll skins (approximately 8 inches square), defrosted
- 1 tbsp. flour
- 1 tbsp. water
  oil for frying

Filling:
- 1 small onion, minced
- 1 leek, cleaned and chopped
- 2 tbsp. olive oil
- 1/2 pound ground beef or lamb
  salt
  black pepper
- 1/2 tsp. cumin or **kebsa** spices
- 2 egg whites, hard-boiled and chopped
  oil for frying

1. Sauté the onions and leek in the oil until transparent. Add the meat, sprinkle with salt and pepper, and cook until done, breaking up lumps.

2. Add the cumin and the chopped egg whites and mix well.

3. Shape and fry as in the preceding recipe for **Libyan Boorak with Two Cheeses**.

Variations

Saudi Arabia, the Gulf States: Add toasted pine nuts to the filling.

Syria, Lebanon, Palestine, Jordan: Omit the leeks and eggs; substitute allspice for the cumin or *kebsa* spices.

Baghdadi Crepes with Meat Filling

Boorak (IRAQ)

The filling of this meat pastry is the flavorful Fertile Crescent standard of ground meat steamed with spices and tossed with fresh parsley and minced green onions. But its packaging is extraordinary: an uncommon dough akin to French crepes that is rolled up in the fashion of a large Chinese egg roll.

Crepes:

- 2 eggs
- ²/₃ cup flour
- 1 cup low-fat milk
- salt

Meat filling:

- ¹/₄ pound ground beef
- 2 tbsp. olive oil
- salt
- black pepper
- ¹/₄ tsp. allspice or **kebsa** spices
- ¹/₄ cup minced parsley
- 2 green onions, minced
- oil for frying

1. Whirl the crepe ingredients in a blender or food processor until smooth. Set aside for at least 1 hour.

2. For the filling, sauté the ground beef in the oil, sprinkling with salt and black pepper. Stir to break up all lumps. When the meat is cooked, drain off the fat in a sieve. Toss with the remaining ingredients.

3. Brush an 8–10-inch nonstick skillet lightly with a bit of oil. When it is hot, pour some batter into the center of the pan. Tip the pan around to spread the batter over the surface. Cook about 30 seconds and flip to cook the other side for 15–20 seconds. Repeat until all the crepes are done.

4. To form the rolls, place several crepes on your work surface, bubbly side up. Put about 2 rounded tablespoons of filling on the lower half of each crepe. Fold the bottom edge up, and the left and right edges over toward the middle, thus closing three sides of the package. Roll up like an egg roll. Repeat the process with the remaining crepes.

5. Heat oil for frying in a skillet. Transfer the rolls to the skillet, lightly sauté them until golden crisp, and drain on paper towels.

Spinach Pies

Fatayr (ARAB STATES)

In the Levant, exquisite pies filled with meat, cheese, or spinach are a product of commercial ovens. Rarely served at home except on special occasions when a massive amount is ordered from a bakery, they are among my family's very favorite dishes.

Housewives in the Gulf States have available from Western-style supermarkets all sorts of frozen dough (both imported and local) from which to prepare these and other traditional pastries. Different effects are obtained by using puff pastry, *filo*, short-crust dough, or yeast (pizza) dough.

Here in the United States, many Arab women select the ordinary biscuit doughs available in tubes from the dairy case, but I find these completely unacceptable in flavor and texture and totally dissimilar to the original Middle Eastern doughs.

I've experimented with frozen yeast dough (Parker House-style rolls) and frozen bread dough, and in a pinch, I'll even use the ready-to-use pizza dough sold in tubes. But I highly recommend the yeast-based prepared mix for rolls and pizza, packaged under various names and labels and marketed in a box next to your supermarket's cake mixes. It's so easy that my children ready the dough while I'm combining the filling ingredients. The texture is smooth and light with a polished surface, making it ideal for these triangular spinach pies and most Middle Eastern savory pastries.

1 package (16 oz.) quick-rise roll mix

Filling:
2 tbsp. olive oil
2 tbsp. pine nuts

1 onion, chopped

²/₃ bunch spinach

1 tsp. water

salt

2 tsp. sumac

juice of ¹/₂ lemon

1. Prepare the dough according to package instructions and set aside to rise.

2. Heat the olive oil almost to smoking and toss in the pine nuts. Immediately remove from the heat. Stir occasionally until the nuts are evenly browned. Remove with a slotted spoon.

3. Add the onion to the oil and sauté until soft and transparent.

4. Rinse the spinach and coarsely chop the leaves. Discard the stems or save them to be added to a salad or a pilaf. Add the spinach leaves to the onion, along with the water. Cover and steam for about 5 minutes, until leaves are wilted, stirring frequently so that they do not stick to the pan. If any liquid remains in the pan, raise the heat cautiously to dry it up.

5. Stir in the reserved pine nuts, the salt, sumac, and lemon juice. Taste and adjust seasoning.

6. Shape the dough into lemon-sized balls. Roll out each ball on a floured board.

7. Spoon about one rounded tbsp. of the filling on the center of each round of dough. Draw up the three sides of the round to the center and pinch them tight, forming a rounded triangle. Cover with a cloth and let rise in a warm place for about 30 minutes.

8. Preheat oven to 350 degrees.

9. Bake about 12–15 minutes, or until golden brown.

Variations

Lebanon: Add crumbled feta cheese to the spinach filling.

Andalusia: Add raisins to the spinach filling.

Zatar Bread

Manaeesh (LEBANON, ARAB STATES)

~~~~~~

My children loved to escape from the desert sun in one of Al Khobar's juice shops, sipping from tall glasses of fresh orange juice served over crushed ice, and staring with amazement as their order of *manaeesh* was popped into the roaring open oven. In its original form this savory pastry looks rather like a small pizza minus the cheese. Actually, the topping is nothing more than olive oil with a generous sprinkling of a special spice mixture known as **zatar**.

Don't confuse this term with the same word that refers to the thyme plant that grows wild over the dry hills of the northern Arab regions. **Zatar** from Syria or Lebanon, sold in 1-pound bags in import groceries, is a mixture of four to six spices, including thyme, sesame seeds, and sumac. Use it as is, or add the optional spices I've listed below.

1   package (16 oz.) quick-rise roll mix

Topping:

2   tbsp. olive oil

2   tbsp. **zatar** spice mixture

½   tsp. sumac (optional)

½   tsp. red pepper (optional)

1   tbsp. lemon juice (optional)

1. Prepare the dough according to package instructions and set aside to rise.

2. Preheat the oven to 400 degrees.

3. Roll dough into circles. (They can be individual snack-sized or as large as a flat loaf of Arabic bread.)

4. Transfer the circles to greased baking sheets. Combine the topping ingredients and brush the mixture onto the dough.

5. Bake for 8–10 minutes.

Grape Leaves with Sweet Herbs and Olive Oil

Zaytinagly Yaprak Dolmasi (TURKEY)

Grape vines are defoliated early in the season to expose the grape clusters to the sunshine. Of course, in this region no food product is ever wasted, and from this humble origin are derived some of the most memorable dishes of the Middle Eastern table. The leaves are rolled and stuffed with rice, or pickled for use later in the year. Tender fresh leaves are softened by soaking in warm water for about 10 minutes, while tougher leaves require blanching in boiling salted water for 5 minutes. Commercially pickled grape leaves need only be rinsed.

This fragrant dolma recipe bears a suggestion of sweetness from currants, allspice, and fresh herbs, a light fruity touch still evident in cuisines from the western (Andalusia and Morocco) and far eastern (Turkey, Iraq, and Iran) edges of the old Islamic empire. Prepared with olive oil, it should be served slightly chilled or at room temperature, with a side dish of yoghurt.

Meatless grape leaves are best when made a day in advance, which is one of the reasons they are ideal as an appetizer or for a dinner buffet. The Lebanese and Syrians are fond of a grape-leaf appetizer filled with chickpeas, rice, and fresh vegetables, but I think it wanes in comparison to this sensuous temptation from the Seraglio.

   1 jar (10 oz.) grape leaves
   1 large ripe tomato, sliced
   2 cups water
      salt
      juice of 1/2 lemon
1/4 cup olive oil

Stuffing:
   2 onions, finely chopped
1/2 cup olive oil
   3 tbsp. pine nuts
   1 cup short-grained Egyptian rice, soaked in hot water for at least 2 hours
   1 cup water

1 large ripe tomato, chopped

2 tbsp. currants

juice of $\frac{1}{2}$ lemon

salt

black pepper

$\frac{1}{2}$ tsp. allspice

$\frac{1}{2}$ tsp. sugar

1 tbsp. crushed dried mint, or:

$\frac{1}{4}$ cup minced fresh mint

$\frac{1}{2}$ cup minced parsley

1. Carefully unfold the grape leaves and soak in water to remove the sour pickling liquid. Change the water at least once, gently moving the leaves to rinse thoroughly. Drain.

2. For the stuffing, sauté the onions in the $\frac{1}{2}$ cup olive oil with the pine nuts for about 5 minutes. Add the drained rice and cook for about 5 minutes, stirring to keep it from sticking. Stir in 1 cup water, chopped tomato, currants, juice of $\frac{1}{2}$ lemon, salt, pepper, allspice, and sugar. Cover and simmer for 10 minutes. (The rice will be partially cooked.) Gently stir in the mint and parsley.

3. Line the bottom of a large saucepan with the sliced tomato, which will protect the leaves from sticking and discoloring.

4. To stuff a grape leaf, place it on a tray with the dull side facing you and the stem down to the 6 o'clock position. Pinch off the stem. Place a tsp. of stuffing in the lower third of the leaf and squeeze it into a tubular shape. Fold the stem part of the leaf over the filling. Then fold each of the sides over to encase the filling. Roll tightly away from you toward the pointed end of the leaf. A normal-sized leaf will roll into a cylinder about $2\frac{1}{2}$ inches long; a large leaf will be longer but of equal diameter.

5. As each leaf is stuffed, place it in the pan, seam side down. Arrange the leaves in neatly layered rows.

6. Place an inverted plate or two over the leaves and weight down with a smooth stone reserved for this purpose, a weight, or a pottery bowl filled with water. Very carefully pour on water to cover. Add salt, juice of $\frac{1}{2}$ lemon, and $\frac{1}{4}$ cup olive oil, and bring to a boil. If the plate floats up, the weight is not sufficiently heavy, and the rolled leaves may begin to unroll. Cover, reduce heat, and simmer for $\frac{1}{2}$ hour.

7. Immediately pour off the liquid and cover the pot with a large dish or a round serving platter. Flip upside down to release the grape leaves. The tomato slices are usually removed and discarded.

8. Serve at room temperature or slightly chilled, with yoghurt.

Stuffed Grape Leaves with Meat

Dolma Yalanchi (ARMENIA)

This is my favorite recipe for grape leaves, with a simple flavorful filling of meat and rice. For a family supper or as one of many dishes on a party buffet, it's best when presented steaming hot. Most restaurants offer only meatless Turkish or Lebanese versions cooked in olive oil, which are easier to serve cold, so it's not well known in this country.

In the Middle East meat is used sparingly and it's nearly invisible in this stuffing, but the lingering flavors of garlic and red pepper will keep it from being missed. Of course, you may add more beef if you prefer a meatier dish.

If you have never before tried your hand at rolling grape leaves, this recipe is the one with which to begin. Just decrease the specified amount of rice and increase the ground beef until you have a cohesive, sticky mixture that is easy to work with. Slowly adjust the proportions each time you prepare this dish, until you are comfortable with a mixture that is mostly rice.

 1 jar (10 oz.) grape leaves
10 to 20 cloves garlic
    water
    salt
 3 tbsp. butter, or:
    olive oil
    juice of 1 lemon

Stuffing:
 1 cup short-grained rice, rinsed
1/4 pound ground beef
 1 tsp. garlic powder

salt

1 rounded tbsp. tomato paste

1/2 tsp. sweet paprika, or:

red pepper

1/2 small onion, finely minced

1. Prepare the grape leaves as in step 1 of the preceding recipe.

2. Knead together the stuffing ingredients.

3. Stuff the grape leaves as in step 4 of the preceding recipe.

4. As each leaf is stuffed, place it, seam side down, in a large saucepan. (The bottom of the pan may be lined with extra grape leaves, a row of tomato slices, or lamb bones, to protect the first row of leaves from scorching.) Arrange the leaves in nearly layered rows and insert the garlic cloves between them.

5. Place an inverted plate or two over the leaves and weight it down with a smooth stone reserved for this purpose, a weight, or a pottery bowl filled with water. Very carefully pour on water to cover. Add salt, butter or olive oil, and lemon juice, and bring to a boil. (If the plate floats up, the weight is not sufficiently heavy, and the rolled leaves may begin to unroll.) Cover, reduce heat, and simmer for 1 hour. As the water is absorbed, the leaves must remain covered with liquid. Pour on additional water as necessary.

6. When the cooking time is complete, sample one of the grape leaves to ascertain that the rice stuffing is completely cooked. If it is still a bit chewy, simmer for 5 or 10 more minutes.

7. As soon as the grape leaves are done, immediately pour off the liquid. Cover the pot with a large dish or a round serving platter and flip upside down to release the grape leaves. Serve warm.

Variations

Kurdistan: Omit the garlic; add 1 large rib of celery (minced), 2 minced green onions, 1 small minced tomato, and 1 tsp. *kebsa* spices or *garam masala*.

Syria: Omit the garlic; substitute cinnamon and allspice for the red pepper; add 1 ripe minced tomato and 1/4 cup minced parsley.

Iraq: Omit the garlic; substitute turmeric for the red pepper; add 1 ripe minced tomato, $1/4$ cup parsley, and 1 tsp. tamarind paste.

Mixed Vegetable Pickles

Mhellal (PALESTINE, ARAB STATES)

A crunchy melange of pickles, called *turshi* or *mhellal,* is a must for every *mezzeh* or buffet table. As with most other Arab dishes, there are no hard-and-set rules to making Middle Eastern pickles, and every household treasures its own traditional combination of spices and brine. Try your hand at pickling carrots, green tomatoes, cauliflower, zucchini or *koosa*, green beans, or even fresh thyme branches and grape leaves. Chunks of eggplant, celery, and cabbage are also delicious.

   3 cups water
   3 tbsp. pickling salt
$1/3$ cup wine vinegar, or:
   8 fresh grape leaves
   2 pounds small cucumbers or a combination of pickling vegetables, as
      described above
   2 to 4 cloves garlic
   5 black peppercorns
   1 or 2 serrano or jalapeño chilis

1. Dissolve the pickling salt in the water and add the vinegar. (Some cooks add the salt to boiled water.) Fresh grape leaves snipped from a vine add an equally sour flavor and can be used instead of vinegar; place the leaves on top of the vegetables at step 3.

2. Scrub and prepare the cucumbers or other vegetables, trimming off the stems. Peel carrots and turnips and cut into wedges or thick slices.

3. Clean the jars in very hot water and pack them with vegetables and seasoning ingredients, pouring on sufficient brine to cover completely. Cap tightly and refrigerate. Turnips, cabbage, and cauliflower can be eaten in less than a week, but cucumbers require at least 2–3 weeks.

Variation

For pickled turnips, use 1 pound peeled, cut up turnips and 2 small raw or cooked beets.

Kurdish Mixed Pickles

Torshi (KURDISTAN)

A striking combination from my friend Basna (see p. 294), these pickles are especially colorful and contain no salt.

- 1 pound cauliflower florets, broken into small pieces
- 1 pound cabbage, shredded $1/3$–$1/2$ inch wide and up to 2 inches long
- 1 pound carrots, pared and cut into thin rounds
- 5 black peppercorns
- 1 serrano chili (optional)
  about 3 cups apple cider vinegar

Clean the jars in very hot water and pack them with the vegetables, peppercorns, and optional serrano chili. Pour on sufficient vinegar to cover completely. Cap tightly and refrigerate for about a week before serving.

Mixed Nuts

Mukassaraat (ARAB STATES)

One of the numerous symbols of Arabian hospitality, combinations of nuts are set out to honor the guests while the food is being prepared. These mixtures are usually purchased from the nut and candy section of the spice souk, where each vendor offers his own flavorful spice combination. A wealthy family would serve only the finest quality large plump roasted nuts, while in a working-class home the humble blend of seeds might not include any of the more expensive items.

Prudent Middle Eastern housewives frugally save watermelon and pumpkin seeds, spreading them out on trays on their sunny flat roofs to dry until a sufficient quantity has been accumulated. Then they are roasted and stored in glass jars until needed.

The quantities in this recipe are approximate; as with most Middle Eastern dishes, you can increase the measure of your favorite ingredients or omit those you don't favor.

> 1 cup chickpeas, soaked overnight and drained
> 1/2 cup watermelon seeds
> 1/2 cup pumpkin seeds in their shells
> 2 tbsp. olive oil
>   salt
>   black pepper
> 1 tsp. red pepper
> 1 tsp. cumin or sweet paprika
> 1/2 cup almonds, not blanched
> 1 cup green pistachios in their shells

1. Toast the chickpeas on an ungreased baking sheet in a 350-degree oven for 20 minutes. If the watermelon and pumpkin seeds are untoasted (that is, if you have saved them from a previous summer or Thanksgiving feast), they should be added to the chickpeas after about 10 minutes.

2. Combine the olive oil, salt, black and red peppers, and cumin. Toss the chickpeas, seeds, almonds, and pistachios in this mixture and spread on the baking sheet.

3. Return to the oven, and roast the mixture for about 10 minutes, stirring and redistributing every 7–10 minutes so that it does not burn.

Salads

Jt's no surprise that in Arabic cookbooks the lines between salads, *mezzeh* appetizers, dips, and vegetable dishes overlap. Their array of fresh ingredients is nearly unlimited: crisp herbs and greens, flavorful ripe vegetables, legumes, and seafood, even juicy oranges and lemons. Virtually any type of produce, legume, or seafood, it seems, may be cut up and steamed with spices and the Mediterranean's cherished olive oil, or mashed and dressed with lemon and olive oil. Only the finest beets, potatoes, carrots, or green beans will do for these unexpectedly appealing cooked salads.

The most common *salata*, the prime choice across the twenty-one countries of the Arab world, is nearly identical to the honest peasant dish my Italian mother prepared every hot summer day from vegetables just snipped from their vines: crisp, tender cucumbers, tomatoes still warm from the sun's caress, and green peppers, moistened with a light vinaigrette and a touch of herbs. Of course, the regional variations are many: In Morocco these vegetables may have been roasted, while in neighboring Libya and Egypt radishes are added. Palestinians tend to mince their salad vegetables; Saudis add a zesty green chili.

The usual dressing of finest-quality virgin olive oil blended with a little vinegar or lemon juice varies across the region only in the addition of fresh herbs (parsley, purslane, mint, cilantro) and spices. In Lebanon, with its eminent European influence, *tahini* or yoghurt may flavor the classic vinaigrette, while in North Africa the seasonings are more fragrantly evocative: garlic, cumin, sweet and hot red peppers, and pungent herbs. Commercially prepared dressings are available only in the wealthy Gulf States, and the high-calorie ingredients common to many of our popular dressings are unknown.

In winter, when seasonal vegetables are expensive or unavailable, beans are slowly simmered and moistened with herbed dressings. Some of these are substantial and nutritious enough to serve as a complete meal: fava bean salad, the national dish of Egypt, is even enjoyed for breakfast. The rich brown beans, which used to be cooked all night in a large clay pot, are now available in cans as well as dried. My favorite Turkish salad is no more than a platter of shredded romaine wearing a coronet of tiny white beans. Lentils or hearty chickpeas, liberally marinated in a tangy red pepper dressing, are other economical and healthy additions to a family meal, yet tasty enough to honor a guest.

In recent years, the greatest of all Arab salads has become increasingly popular with gourmets as well as health-food advocates. **Tabbooleh** juxtaposes nutritious and intensely aromatic minced parsley with an equal amount of small-grain *burghol*, a crushed wheat grain high in fiber. As **Tabbooleh**'s texture and flavor never fail to charm family and visitors, the Middle Eastern wife prepares it to judiciously soothe egos affronted in a domestic squabble, as well as for every sumptuous holiday feast.

Fettoosh Salad also holds a special appeal for Americans because of its similarity to our mixed green salad. Ribbons of lettuce are tossed in a light olive oil vinaigrette dressing with tomatoes and cucumbers, garlic, and fresh herbs. Crisp bites of toasted Arabic bread, the original crouton, add an excitingly different element to the dish.

Some Middle Eastern salads, looking more like dips, appear in the preceding *Mezzeh* section. Others are vegetable-based but lack the familiar dressing and seem to belong in the Vegetables chapter. And when no other salad is available, the Arab hostess will simply slice some tomatoes and sprinkle them with herbs, feta cheese, or lemon salt, or set out small dishes of crudités or pickles.

A Christian neighbor in our village showed me the light lunch of delicious leftover **Kibbeh** she had set out for her hurried husband, with a small mound of glistening olives on a miniature oval tray, alongside a larger metal oval laden with fresh thyme branches, crisp green onions, and velvety purslane. "If you loved it when it was freshly picked from the garden," she recommended, quoting a famous proverb, "you'll like it even more when it comes in from the kitchen!"

In the Western world, the word "salad" is usually synonomous with "lettuce," suggesting a bowl of fresh greens coated with a smooth, creamy dressing. I quickly grasped this fact one day in Jeddah when my Dutch neighbor noticed me throwing on my black veils to walk over to Happy Family Supermarket. "Bring me some salad," she called across the low wall that divided our identical houses.

In contrast, lettuce is the least important element of a Mediterranean salad. In the Arab world, romaine leaves may be trimmed and nibbled on, or used to scoop up **Tabbooleh** or a mixed vegetable salad, but a plate of dressed mixed lettuce would be simply preposterous.

Where vast quantities of wholesome vegetables and greens are served alongside hardy grains and legumes at every meal, one's eye focuses naturally on the sun-drenched main dishes bursting with passionate flavors. The wonderful variety of delicious salads are pleasant side dishes intended to complement and enhance the main dish, but not to precede it. And because the entire Mediterranean menu is nutritious and well-balanced, there is no need to rely on this one dish for healthy eating.

In the villages there are few set rules for these extraordinary yet rustic salads, which are often thrown together at the last minute from whatever greens or vegetables happen to be on hand. There are no strictly marked culinary boundaries here, so don't feel bound to use the suggested dressing each time you prepare a favorite salad. And remember that the following salad recipes are offered merely as guidelines, examples of the nearly limitless possibilities you can look forward to exploring.

Tabbooleh

Tabbooleh (SYRIA, LEBANON, ARAB STATES)

~~~~~~

This unique salad, rich with fresh spring parsley and the first green onions of the season, is the Arab dish most widely known in this country: fluffy morsels of *burghol*, a crushed parboiled wheat, tossed in a penetrating minty lemon dressing with bits of juicy red tomatoes and minced parsley.

Avoid the deli department facsimiles and supermarket plastic packages of something labeled "Tabbouleh Mix." A plate of glistening, refreshing **Tabbooleh** requires only 10 minutes of preparation, and the resulting compliments will resound in your ears all evening. Just remember to use fine-grain *burghol* and to be sure that the wheat is at least equal in proportion to the minced parsley. Traditional Arab flat-leafed parsley (often labeled "Italian" parsley here) is more flavorful than our curly American variety, but may be more expensive and difficult to find. The widely available standard variety is an acceptable substitute and can even be minced in the food processor.

If you wish, you may increase the quantity of parsley listed below, as some Lebanese restaurateurs do, to as much as 9 parts to 1 part wheat. Personally, I envision the perfect **Tabbooleh** as one in which parsley's sweetness and bracing aroma is equally balanced by the nutty earthiness of *burghol*.

3/4 cup fine-grain **burghol**

  3 cups finely minced fresh parsley

  2 to 3 tomatoes, chopped

  4 to 5 green onions, minced

 15 fresh mint leaves, chopped, or:

  1 tbsp. dried mint

Classic Lemon Vinaigrette: (double recipe, p. 86)

1. Rinse the *burghol* several times and cover with about 2 or 3 times as much water. Set aside to soak.

2. The parsley should be relatively dry before it is minced, and it must be chopped very fine. I merely soak the bunches briefly in a large quantity of water and repeat the step as necessary, inspecting carefully until the

water is clear. Give each bunch a vigorous shake to remove excess water. (My husband believes that I should separate the stems and pinch off each individual leaf before rinsing.) American (curly-leafed) parsley can be minced in a food processor if it is done in moderate quantities and not overprocessed. In the Middle East a large wooden cutting board and sharp chopping knife are required because the flat-leaf parsley grown in the region is easily bruised by the food processor.

3. Squeeze the water out of the *burghol* by handfuls and combine with the parsley and remaining ingredients.

4. Pour on the lemon dressing (vinegar is not used for **Tabbooleh**) and mix well. American parsley requires more dressing than flat-leafed Arab parsley, so be sure the salad is moist with vinaigrette. This dish is best when prepared about an hour in advance so that the wheat and parsley can absorb the dressing; the onion flavor will intensify and unbalance the flavors if the **Tabbooleh** is more than 4 or 5 hours old.

5. Arabs frequently serve this salad on a platter with an accompanying small tray heaped with the crisp inner leaves of romaine. The lettuce is used as a spoon to scoop up the salad from the serving dish.

Fettoosh Salad

Fettoosh (SYRIA, LEBANON, ARAB STATES)

A meal without bread is unthinkable for the Arabs, who consume large quantities of flat bread every day. Arabian cuisine abounds with delicious recipes like this one that are designed to use excess scraps of bread as well as the leftover pulp of vegetables that have been hollowed out and stuffed with rice and meat.

Lettuce is not an essential part of this vegetable salad with its added Arab "croutons" and tangy sumac dressing. If you wish to include it, be sure to use romaine, whose firm texture balances the juicy flesh of the ripe tomatoes and cucumbers.

2 cups romaine lettuce, torn into small pieces or cut into ribbons

2 tomatoes

2 small cucumbers, peeled

1 green pepper

3 green onions, minced

15 mint leaves, chopped, or:

1 tbsp. dried mint

1/4 cup chopped parsley

2 tbsp. chopped purslane or chickweed (optional)

1 to 2 cups Arabic bread, torn into pieces

Classic Lemon Vinaigrette: (double recipe, p. 86) with added:

1 to 2 tbsp. sumac

1. Cut the vegetables into pieces of relatively similar size. Occasionally, a cook may coarsely dice them, but usually they are of standard bite size.

2. If no dry bread is on hand, split loaves of Arab bread by separating the top and bottom of the "pocket," and crisp in a microwave or regular oven. (You may place the pieces of bread in a plastic bag, sprinkle with drops of olive oil, and shake well before baking.)

3. Prepare the dressing with the added sumac and toss all ingredients in a salad bowl.

Variation

Add 1–2 tbsp. *hamod er rummaan* pomegranate syrup to the dressing.

Shepherd's Vegetable Salad with White Cheese

Salatet Khodar (PALESTINE)

This humble dish is a salad lover's dream, as rich and exciting as **Tabbooleh**, a vivid palette of warm Mediterranean hues. Lebanese and Greek restaurateurs in the United States have adjusted to local tastes by serving this traditional combination of vegetables, cheese, olives, and fresh herbs on a bed of crunchy romaine leaves, and I can't say that I mind in the least!

It is worth a special trip to an import food store to look for a fine Bulgarian or creamy Greek feta. You may also find other types of defatted white Arab cheeses, all of which are concentrated sources of energy and rich in protein. For variety, after the salad has been scented with garlic and olive oil, distribute it onto 4 or 5 salad plates, and dress each plate with a light halo of white cheese that you have pressed through a coarse sieve.

- 4　cups romaine lettuce, torn into small pieces or cut into ribbons
- 1　tomato, cut into wedges
- 1　green pepper, sliced into rings
- 1　cucumber, peeled and sliced
- 1/2　serrano chili, seeded and minced
- 2　green onions, chopped
- 1/4　cup minced fresh parsley

Classic Lemon Vinaigrette: (p. 86)

Garnish:
- 12　purple or black Middle Eastern olives
- 1/2　cup feta cheese (or other white Middle Eastern cheese), crumbled
- 4　radishes, partially peeled in attractive strips or carved into flowers

1. Toss the salad ingredients with the dressing.

2. Arrange the salad on serving plates and top each with olives and feta cheese. Garnish with a radish.

Variation

Andalusia: Use green olives and substitute minced hard-boiled eggs for the feta cheese.

Vegetable Toss Salad

Salatet Khodar (ARAB STATES)

Across the Arab world, this colorful and endearing peasant salad is the one served nearly every day. Because it is so popular, innumerable regional variations for *Salata* introduce fresh textures and flavors. Palestinians, Kurds, and southern Arabs of the Arabian peninsula and the Gulf States usually prefer it coarsely chopped rather than cut into bite-sized pieces. When lettuce is available, a small amount of romaine may be added, but it's not essential.

- 2 cucumbers, peeled
- 2 large tomatoes
- 2 green peppers (optional)
- 3/4 cup chopped parsley

Classic Lemon Vinaigrette: (p. 86) prepared with added:
- 3/4 tsp. dried mint

1. Peel the cucumbers and cut into rings. Some cooks cut the rings into halves or quarters.

2. Wash the tomatoes and cut into bite-sized pieces.

3. Toss the vegetables with the parsley and the dressing.

Variations

Syria: Add 2 cups torn or shredded romaine lettuce.

Libya: Substitute radish wedges for the cucumbers.

Morocco: Substitute green olives for the cucumbers, or substitute hard-boiled eggs for the tomatoes.

Tunisia: Omit the tomatoes and parsley; dress only with lime juice.

Saudi Arabia: Substitute cumin for the mint; use only tomatoes and onions.

Egypt: Substitute **Yoghurt Dressing** (p. 88) for the **Classic Lemon Vinaigrette**.

Andalusia: Add several cut up anchovy fillets.

Tomato and Roasted Pepper Salad

Mishweeyeh (MOROCCO)

Tangy with cumin and red pepper, this vibrant salad is as dazzling and intense as the Mediterranean sun, and boasts a high fiber content and more vitamin C than oranges. Food historian Paula Wolfert believes that it must be the origin of Spanish gazpacho.

In North Africa, salad vegetables are frequently parboiled or lightly roasted over the cooking fire. Exposing the peppers to the flame softens the flesh, heightens the flavor, and imparts a subtle smokiness that many Americans recognize in the eggplant dip known as *baba ghanooj*.

- 3 large green peppers
- 3 large firm tomatoes

Picante Vinaigrette with Herbs: (p. 87), prepared with wine vinegar

Garnish:

   minced parsley

1. I prefer to grill the peppers under the broiler, about 1 inch from the heat. Placing each pepper directly between two parallel heating elements ensures even charring. As the surface blisters and turns black, rotate the peppers until tops, bottoms, and all sides are rather evenly cooked. (If you own a gas stove you can do this directly on the burner.) Remove from the flame and plunge into cool water. Under running water, rub off the charred skin. (Some cooks recommend leaving the peppers for 10 minutes in a paper bag to facilitate this step.) Remove the seeds. Cut peppers into pieces about 1 inch square.

2. Prepare a pot of boiling water and drop in the tomatoes. Cook for 1–2 minutes, then transfer to a bowl of cold water. Remove the tomato skins and cube the flesh. (Some cooks omit this step, while others roast the tomatoes over a flame and peel them.)

3. Add the vegetables to the dressing and gently toss. Marinate for at least 1 hour. Serve chilled or at room temperature. Garnish with parsley.

Variations

Armenia: Add red pepper and cumin.

Saudi Arabia: Roast a serrano chili with the green peppers; add $1/3$ cup minced cilantro.

Morocco: Garnish with the minced peel of $1/2$ preserved lemon (see p. 85).

Egypt: Add 3 minced green onions.

Sliced Tomato Salad

Salatet Benadora (KURDISTAN, IRAQ, ARMENIA, SAUDI ARABIA)

With a sprig of parsley or mint and a few sprinkles of white feta or Halloomi cheese, a plate of sliced tomatoes adds a spirited accent to any meal. Across the Mediterranean, this simple earthy food graces linen-robed tables as well as plastic sheets spread on the floor. The following version was shared with me by Um Khalil, a beautiful Kurdish mother of eight children.

    4 large tomatoes, sliced
       lemon salt, or:
       lemon juice plus salt
       curly lettuce leaves (optional)

Garnish (optional):
       feta cheese, crumbled
       parsley or mint sprigs
       onion rings
       green onions, chopped

1. Arrange the tomatoes attractively on several small plates and sprinkle with the lemon salt (or lemon juice and salt). For additional color you may display the tomatoes on leaves of curly lettuce.

2. Um Khalil does not garnish this dish, but a garnish of cheese and sprigs of mint or parsley contrasts nicely with the intense red of the tomatoes. My Saudi friends scatter thinly sliced onion rings or bits of green onion over the tomatoes.

Cucumber Yoghurt Salad

Salatet Leban (ARAB STATES)

This classic yoghurt salad with its understated minty flavor and soothing mildness is also a basic element of cuisine in Iran, Afghanistan, and on eastward into Pakistan and India. A required side dish with many Middle Eastern entrées, it is a favorite because the ingredients are few and are always on hand. Especially popular with children, and a health food for the elderly of the region, **Cucumber Yoghurt Salad** is also easy to throw together in a minute.

Which is precisely what I did one Arabian Friday just before the midday prayer, when we were suddenly favored by the unplanned visit of no less than eight Syrian truck drivers. They were cousins, of course, and wouldn't have dreamed of intruding on a weekday when they might have caught me alone at home. But on Friday, the Muslim sabbath, they knew that my husband Ma'Amun would be available. Having just finished unloading their cargoes of fresh vegetables in Jeddah, they brought us news from the village before turning northward for the hot and dusty three-day return trip through the desert.

What did one serve an army of hungry men when there was little on hand and all local markets were closed?

A huge bowl of this refreshing yoghurt salad, of course, with lots of fresh fruit, and crisp homemade pickles, plates of **Sliced Tomato Salad**, plus the usual olives and cheese that were the mainstay of every morning and evening meal…and 10 garlicky grilled chickens Ma'Amun picked up from a modest fast-food establishment on the seaside corniche. I recall being so nervous and uncertain about the parameters of modest behavior and the challenge of traditional Arab hospitality that I accidentally dumped at least half a cup of mint in the yoghurt!

  2 cucumbers, peeled and diced

2¹/₂ cups low-fat yoghurt

  2 cloves garlic, crushed with salt

  2 tsp. dried mint

Combine all ingredients and stir to blend well. Served slightly chilled.

Sultan's Salad with White Beans

Fasooliye Peeyazuh (TURKEY, ARMENIA, SAUDI ARABIA, ARAB STATES)

This salad was one of the specialties of our favorite Istanbul restaurant, situated across from the Sultan Ahmet (Blue) Mosque. It's very similar to the ordinary American dinner salad, but with a topping of delicate white beans. In Turkish restaurants, the dressing and aromatic Middle Eastern red pepper are usually served separately, so that each person sprinkles the desired amount over his or her salad. A plate of crisp mildly hot peppers, long and pale green like slender Anaheim chilis, finishes off the first course.

To be quite honest, when dishes require a small quantity of beans, I simply don't think it's worth the bother to cook them from scratch. The slightly reduced cost does not seem to justify the energy required to soak and simmer the cup of beans to adorn this salad. Of course, throughout the Mediterranean states, where quantities of food are always more than ample and 10 or 15 relatives and friends may gather around the dinner table, it is both practical and economical to begin with dried beans.

> 4 cups romaine lettuce, cut into ribbons
> 1/4 cup minced parsley
> 1 cup cooked navy or cream beans, or other small white beans
> (to taste) Middle Eastern red pepper
> 1 tomato, cut into wedges or minced

Classic Lemon Vinaigrette: (p. 86)

Garnish:
> 2 hard-boiled eggs, sliced (optional)
> purple or black Middle Eastern olives

1. Just before serving, toss the lettuce and parsley with half the dressing. Arrange the greens on salad plates.

2. Toss the beans with the remaining vinaigrette and distribute evenly in the center of the individual salad plates lined with shredded lettuce. Sprinkle with red pepper.

3. Arrange the tomato artistically on each plate. Garnish with egg and olives and serve with a dish of fresh mild chilis.

Variations

Armenia: Add 1 chopped green pepper and 2 minced green onions.

Saudi Arabia: Substitute cilantro for parsley.

Two Bean Salad

Salatet Fool (EGYPT, SYRIA, LEBANON)

This is a variation from the northern Arabs on the famous Egyptian *Fool Mdammas* prepared with the rich dark fava beans so popular in the Nile delta. Throughout the early and midmornings, shopkeepers of the Damascus and Amman souks send their young sons or assistants out for paper bowls of this nutritious steaming breakfast. Drained of its rich cooking liquid, *foul* is transformed into an exciting salad when other vegetables and dressing are added.

1³/₄ cups cooked **foul** (fava) beans

1 cup cooked chickpeas

4 green onions, minced

2 tomatoes, chopped

1 cup minced parsley

Classic Lemon Vinaigrette: (p. 86) prepared with added:

2 cloves crushed garlic

1 tsp. cumin

1. Heat the beans in their liquid, either on the stovetop or in a microwave. (Warm beans will absorb the dressing more thoroughly.) Drain and rinse with hot water.

2. Toss the beans with the remaining ingredients and the dressing.

Baleela

Baleela (SAUDI ARABIA)

We first encountered this bean salad one sunset as we strolled barefooted along Jeddah's corniche, watching the huge red sun suddenly drop into the sea. Our young son dashed ahead, laughing, teasing the waves that pounded against the rocks and splattered us with foam.

In the far distance a lonely figure advanced rapidly, straining to push his big-wheeled cart through the sand. Scarcely taller than his wagon, the Yemeni sported a fluorescent green *kaffiyeh* headdress with hot-pink fringe tied into a rakish turban. *"Baleelaaaah!"* he chanted, and our mouths and eyes began to water at the thought of tender warm chickpeas with their exquisite splashes of vinegar and fiery *shata* dressing.

He filled each plastic cup with a ladle of plump peas drawn up from the cavernous depths of the pear-shaped bean pot, and sprinkled on the requested quantity of *shata* and garnishes. The sensuous delight of that tropical evening comes to mind every time I make this dish.

1¼ cups chickpeas, soaked overnight, or:

- 2 (14–16 oz.) cans chick-peas
- 6 cups water
- 1 tsp. baking soda (optional)
  salt

Garnish:

- ½ cup wine vinegar
- ½ tsp. Tabasco sauce, or to taste
- 2 tsp. cumin
- ¼ cup onions, chopped
  dill pickle spears

1. Drain and rinse the soaked chickpeas. Bring the water to a boil and add the chickpeas and optional baking soda. Cover and simmer the beans until tender, about 1½ hours or longer. (If you are using canned beans, heat them on the stovetop or in the microwave.) Drain and transfer to bowls, adding salt as necessary.

2. Pour vinegar to taste over each serving, generously splash on the Tabasco sauce, and sprinkle with cumin. Garnish with onions and dill pickles.

Spring Carrot Salad

Slatit Finari (MOROCCO)

~~~~~~

Morocco's exotic blend of fragrant and hot spices combines beautifully with sweet juicy carrots, while regional cuisines of North Africa offer us diverse fragrant and evocative ways to present this familiar staple. Inexpensive and remarkably easy to prepare, this salad's flavor will intensify as the hours pass. Each serving contains only 4 grams of fat, while delivering 3 times the recommended daily allowance of beta carotene.

$^1/_2$ cup water
   salt
 1 pound carrots, pared and sliced (tiny baby carrots are lovely for this dish, and ready to steam)
    fresh parsley, minced

Picante Vinaigrette with Herbs: (p. 87)

1. Bring the water to a boil. Add the salt and carrots, and steam over medium heat until tender-crisp, about 10 minutes. Drain, reserving $^1/_4$ cup of the cooking liquid.

2. Prepare the **Picante Vinaigrette with Herbs**, using your choice of lemon juice or wine vinegar. Stir the dressing and the reserved cooking liquid into the carrots, cover, and simmer about 7 minutes. (The carrots will be soft. If you prefer them crispy, reduce the cooking times in both steps 1 and 2.) Add the parsley and toss.

3. Serve chilled or at room temperature. (This dish can be prepared several hours in advance.)

Variation

Morocco: Add cinnamon and 1 tbsp. sugar.

Iraq: Instead of **Picante Vinaigrette**, dress with vinegar, olive oil, crushed garlic, and caraway seeds.

Oriental Green Bean Salad

Fasooleyah Khodra bi Zeit (SAUDI ARABIA)

This type of simple cooked salad is popular in the eastern Mediterranean and throughout the Gulf, where carrots, green *koosa* squash, beets, spinach, and potatoes are prepared in similar fashion. Subtly blended with the fruitiness of olive oil and the refreshing tartness of lemon, any vegetable at the peak of its season becomes a healthy accompaniment to a main dish. Permutations and modifications are endless: some cooks take a shortcut by omitting the onions, while others eliminate the chili or add a favorite regional herb or spice.

1 pound green beans, fresh or frozen (cut into pieces, or French-cut)
2 onions, chopped
2 tbsp. olive oil
1 serrano chili, seeded and chopped
1/4 cup water
1/2 tsp. salt
   juice of 2 lemons

1. If you are using fresh beans, steam them until crispy-tender. Drain.

2. Sauté the onions in the olive oil until softened and transparent.

3. Add the drained fresh green beans or the frozen beans and the chili, stirring to mix well. Sauté for 2 minutes.

4. Stir in the water and the salt and bring to a boil. Reduce the heat, cover, and steam for about 7 minutes, until the beans are tender. Uncover and raise the heat to evaporate as much of the water as possible.

5. Toss with the lemon juice. Taste and adjust seasoning. Serve at room temperature or slightly chilled.

Variation

Armenia: Substitute 1 large minced tomato for the chili and add 2 tbsp. olive oil and red pepper to the lemon juice.

Cauliflower or Potato Tahini Salad

Salatet Zahra bil Tahini (JORDAN, IRAQ, SAUDI ARABIA)

~~~~~~

The addition of juicy tomatoes and the nutty flavor of creamy tahini to the previous recipe produces yet another type of traditional vegetable salad—in this case, prepared with cauliflower or potatoes. Beets, eggplant, asparagus, or green beans are also ideal for this type of dish.

  1 head cauliflower, broken into florets, or:

  4 large potatoes, peeled and cut into chunks

  2 tomatoes, coarsely chopped

$3/4$ cup minced parsley

Tahini dressing: (p. 88)

Garnish:
    minced parsley
    Middle Eastern red pepper

1. Steam the cauliflower or potatoes in salted water until crispy-tender.

2. Toss the cooked vegetables with the tomatoes, parsley, and the dressing. Arrange on a platter and garnish with parsley and red pepper.

Wilted Spinach with Preserved Lemon

Bekkooleh (MOROCCO, LIBYA)

~~~~~~

After one brief visit to Marrakesh, I've fallen under the spell of its enticing panoramas and evocative flavors. The charm of this wilted Moroccan salad results from its unique combination of fresh herbs and leafy greens. Although related to the cooked salads of the eastern Arab world, *Bekkooleh* offers an exciting Andalusian touch.

Although the original recipe calls for a specific green leaves not available here, spinach imparts a similar taste and texture. In neighboring Libya, the salad is prepared from the high-iron combination of cabbage with Swiss chard.

    1 pound purslane leaves, or:
    1 bunch fresh spinach, cut into coarse ribbons
1 1/2 cups chopped parsley
    1 cup chopped cilantro
  1/4 cup water
       salt
    3 cloves garlic, minced
  1/4 cup olive oil
    1 tsp. sweet paprika
  1/2 tsp. Middle Eastern red pepper
  1/3 cup lemon juice

Garnish:
       purple or black Middle Eastern olives
       peel of 1/2 preserved lemon (p. 85)

1. Steam the spinach or purslane, parsley, and cilantro with the water until limp, about 7 minutes. Transfer the greens to a sieve to drain.

2. In the same pan, lightly sauté the garlic in the olive oil, adding the paprika and red pepper. Cook over medium heat just until the garlic begins to turn color.

3. Stir in the lemon juice and turn off the heat. Add the cooked greens and toss to combine flavors. Taste and adjust seasoning.

4. Serve at room temperature or slightly chilled, garnished with olives and slivers of preserved lemon peel.

Variation

Libya: Use cabbage and a few leaves of Swiss chard and wedges of fresh lemon.

Tunisian Salade Niçoise

Salata Mishweeyeh (TUNISIA, LIBYA)

Tunisian *mishweeyeh*, or grilled vegetable salad, usually differs from the Moroccan version that appears on p. 73 in that tuna is added to the dish. I love the dramatic contrast of the tuna atop the colorful pepper salad, sprinkled with flecks of white feta and lustrous purple or black olives. It's beautiful enough for a sumptuous buffet, yet nutritious enough for a summer lunch.

2 green peppers
4 firm tomatoes
2 small onions
1/2 serrano chili
1 can (7 oz.) water-pack tuna, drained
1/2 cup feta cheese, crumbled
2 hard-boiled eggs, chopped

Classic Lemon Vinaigrette: (p. 86) prepared with added:
1 tsp. oregano or mint
1/2 tsp. black pepper

Garnish:
   minced parsley
   minced fresh mint
   fresh red onion rings
   Middle Eastern olives (any color)
   radish roses

1. Roast the peppers, tomatoes, onions, and chili pepper according to the directions in step 1 of **Tomato and Roasted Pepper Salad** (p. 73). When the vegetables have cooled and their skins have been removed, chop them into small pieces, discarding the seeds and veins of the peppers.

2. Combine the dressing ingredients and pour it over the vegetables, reserving about a fourth of the liquid. Toss to coat well.

3. Stir the reserved dressing into the drained tuna and press into a small bowl. Turn over to unmold in the center of a serving dish. Arrange the vegetables around the tuna. Sprinkle the cheese and egg over the top, and garnish liberally.

Libya: Mash together the tomato and garlic, add green pepper, tuna, and dressing.

Lemony Fisherman's Salad

Salatat Semak (SAUDI ARABIA)

Poached fish, flaked and moistened with a lemony vinaigrette, is a regional specialty of Saudi Arabia and the Gulf. The Saudis are particularly fond of seafood scented with the aromatic perfume of cardamom, while northern Arabs of the Levant, unaccustomed to preparing the sea's bounty, would find this type of dish quite foreign.

Fish:

  2 cups water
     salt
 1/4 lemon, sliced
  1 pod cardamom
 1/2 onion
 3/4 pound fish fillet

     juice of 1 or 2 large lemons
  1 large tomato, chopped
 1/3 cup chopped parsley
 1/3 cup chopped cilantro
     romaine lettuce, cut into ribbons

1. Place the water, salt, lemon, cardamom, and onion in a saucepan and bring to a boil. Add the fish and gently poach for about 3–6 minutes, depending on the thickness of the fillet.

2. Remove the fish, dry with paper towels, and flake into small pieces.

3. Squeeze the fresh lemon juice over the fish and toss with the chopped tomato and herbs. Taste and adjust seasoning. Serve on a bed of romaine.

Preserved Lemons

Hamod Msyiar (MOROCCO)

~~~~~~

In the Gulf, we used to buy these Moroccan lemons in the deli section of the local supermarket, alongside overflowing barrels of hot-pink turnip pickles and fat, shiny olives. They add a unique flavor to Moroccan cooking, especially to salads, some of which are garnished with strips of pickled lemon rind, while others include juicy bits of pickled lemon among the vegetables.

This recipe doesn't keep as long as another version that calls for packing the cut lemons with salt. Unless you use preserved lemons with great frequency, this simpler method will serve you well.

3 lemons

$1/2$ cup water

$1/4$ cup lemon juice

$1/4$ cup pickling salt

3 peppercorns

$1/2$ serrano chili (optional)

$1/2$ small cinnamon stick

1. Cut 6 lengthwise incisions into each lemon, taking care not to pierce the pulp. Alternatively, quarter the lemons lengthwise without cutting through the stalk end, so they are still joined. Place all ingredients in a large saucepan and bring to a boil. Boil about 8 minutes, until the peels are slightly softened.

2. Transfer the lemons to glass jars that have been rinsed with very hot water. Let the liquid cool slightly and pour over the lemons to completely fill the jars. Cover tightly and refrigerate.

3. The lemons are ready after 4 days. Use within 1 month.

Classic Lemon Vinaigrette

Titbeelit Leimoon (ARAB STATES)

Most Middle Easterners prefer the lightly stimulating flavor of fresh lemon juice in their salad dressing rather than vinegar. I think this is probably because fresh lemons are a standard provision even in the humblest households, and because lemons are perceived as an exceptional health food that even cures nausea and headache.

In the prosperous Gulf, every sort of exotic food imported from the West graces the groaning supermarket shelves. Imported lemons are available year-round, and consumers worry about their freshness and the amount of juice they hold rather than the price.

¼ cup lemon juice
¼ cup olive oil
  salt
  pinch Middle Eastern red pepper (optional)

1. Combine all ingredients in a jar with a tight-fitting lid, cover, and shake to blend.

Garlic Vinaigrette

Titbeelit Khel (ARAB STATES)

You can use either lemon juice or wine vinegar in this dressing, but I find the brightness of vinegar combines well with garlic's zest. The standard vinegar around the Arab Mediterranean (called wine vinegar in this country) is an unassuming homemade product. Ledges of city balconies and flat roofs of village homes alike are dotted with net-covered pots of ripe red grapes being converted to vinegar. "I watch the vinegar carefully," giggled my village friend Sabah, "or it will turn to wine!" Of course, she had the tale backward.

Once the supply produced during the previous grape season is exhausted, only a limited number of city people will spend cash on something that requires only the sun's labor and that is almost free during the early fall months. Vinegar does tend to be used more frequently in winter, when fresh lemons are expensive and hard to find.

In the Arabian peninsula, vinegar is imported from abroad. Because of the Qur'anic injunction forbidding alcoholic consumption, wine vinegar in these countries is relabeled by its American manufacturers and sold as "red grape vinegar."

 1 clove garlic, crushed with
    salt
¹⁄₄ cup wine vinegar or lemon juice
¹⁄₄ cup olive oil
    pinch Middle Eastern red pepper (optional)

1. Combine all ingredients in a jar with a tight-fitting lid, cover, and shake to blend.

Picante Vinaigrette with Herbs

Leimoon au Khal oo Zeit (NORTH AFRICA)

Moroccan cuisine frequently delights us with an unanticipated combination of flavors, and these unusual alliances are never more exciting than in its vegetable salads. Whether you use this dressing in a North African recipe or over a more familiar Western salad, you'll be seduced by its superb blend of spices. The richness of sweet paprika and the sharp bite of aromatic hot red pepper appear in the usual 4:1 ratio. Cumin adds its subtle mystery but does not dominate as in other cuisines of the North African Mediterranean.

 1 clove garlic, crushed with
    salt
 3 tbsp. lemon juice or wine vinegar
¹⁄₄ cup olive oil
¹⁄₂ tsp. sweet paprika
¹⁄₄ tsp. cumin
¹⁄₈ tsp. Middle Eastern red pepper (or more)
 2 tbsp. minced parsley
 2 tbsp. minced cilantro
 1 tbsp. grated lemon peel (optional)

1. Combine all ingredients in a jar with a tight-fitting lid, cover, and shake vigorously.

Variation

Sometimes ground coriander and/or sugar are added to the above spices.

Yoghurt Dressing

Titbeelit Leban (LEBANON, EGYPT)

This is similar to a thin ranch dressing and is a base to which a feta or other crumbled low-fat cheese can be added. It can be substituted for the traditional **Classic Lemon Vinaigrette** in most recipes but is especially delicious over green salads.

1/4 cup olive oil
2 tbsp. wine vinegar
salt
black pepper
1/2 cup low-fat yoghurt

1. Combine all ingredients in a jar with a tight-fitting lid, and shake to blend. Or puree in a food processor.

Tahini Dressing

Titbeelit Tahineh (LEBANON, EGYPT)

Sesame seed tahini is a regional favorite of Lebanon, adding a unique flavor to this salad dressing. A similar tahini sauce called *Tarator* is the preferred way of seasoning fish in the Levant region. Sesame may be the oldest condiment known to man, as records have been found of sesame production in the Tigris and Euphrates valleys in 1600 B.C.

2 cloves garlic, crushed with salt

¼ cup lemon juice

¼ cup tahini

¼ cup olive oil

¼ cup low-fat yoghurt or milk

1. Combine all ingredients in a jar with a tight-fitting lid, cover, and shake to blend. Or puree in a food processor.

Crudités

El Khodra (ARAB STATES)

Throughout the Levant and neighboring countries, no table is complete without a salad of some sort. When time doesn't allow preparation of a cooked vegetable salad, or when the last tomato has disappeared, a small tray heaped with raw herbs and greens is offered to the guests. Even amid the myriad of wondrous dishes of the *mezzeh* table, a dish of crudités refreshes the palate.

You might try an artistic arrangement of carrot sticks, green pepper slices, cauliflower florets, celery, radishes, or whatever is available, heaped artistically on a bed of fresh mint or dill. When guests are invited, this attractive presentation is recommended even when another salad is set out. The only rules pertaining to a tray of crudités are that they be fresh, colorful, and generous in quantity.

Saudi Arabian Tea

Soups

In the countries that skirt the Arab Mediterranean, soups are traditionally a substantial part of the family's winter cuisine rather than a first course to festive meals. Village matriarchs, guardians of everything precious, confront the frigid winter winds with an arsenal full of warm nutritious weapons certain to vanquish their frosty foe. The wafting aromas from enormous cauldrons of chicken or lamb bones, steaming with vegetables or legumes, welcome husbands home from the fields. Children arriving from an unheated schoolroom sneak into the kitchen to steal a ladleful of comforting broth, to wrap themselves in the warm blanket of mother's love.

A meal in themselves, soups are usually served at midday with lots of bread and perhaps a side dish of winter salad or a smooth-textured bean dip. They are also enjoyed as a late-evening supper, accompanied by the usual tiny oval platters of assorted olives, cheeses, and homemade preserves that also appear on the breakfast tray. North African soups, replete with grains and legumes, make a bracing breakfast. Only during the blessed Ramadan month of daytime fasting are soups offered as an introductory course to a full meal, one that gently soothes a stomach shrunken by 14 or 16 hours passed without food or drink.

From the Coptic and Orthodox communities across the region appear numerous meatless vegetable soups reserved for the Lenten and Advent seasons while in Turkey a bit of fresh yoghurt, with lemon or mint "cools" brothy soups.

Nourishing soups prepared from legumes are especially common across the Middle East during the months when fresh vegetables are unavailable. Peas, lentils, chickpeas, and dried beans are slowly cooked in a simmering meat or bone stock and enlivened with fragrant spice combinations, a dash of lemon juice, or *hamod er rummaan* pomegranate syrup. Hearty Armenian and Gulf soups with whole-grain wheat are healthful, tangy, and tart. Sensationally seasoned with onions, garlic, fresh herbs and spices, legume and grain soups thicken naturally without the addition of cream or eggs. The complete proteins formed when these legumes are accompanied by a sourdough or whole-wheat bread are yet another example of healthy eating.

Lean and lovely, yet high in fiber and vitamins, some soups are simmered for hours, while others are ready as soon as the flavors have blended. **Easy Meatball Soup** and **Saffron Garlic Broth with Diced Potatoes** are quick, nutritious broths that require only a few minutes of preparation time and just a little longer for cooking.

When numerous flavorful ingredients and seasonings are to be added to a soup, as in **Quick Tomato Broth with Noodles**, even villagers occasionally substitute a cube or spoonful or two of bouillon for stock. No compromise of vibrant flavor is noticeable, and much time is saved, but it is wise to check the label first (see General Cooking Tips, p. 27). Bouillon can also be a convenient extender for a homemade stock and is helpful in intensifying the flavors of simple dishes like **Cream of Chickpea Soup**.

Although today's soups are sophisticated foods, carefully blended and seasoned, many are of humble origins. Villagers still prepare rich vegetable and legume soups from whatever odds and ends are on hand, and my husband recalls the days of his youth, when leftover *burghol*, rice, or stewed vegetables disappeared into the steaming cauldron of tempting broth.

Even today, Christians and Muslims alike agree that food is God's greatest gift. A good cook is not only frugal but also creative in turning the simple blessings of the earth into lovely soups whose exciting flavors and textures are sure to brighten any day.

Lamb Broth

Shorabit Lahme (ARAB STATES)

On those special days when my husband Ma'Amun strode into our Jeddah kitchen carrying a small frozen lamb, imported from Uruguay or New Zealand, both the cat and the children came running in expectation of the upcoming feast. We hung the carcass by its leg from the butcher's hook suspended from the kitchen ceiling, and as soon as it was soft enough to be cut, Ma'Amun went to work. I placed our largest aluminum tray on the floor, and the cat patiently took up her position next to it, waiting for tidbits to be tossed her way.

That evening, we charcoal-grilled the lamb fillet and cut most of the meat into cubes, to be frozen. Bones were broken up and frozen, too, to be turned into delicious soups.

Meanwhile, I filled a gigantic soup pot with water and brought it to a boil. Into the cauldron Ma'Amun tossed the larger bones, along with a few scraps of meat. Seasoned only with salt and pepper, this rich stock was a superb base for more complex soups, but I must admit that in our house it never lasted long enough for that. As the cat sat, licking her paws, satiated, and the delicious aroma began to tantalize the children, we could hardly wait for the broth's healthy goodness to warm our throats and tummies.

> 3 to 5 pounds lamb bones
> 8 to 12 cups water, depending on the amount of bones
> salt
> black pepper

Garnish:
> minced parsley
> black pepper

1. Place the bones in the largest available pot and cover with water. Add the salt and pepper and bring to a boil. Skin the foam for as long as necessary. Cover, reduce heat, and simmer for about $2^1/2$ to 3 hours.

2. If you are not serving the broth immediately, refrigerate it so the fat that rises to the surface may be lifted off.

3. Taste and adjust seasoning. Sprinkle each bowl or cup with freshly ground black pepper and parsley.

Classic Red Lentil Soup

Shorabit Addas (ARAB STATES)

This creamy light classic is served at dusk in Syria, Lebanon, and Saudi Arabia to break the strenuous daylong fasts of the month of Ramadan. In accordance with Islam's emphasis on sharing God's blessings with neighbors and friends, my Saudi neighbor Nadia would often send her Pakistani houseboy over to my house just before the cannon sounded to mark the end of the long hot daylight hours, carrying a large tray bearing red lentil soup and other special treats.

Although its name suggests otherwise, the dish is prepared with brilliant orange-colored lentils, which slowly disintegrate into a soft yellow cream without pureeing. Neither milk nor cream is added to produce the rich texture, which, according to a proverb from Fez, should be "as smooth as silk." It is one of the healthiest and easiest of the great Middle Eastern dishes: low in calories and fat, high in vitamins and fiber.

Claimed by every nationality and ethnic group in the Arab world, this soup boasts innumerable variations, each of which is noteworthy—more proof that nearly any compatible ingredient may be thrown into the cauldron. Our personal favorite is to add garlic, carrots, a bit of celery, and Middle Eastern red pepper.

    8 cups water
    2 pounds lamb bones and meat
 1¹/₂ cups red lentils, rinsed
    1 small onion, chopped (optional)
       salt
       black pepper

Garnish:
       minced parsley or cilantro
       lemon wedges

1. Place all ingredients in a large saucepan and bring to a boil. (I like to sauté the onion lightly in a bit of olive oil, but this is not necessary. Some cooks even omit the onion.) Reduce heat, cover, and simmer for 1¹/₂ to 2 hours. Stir occasionally to keep the lentils from sticking to the bottom of the pan.

2. Taste and adjust seasoning. More water may be added if you prefer a thinner soup. For a thicker broth, uncover the pot and cook a bit longer to reduce the liquid.

3. Garnish and serve with a generous squeeze of fresh lemon juice.

Variations

Turkey: Add 1 rounded tsp. tomato paste, 1/4 cup uncooked rice or *burghol*, mint, and paprika.

Kuwait: Add 1/4 cup uncooked rice, 2 cloves garlic, cumin, and ground coriander.

Gulf States: Add 2 chopped tomatoes, fettuccine noodles, *loomi*, and *kebsa* spices.

Iraq: Add 1 rounded tsp. tomato paste, turmeric, and cumin.

Saudi Arabia: Add 1 chopped potato, 2 chopped carrots, 2 chopped tomatoes, and cumin.

Egypt: Add 1 chopped tomato, 2 ribs chopped celery, 2 cloves garlic, cumin, and red pepper.

Libya: Add 1 rounded tsp. tomato paste, 1 chopped potato, 2 chopped carrots, cumin, and cardamom.

Morocco: Add 2 chopped tomatoes, 2 chopped carrots, turmeric, cinnamon, ground ginger, paprika, saffron, and 1 cup cooked chickpeas.

Lebanon: Add 1 chopped leek.

Syria: Add 1/3 cup uncooked rice.

Armenia: Add 1/4 cup *jareesh*, 1 rib chopped celery, 2 chopped carrots, and red pepper.

Yemen: Add 2 chopped tomatoes.

"He Burned His Fingers"

Shorabit Addas ma Shayreeyeh (LEBANON, SYRIA)

This wonderful dish is a traditional favorite across the northern Arab countries. Legend has it that one cold winter day, someone couldn't wait until the robust broth was cool enough to indulge himself. Dashing off to the simmering pot to fill his bowl with this soup flavored with sweet-sour pomegranate syrup, he burned his fingers.

This substantial dish combines the dried legumes common to winter soups with Swiss chard (*silik*), one of the first fresh greens of spring. I find the long crimson-stemmed American variety so unlike Middle Eastern *silik* that I prefer to substitute spinach. The flat-leafed spinach that is usually found tied in neat little bunches is more like the original ingredient than the curly-leafed prebagged type sold in supermarkets.

2 tbsp. olive oil

1/2 onion, thinly slivered

2 cloves garlic, minced

8 cups beef, lamb, chicken, or vegetable stock

3/4 cup brown or green lentils, rinsed

3 ounces fettuccine noodles

1/3 bunch fresh spinach, cut into ribbons, or:

1 package (10 oz.) frozen chopped spinach

1/2 cup minced cilantro

2 tbsp. **hamod er rummaan** pomegranate syrup

1. In a large soup pot, sauté the onion in the olive oil until transparent and softened. Add the garlic and cook for another minute.

2. Add the stock and the lentils and bring to a boil. Reduce heat, cover, and simmer until the lentils are almost tender. Cooking time will vary according to the type and the age of the lentils, probably about 1 hour; do not allow them to get mushy.

3. Add the remaining ingredients, cover, and simmer until done, about 15 minutes, or according to the suggestions on the fettuccine package. Taste and adjust seasoning.

Split Pea and Potato Potage

Soopeh Goosfand (Kurdistan)

~~~~~~

In the mountainous regions of remote eastern Kurdistan, this is a favorite hearty dish that is served in a unique manner. Seated on the floor around a spotless white cloth in the traditional dinner style known as *sufra*, the family first drinks the thick pea broth, enriched with the flavors of meat and vegetables. The new potatoes and the chunks of lamb, which have been lifted out of the soup, are smashed in a stone *jarren* (mortar) along with one raw chopped onion. This beaten mixture, which is similar to the Saudi Arabian *jareesh* (smashed wheat and meat popular during Ramadan), is placed on a tray and brought to the tablecloth on the floor, to be scooped up with thick pieces of homemade Kurdish flat bread.

Yellow split peas are nothing more than the insides of hulled dried green peas. They cook quickly yet retain the high nutritive value of peas, and like lentils, do not require soaking.

> 1 large onion, chopped
> 2 tbsp. olive oil
> 1 large (2 pounds or more) lamb shank
> 10 cups water
>   salt
>   black pepper
> 1¹/₂ cups yellow split peas, rinsed
> 8 small (about 1 pound) new potatoes, washed but not peeled
> 1 rounded tbsp. tomato paste (optional)
> 1 tsp. turmeric

Garnish:
>   minced parsley
>   lemons

1. In a large soup pot, lightly sauté the onion in the olive oil until softened. (Often the onion is not sautéed.)

2. Add the lamb, water, and peas and bring to a boil. Reduce heat, cover, and simmer for 1¹/₂ hours, stirring occasionally to prevent the peas from sticking to the bottom of the pan.

3. Add the potatoes and optional tomato paste and cook until the vegetables are tender, about 1/2 hour longer. Stir in the turmeric during the last 10 minutes of cooking to give the soup a lovely golden color.

4. The soup may be served at this point. Or, the vegetables may be pureed in a blender and returned to the pot to simmer with the meat for about 5 minutes. Taste and adjust seasoning. (Traditionally, the soup is served as described in the introduction.)

5. Garnish with parsley and serve with a generous squeeze of fresh lemon juice.

Variations

Syria: Add 1 rib chopped celery, 1 chopped carrot, and 1 chopped leek.

Iraq: Substitute 1 1/2 cups egg noodles for the potatoes.

Cream of Chickpea Soup

Leblebi (TUNISIA)

Across the southern Mediterranean, soups made from the dried beans and onions stored in the family's cool pantry are inexpensive dishes infused with the appealing flavors of the cook's favorite spice mixture. The original cream of chickpea soup is a very nutritious and popular peasant dish consumed for breakfast or as a midday snack in winter, when fresh vegetables are unavailable. Whenever possible, a large bone is added for heartier flavor, or olive oil is drizzled atop the smoothly textured soup for additional energy. The yoghurt with which it is combined is appealingly tart, while fresh lemon juice sharpens the flavor. Tunisians love the fire of hot peppers even more than their North African neighbors, and always serve a bowl of blazing *harissa* salsa on the side.

Nutritionists recommend overnight soaking of legumes in order to retain all the vitamins and the benefits of the fiber; chickpeas will not cook properly with a briefer soaking time. Arab cooks always pour off the soaking water, and usually add baking soda during the simmering to ease digestion and to improve the texture, taste, and quality of the dish. If flatulence remains bothersome, it is suggested that the cook drain the cooking water after the first hour of cooking. Add your seasoning ingredients to fresh water or broth, as described in the recipe.

Often, when I'm cooking a pureed soup like this one, I'll save a step by substituting a rich beef or lamb broth for the traditional bone and water. Or I'll use bouillon made from real meat to intensify the flavor.

1¼ cups chickpeas, soaked overnight
1 tsp. baking soda (optional)
1 large onion, coarsely chopped
2 tbsp. olive oil
5 cloves garlic, minced
1 carrot, coarsely chopped
1 stalk celery or leek, thinly sliced
8 cups beef or lamb broth or water with beef bouillon
½ tsp. Middle Eastern red pepper
1 tsp. caraway seeds
1 cup low-fat yoghurt
salt

Garnish:
minced cilantro
Harissa Red Chili Paste (p. 41)
cumin

1. Soak the chickpeas overnight in water to cover.

2. Drain the chickpeas and cover again with water to which you have added the baking soda. Bring to a boil, reduce heat, and simmer for 1 hour. Drain.

3. Sauté the onion in the olive oil until softened and transparent. Add the garlic, carrot, and celery or leek and cook for another 3–5 minutes. (This step is sometimes omitted.)

4. Add the drained chickpeas to the vegetables, along with the broth, red pepper, and caraway seeds. Bring to a boil. Cover and simmer until chickpeas are tender, about 1 hour.

5. Use a slotted spoon to lift the vegetables from the broth and transfer them to a blender. Add the yoghurt and as much cooking liquid as necessary to blend to a smooth puree.

6. Return the pureed mixture to the cooking pot, stirring it into the remaining cooking liquid. Because the yoghurt has been broken up in the blender, it usually does not separate. Stir until smooth, adding additional water if the soup is too thick. Taste and adjust seasoning.

7. Garnish and serve. The authentic manner of enjoying this soup is to pour it over dry or toasted Arabic bread.

Navy Bean Soup with Onions and Tomatoes

Shorabit Fasooleeyeh Beida (JORDAN)

This peasant soup is a feast for the eye as well as the palate with its bright bits of tomatoes, tiny white beans, and a lacy sprinkling of crisp green parsley. It's another delicious classic of regional cooking that reminds me of the masterpieces my Italian aunts used to create from the most inexpensive ingredients.

As in the previous recipe, a bone with a small amount of meat can also be added to this soup. If the amount of liquid is reduced somewhat, it becomes a well-balanced vegetable stew to serve with *burghol* pilaf.

In the following version, olive oil adds body and nourishment, making it perfect for the Orthodox Christian meatless days that seem to include nearly half of the yearly calendar.

An added benefit is that this dish also provides nearly all the fiber required for a day of healthy eating.

½ pound navy beans, soaked overnight
1 large onion, chopped
2 stalks celery, chopped (optional)
2 tbsp. olive oil
2 cloves garlic, minced
2 tomatoes, skinned and chopped
2 rounded tbsp. tomato paste
salt

black pepper

generous pinch sweet paprika

pinch Middle Eastern red pepper

1 bay leaf

¼ cup parsley, minced

1. Cook the soaked, drained beans according to package instructions, leaving them just slightly undercooked.

2. In a large pot, sauté the onion and the celery in the olive oil until soft and transparent. Add the garlic and cook for another minute.

3. Stir in the chopped tomatoes and simmer for a few minutes. Add the remaining ingredients, plus the beans and 7 cups of their cooking liquid. (If there is not enough cooking liquid, add water to make 7 cups.) Mix well, cover, and cook another 20 to 30 minutes to blend flavors. Remove bay leaf. Taste and adjust seasoning.

Fish Stock

Of the many delicious fishes of the southern Mediterranean, the Arabian Gulf, and the Red Sea, those in the grouper family are ideal for a flavorful fish stock on which a variety of soups can be built. These fish are easily identifiable by their large heads. Red snapper is perfect, as is any large-mouthed bass or similar, meaty fish. The heartiest and most economical stock is prepared from scraps such as the head, tail, and backbone, although whole fishes and fillets will work just as well.

Many American supermarkets and fishmongers receive regular shipments of whole fish, which they fillet or cut into steaks, discarding the head with the tail and spine connected. The seafood department is usually willing to save a bag of these scraps for customers. Ask if this is possible and you'll probably discover that there is no charge.

This recipe should produce about 6 cups of fish stock, to be used in one of the regional soups that follow. I like to keep stock on hand in the freezer, to be quickly turned into a fragrant fish soup for an easy family meal.

1 pound (or more) fish bones, tails, and heads

2 quarts water

salt

1. Place the ingredients in a large saucepan and simmer for 30 minutes or longer.

2. Strain the stock.

3. Return any chunks or bits of fish to the broth. Use as a base for fish soup.

Mediterranean Fish Soup

Sharbat Hoat (LIBYA)

Many elements of Arab and North African cooking are identical to the well-known dishes produced just across the Mediterranean Sea in Italy, Provence, and Spain. Except for the cumin that marks this soup as Libyan, the garlic and tomato might suggest that it is Spanish, Provençal, or Neopolitan.

1/4 onion, chopped

2 tbsp. olive oil

1/4 tsp. Middle Eastern red pepper

4 cloves garlic, minced

6 cups **Fish Stock** (see previous recipe)

1 rounded tbsp. tomato paste

1 tsp. oregano

1 tsp. cumin

1/2 pound fish fillets, cut into pieces

lemons

1. Sauté the onion in the olive oil until softened and transparent. Add the red pepper and the garlic and cook for another minute.

2. Add the fish stock, tomato paste, oregano, and cumin, and bring to a boil.

3. Drop in the fish and simmer for about 10 minutes, until tender. Taste and adjust the seasoning.

4. Serve with a generous squeeze of fresh lemon juice.

Variation

Lebanon: Substitute basil for the cumin; add $1/3$ pound shrimp and $1/3$ pound scallops.

Savory Fish Soup

Shorbat al Samak (SAUDI ARABIA, THE GULF STATES)

Ground *loomi*, dried lime from the Gulf, is included by some families in their *kebsa* mixture (p. 25). We like the pungent citrus tang it adds to many soups and stewed dishes. If you can't find *loomi*, just proceed without it.

$1/4$ onion, chopped

 2 tbsp. olive oil

$1/2$ tsp. Middle Eastern red pepper

 4 cloves garlic, minced

 1 large, ripe tomato, chopped

 1 tsp. **asfor**, or:
   pinch saffron

$1/2$ tsp. **kebsa** spices

 6 cups fish stock

 1 rounded tbsp. tomato paste

$1/2$ pound fish fillets, cut into pieces

$1/4$ pound shrimp, shelled

Garnish:
   minced cilantro

1. Sauté the onion in the olive oil until softened and transparent. Add the red pepper, garlic, tomato, and spices and cook for another minute to release the flavors.

2. Add the fish stock and tomato paste and bring to a boil.

3. Drop in the fish and shrimp and simmer for about 10 minutes, until tender. Taste and adjust the seasoning.

4. Serve garnished with cilantro.

Tangy Chicken Noodle Soup Avgolemono

Shorabit Djaj ma Shareeyeh (MOROCCO)

I cannot resist the brilliantly flavored North African combination of fiery red peppers dried in the dazzling Mediterranean sun, sweet spices, and fresh herbs. Here it's all added to a classic chicken soup served avgolemono style: lemon juice whipped into eggs is added in the final minute of cooking to thicken the broth.

  1 large onion, chopped
  2 tbsp. olive oil
  8 cups water
  1/2 (or more) chicken, cut up
  1 cinnamon stick
  1/4 tsp. Middle Eastern red pepper
  1/4 tsp. black pepper
    salt
1 1/2 cups cooked chickpeas
1 1/2 cups **fideo** vermicelli
  1/3 cup minced parsley
  1/3 cup minced cilantro
    juice of 1 lemon
  3 egg yolks, or:
  1 egg plus 1 egg white

1. Sauté the onion in the olive oil until softened and transparent but not browned. Add the water and bring to a boil.

2. Rinse the chicken and add it to the pot, along with the cinnamon, peppers, and salt. Cover and simmer, skimming the foam, until the chicken is tender, about 1 hour.

3. Lift the cooked chicken pieces from the stock and set aside to cool for a few minutes. Meanwhile, add the chickpeas, noodles, parsley, and cilantro to the stock.

4. While the noodles are cooking, taste and adjust the seasoning. When chicken is cool enough to handle, remove the meat from the bones, discarding the skin, and return the chicken to the simmering broth.

5. Beat the lemon juice into the egg yolks (or egg plus egg white) and incorporate $1/2$ cup or more of the hot soup. Return this mixture to the pot, stir to blend well, and simmer for a minute or two before serving.

Variations

Egypt: Flavor with cumin.

Palestine: Omit the chickpeas and substitute rice for the noodles.

Chicken Yoghurt Soup

Yoghurtlu Tavuk Chorbasi (TURKEY)

Even our youngest daughter, Leila, who was 7 at the time, fell in love with Istanbul, but for rather curious reasons. Leila is captivated by any cuisine rich in soups, and even more so when the restaurant's ambiance includes a family of felines. We learned to slow our pace when from around every charming corner, in every splendid garden, in the doorway of each little shop, as if in answer to the Pied Piper's call, pranced a procession of cats to lick her caressing fingers and nuzzle her cheek. Turks believe that he who harms or kills a cat will suffer nine years of bad luck.

So, while my fond memories evoke exquisite pilafs with pine nuts, currants, and bits of chicken liver, offered in the shadow of the Topkapi's

Seraglio, Leila giggles, remembering her yoghurt soups and the 244 cats that responded to her greetings: "an average of 31 per day!"

Sometimes the following light soup is prepared in a more European manner, with 1 cup cream blended with 2 or 3 egg yolks (and sometimes lemon juice) instead of the yoghurt. Yoghurt, however, offers the same smoothness with $1/25$ the saturated fat and $1/4$ the calories. I especially enjoy the counterpoint of its soothing coolness and the perfumed passion of Turkish red peppers.

- 1 small onion, minced
- 2 tbsp. olive oil
- 8 cups water
- $1/2$ chicken, cut up
  - salt
  - white pepper
- $1/8$ tsp. (or more) Middle Eastern red pepper
- $1/2$ tsp. (or more) sweet paprika
- $1^1/2$ cups low-fat yoghurt
- 1 egg
- $1/3$ cup flour

Garnish:
- minced parsley, or:
- mint, fresh or dried

1. In a large saucepan, sauté the onion in the olive oil until softened. Pour on the water and add the chicken, salt, peppers, and paprika. Bring to a boil. Cover and simmer 1 hour or longer, skimming the foam as necessary. Taste and adjust the seasoning.

2. Remove the chicken pieces to a plate. When cool, remove the chicken meat from the bones and cut into bite-sized pieces. Return the chicken to the soup.

3. Use a blender or food processor to mix the yoghurt, egg, and flour until smooth, and gradually beat them into the warm soup. Again, taste and adjust the seasoning. Heat only to simmering, as the egg and yoghurt may curdle.

4. Garnish with minced parsley or mint.

Variations

Turkey: Cook the mint and parsley for a minute in a bit of melted butter.

Egypt: Eliminate the flour and spices but brown the onions until crisp.

Bedouin Wheat Soup

Shorabit al Laham ma Jareesh (SAUDI ARABIA AND THE GULF STATES)

~~~~~~

Also called *Shorabit Habhab* (Soup of Tiny Round Pieces), this dish is prepared with *jareesh*, whole-wheat kernels that look like yellowish barley. (The off-white husked grain requires slightly less time to cook.) Numerous regional variations can be found, the most interesting of which features a cardamom-scented broth thickened with flour and milk.

Jareesh is especially popular in Armenian communities (where it is called *dzedzadz* or *gorgod*) and in the Gulf States. Man's first attempt to cultivate grain was in ancient Mesopotamia (now Iraq), and wheat continues to be the staple of the region today. Both types of *jareesh* are available in import food stores, also sold in health food stores under the name "wheat berries."

1   large onion, chopped

2   tbsp. olive oil

2   cloves garlic, minced

1   pound lamb or beef, with bones
    salt
    black pepper

3/4 cup husked **jareesh** (whole-wheat kernels, sometimes called
    wheat berries)

8   cups water

1   rounded tbsp. tomato paste

1   small stick cinnamon
    salt

Garnish:
    minced parsley
    lemons

1. In a large soup pot, sauté the onion in the olive oil until slightly softened. Stir in the garlic and cook for another minute. Add the meat, sprinkle with salt and pepper, and lightly brown. Add the *jareesh* and cook for 2 or 3 minutes, until it begins to change color.

2. Add the remaining ingredients and bring to a boil. Reduce heat, cover, and simmer until the meat and wheat are tender, about 2 hours. Add additional water if needed, and stir occasionally to keep the *jareesh* from sticking to the bottom of the pan. Taste and adjust seasoning.

3. Garnish and serve with a generous squeeze of fresh lemon juice.

Sun-Dried Meat Soup with Couscous and Rice

Shorabit Cooscoos bil Lahme al Moojaffaf (MOROCCO, LIBYA)

Even today, many kitchens in the Middle East, especially in the agricultural villages and more remote mountain areas, do not contain refrigerators. The investment in such a luxury item is a matter that necessitates serious planning, especially where the electric supply is often sporadic. Many a young bride has sold her gold wedding jewelry to purchase a refrigerator when the first baby arrives, only to discover that even when power is semiregular, fluctuating voltage can blow out the motor of a large electric appliance.

Traditional homes still include a small pantry room attached to or built like a platform jutting out over much of the high-roofed kitchen. Filled with exotic smells, textures, and colors, these storerooms overflow with bags and baskets of dried legumes, nuts, and vegetables. From the rafters dangle twisted braids of garlic, strands of velvety dried baby okra, links of spicy sausage, and strips of sun-dried meat, the staples of a peasant civilization living in harmony with the earth.

In North Africa, whenever a sheep is slaughtered for an *Eid* feast or a special celebration such as a son's circumcision, women of the extended family—aunts, nieces, granddaughters—gather to preserve the excess meat. After the needy have been fed, whatever meat cannot be consumed by the following day is sliced in thin strips, rubbed with salt and garlic, and hung to dry (like Native American pemmican) in the warm sun of the courtyard or on lines strung atop the flat roof.

The following day, the strips are rubbed with red pepper, caraway, coriander, and (sometimes) dried mint, which helps the preservation process and gives the product its typical taste. If flies are abundant, pieces of net or chiffon are hung over the meat. As soon as the strips are completely dehydrated but still tender, they are cut into pieces and fried in the melted tail fat of the lamb mixed with some olive oil. This mixture, called *gargoosh* or *gadeed*, is transferred to big clay jars and sealed with olive oil.

In Syria and the Levant, a similar process produces *bastirma* and *kawarma*. Salted dried meat is such a popular traditional food that even where freezers and refrigeration are available, many people continue to preserve lamb the old-fashioned way.

I've had success in substituting beef jerky, our traditional American sundried beef, for the authentic product in this Moroccan recipe. It works well because they are essentially the same item, although beef jerky tends to become harder the longer it sits on the supermarket shelf, making it difficult to estimate cooking time. The paper-thin dried meat sold in health food stores is of very high quality and is ideal. Or, if *bastirma* is available in your imported food store, try a few slices for a tasty traditional flavor.

  1 large onion, chopped

  2 tbsp. olive oil

  2 cloves garlic, minced

10 cups water

  3 oz. beef jerky, minced or shredded

1/2 tsp. cumin

  1 tsp. sweet paprika

     salt

  2 rounded tbsp. tomato paste

  2 tbsp. **Harissa Red Chili Paste** (p. 41)

1 1/2 cups cooked white rice

1/2 cup uncooked couscous

  2 tsp. dried mint

1/8 tsp. black pepper

1. In a large soup pot, lightly sauté the onion in the olive oil until softened, adding the garlic during the last minute of cooking. Add the water and mix in the beef jerky, cumin, paprika, salt, tomato paste, and *harissa*. Bring to a boil. Cover, reduce heat, and simmer until the dried meat is tender. This may take from 1 to 2 hours, depending on the thickness of the jerky slices and the cut of meat from which it has been prepared.

2. Stir the cooked rice and the couscous into the broth, continuing to simmer for about 7 to 10 minutes. Season with mint, and taste to adjust the seasoning. As some jerky is quite salty and highly seasoned with red and black peppers, it is difficult to estimate the precise amount of salt and *harissa* you will need for this soup. Add small quantities of each at this point until the spices are to your taste.

Vegetable Soup a la Araby

Shorba (ARAB STATES)

My husband enjoys nothing more than standing watch over a simmering pot of lamb stock, tossing in whatever vegetables and leftovers happen to be available. The soup he creates is slightly different each time, but is essentially indistinguishable from the soup my Italian mother enjoyed as a light and cleansing lunch nearly every day. The hearty, healthy blending of flavors from the earth's bounty seems to refresh the spirit as well as the body.

So many variations of this soup exist that it was difficult for me to select just one. In fact, every Arab country claims this dish as its own, as does, I suppose, most of the world! Make this dish your own by adding your family favorites: cooked chickpeas, *foul* beans or white beans, a tbsp. of tomato paste instead of fresh tomatoes, or chicken soup base in which to cook the vegetables. Nearly any vegetable will add to the flavor. My family's favorite spice combinations are listed below, but you might prefer another regional mixture for a slightly different aroma.

1 (1¼–2 pounds) lamb shank
8 cups water
  salt

1 **loomi**, pierced

pinch Middle Eastern red pepper

1 bay leaf

2 small ripe tomatoes, peeled and chopped

1 large onion, chopped

2 tbsp. olive oil

1 clove garlic, minced

2 potatoes, peeled and cubed

2 carrots, peeled and chopped

1 zucchini or other summer squash, chopped

1 rib celery, chopped

1/2 cup chopped red pepper

black pepper

1 tbsp. **hamod er rummaan** pomegranate syrup

Garnish:

minced parsley

1. In a large soup pot, place the meat in the water and bring to a boil. Add the salt, *loomi*, pinch of red pepper, bay leaf, and tomatoes. Cover and reduce heat. Simmer for about 1 hour, skimming the foam as needed. (If the shank is especially large, allow for an additional 1/2 hour of cooking.)

2. Lightly sauté the onion in the olive oil until softened, adding the garlic during the last minute of cooking. Transfer to the soup pot.

3. The vegetables may be sautéed in the same olive oil, or they may be added directly to the stock.

4. Simmer the soup about 1/2 hour, until the vegetables are tender.

5. Add the black pepper and *hamod er rummaan* syrup, taste, and adjust seasoning. Remove the bay leaf. Serve garnished with parsley.

Variations

Egypt: Season with red pepper and mint.

Saudi Arabia: Add *kebsa* spices, 1 minced leek, 3 cardamom pods, and orzo pasta.

Turkey: Preferred vegetables are leeks, green beans, spinach, and cumin.

Libya: Season with allspice and mint, adding 1 leek, 3/4 cup cooked chickpeas, orzo pasta, 2 additional minced tomatoes, and the juice of 1/2 lemon.

Iraq: Add 1 cup cooked chickpeas, turmeric, and a second *loomi*.

Kuwait: Add *kebsa* spices and 1 peeled, diced turnip.

Morocco: Add 1/2 cup cooked red beans, 1/2 cup cooked chickpeas, 1/3 cup uncooked lentils, turmeric, ground ginger, paprika, and saffron.

Kurdistan: Add 1 cup cooked chickpeas, 1 rib minced celery, and 1 rounded tsp. tomato paste.

Yemen: Substitute cardamom, caraway, and turmeric for the *hamod*.

Mlookheeyeh Soup

Mlookheeyeh (EGYPT)

~~~~~~

Just as **tabbooleh** and *kibbeh* are the classic dishes of the Levant, this great Egyptian soup, which dates back to pharaonic times, symbolizes the unchanging cycle of life, the roots of a great peasant culture. A leafy green vegetable, *mlookheeyeh* (*Corchorus olitorius*) is consumed with pride and pleasure once or twice a day by the Egyptian fellaheen. Although it also is popular in North Africa, Syria, and parts of North Africa, *mlookheeyeh* is really the specialty of the vast peasant villages of the Nile delta.

In Egypt *mlookheeyeh* is prepared as a brothy green soup, which is served over **Vermicelli Rice** (p. 168). Seasonings vary, as does the meat base: Chicken is most common, although lamb is also popular, but rabbit is said to be the favorite.

For this soup, there is absolutely no substitute for the real McCoy, which is slightly glutinous like okra. You'll find dried or frozen *mlookheeyeh* at an imported-food store.

8 cups water

1½ pounds lamb bones and meat, **or** chicken, cut up
    salt

1 large tomato, peeled and chopped

1 onion, chopped

1½ cups dried **mlookheeyeh**, or:

1 package frozen Egyptian **mlookheeyeh**

Tekleeyeh Sauce:

4 cloves garlic
    salt

1 tbsp. olive oil

2 tsp. ground coriander

⅛ tsp. Middle Eastern red pepper
    juice of 1 lemon

1. In a large soup pot, combine the water, meat, salt, tomato, and onion and bring to a boil. Reduce the heat, cover, and simmer until tender—about 2 hours for lamb, 1 hour for chicken. Skim the foam and add water as necessary. (Some cooks remove and discard the vegetables at this point.)

2. If you are using dried *mlookheeyeh* leaves, place them in a bowl while the meat is simmering, and moisten with hot water. When double in bulk, about 20 minutes, drain them and add them to the stock. Fresh chopped or frozen leaves are added without soaking. Cook for 25 minutes.

3. To prepare the garlic sauce called *tekleeyeh*, crush the garlic with the salt and sauté it in the olive oil. When it is golden brown, stir in the coriander and red pepper. Add to the soup.

4. Strip the meat from the bones and add to the pot, along with the lemon juice. Taste and adjust the seasoning.

Quick Tomato Broth with Noodles

Shorabit Ibtisam (SYRIA)

From start to finish, this requires only 2 minutes of preparation and 10 minutes to simmer. The result: a fresh, light bowl of tender noodles in tomato-flavored broth, a healthy Sicilian-style soup with just a hint of meat that is adored by children and appreciated by all.

In Grandfather's village home, we simply call this recipe "Soup." It's an excellent choice for those evenings in Arabia when the house is bursting with the usual eclectic collection of impassioned visitors of every age and political opinion, when supper is almost an afterthought. In the time it takes to straighten up the kitchen and set the table with the traditional dishes of olives, cheese, and *lebneh*, this delicious soup is ready to serve.

1/4 pound tender lean lamb or beef, coarsely chopped
    salt
    black pepper
3 tbsp. olive oil
1 clove garlic, minced
1 rounded tbsp. tomato paste
7 cups beef, lamb, or chicken stock
1 cup **fideo** vermicelli

Garnish:
    minced parsley
    chopped green onion

1. In a large soup pot, sprinkle the meat with salt and pepper and brown in olive oil. Add the garlic. Stir in the tomato paste and cook for another minute.

2. Pour on the stock and bring to a boil. Add the vermicelli and cook until done, about 10 minutes. Adjust seasoning and garnish with parsley and green onion.

Saffron Garlic Broth with Diced Potatoes

Shorabit Batata (SYRIA)

The saffrony Spanish broth with diced potatoes I threw together one evening, tantalizing with the aroma of garlic and onions, turned out to be a Mediterranean cousin of a soup my husband had enjoyed in his youth. "This is one of those great winter soups Mother used to prepare!" he said. "Of course, she added more potatoes, and threw in a handful of chickpeas, too. How could I have forgotten it for all these years!"

His comment on a Syrian village dish, one I knew as Andalusian Garlic Soup, was an unexpected reminder that for 800 years the great Islamic empire included most of Spain and stretched as far eastward as India. Cultural exchanges were the rule during this Golden Age, whose contributions to Western civilization were astounding, and exotic Eastern foodstuffs were introduced into prosperous European households.

1/2 small onion, minced

2 tbsp. olive oil

pinch saffron, or:

1/2 tsp. **asfor**

6 to 8 cloves garlic, minced

1 can (16 oz.) tomatoes, with juice

7 cups chicken stock

3 potatoes, peeled and diced

salt

black pepper

Garnish:

minced parsley

red or black pepper

1. In a large soup pot, sauté the onion in the olive oil until soft and transparent.

2. Add the saffron or *asfor* and garlic, and stir-fry for 2–3 minutes to release the flavors.

3. Pulse the tomatoes and their juice in a food processor until partially pulverized. There should still be little bits of tomato visible.

4. Add the tomatoes and the remaining ingredients to the onion. Bring to a boil and cook about 12 minutes, until the potatoes are tender but not overcooked. Taste and adjust seasoning.

5. Garnish with parsley.

Variations

Kurdistan: Add 1 large diced carrot, 2 ribs diced celery, and turmeric.

Syria: Add 1 cup cooked chickpeas.

Zesty Potato Bisque

Shorabit Batata (SYRIA)

My friend Raghda fondly recalls this robust favorite, which her mother prepared many evenings as chilling mountain winds rattled the French windows of their Damascus apartment. Years later she ordered a bowl of potato soup in a German restaurant and was startled to be served precisely the same nourishing dish!

The technique used for this classic soup is extremely simple: the garlic and onions are not even sauteed before being added to the potato broth, and the ingredients can be pureed in a food processor or blender. The addition of raw onions in the final step produces a surprising zesty flavor, which prompted my children to proclaim this potato soup "far superior to those ordinary ones you usually make with cream and butter."

    3 large potatoes, peeled and cut up
    3 cups chicken stock
    1 cup low-fat milk
  1/2 small onion, coarsely chopped
    2 cloves garlic, minced
       salt
       black pepper
       pinch allspice or nutmeg

Garnish:
> butter (optional)
> minced parsley
> red or black pepper

1. In a large soup pot, boil the potatoes in the chicken stock until tender.

2. Use a slotted spoon to transfer the cooked potatoes to a food processor or blender. Do not discard their cooking liquid. Add the milk, onion, and garlic to the potatoes, and process until smooth.

3. Return the mixture to the liquid in which the potatoes were cooked, and heat, stirring until well blended. Add seasonings to taste and additional water if the soup is too thick.

4. Raghda's mother placed a generous pat of butter in each soup bowl, but this dish can alternately be garnished with parsley and a sprinkle of red or black pepper.

Pumpkin Soup Any Day

Shorabit Yatkeen (ARAB STATES)

I make this unusual soup in November, when I attack our Halloween pumpkin with a knife and transform it into an endless supply of exotic delicacies. Pumpkin is, after all, of the squash family, with a mellow flavor and smooth texture ideal for soups. In the Arab countries, small chunks of pumpkin are simmered until they disintegrate in a lamb-bone broth. The version described below, with canned pumpkin, makes it possible to enjoy this fall treat any day of the year.

> 1 large onion, chopped
> 2 tbsp. olive oil
> 1 pound lamb bones with meat
> 8 cups water
> 1 can (16 oz.) pumpkin
>   salt
>   black pepper
> 3 tbsp. cornstarch
> 1/4 cup water

1. In a large pot, sauté the onion in the olive oil until transparent and softened.

2. Add to the pot the meat, 8 cups water, pumpkin, and salt and pepper. Bring to a boil, cover, and reduce the heat. Simmer for 2 hours, until the meat is tender.

3. Remove the meat and bones from the stock.

4. Dissolve the cornstarch in $^1/_4$ cup water and add to the broth, stirring until it returns to a boil.

5. Strip the meat from the bones and return the meat to the soup. Taste and adjust seasoning.

Variation

Turkey: Use a blender to beat 1 cup yoghurt into the cornstarch and water.

Secret Police Pigeon Soup

During the years of the economic boom in Saudi Arabia, a Saudi neighbor (reputed to be the chief of Jeddah's Secret Police) called in a European decorator to add some pizzazz and elegance to his old two-story concrete-block villa. Soon, heavily carved and hand-painted plaster moldings graced the ceilings of the formal men's *maq'ad* meeting room on the ground floor and the women's and children's rooms upstairs. As the swirls and curls of the Baroque period entwined everywhere, the refrigerator that usually sat just inside the entrance hall was replaced by an impressive fountain of shimmering crystal palm trees. Golden faucets sprouted in the bathrooms, and dramatic chandeliers glimmered wherever a visitor might glance.

However, although my neighbor demonstrated obvious pride in the public symbols of his wealth and Westernization, two conspicious signs of the "old ways" remained. Perched above the second story women's *hareem* floor, where the ladies usually sat sipping tea and shouting at their Filipino housemaids, remained the prefabricated porta-cabin that served as the family's traditional pantry. Once a year the supplies of staples in the storehouse were renewed, the household's brawny Sudanese servants carried up on their backs huge 50-kilo bags of flour and sugar, chickpeas, lentils, beans, walnuts, and *loomi*.

For a long time I naively believed that my Saudi neighbor was a bird-lover because his flat roof also displayed a large conical structure of wood and chicken wire, a dovecote to which masses of wild birds flocked. How disillusioned I was to discover that food was set out daily to attract pigeons, with the intention of catching and grilling them, or turning them into this tasty broth!

2 onions, chopped

2 tbsp. olive oil

4 pigeons, squab, or Cornish hens
    salt

8 cups water

1/2 tsp. peppercorns

1   stick cinnamon

4 pods cardamom

Garnish:

minced parsley or cilantro

lemon wedges

1. In a large pot, sauté the onions in the oil until softened. Remove with a slotted spoon.

2. Wash the pigeons carefully and dry them. Sprinkle with salt and sauté in the same olive oil until golden brown on all sides.

3. Add the water and the spices and bring to a boil. Skim the foam.

4. Cover and simmer until the birds are tender, about 1 hour.

5. Present one bird in each bowl of broth. Garnish and serve with a generous squeeze of fresh lemon juice.

Easy Meatball Soup

Shorabit Kefta (JORDAN, PALESTINE, ARAB STATES)

This popular meatball soup is complex in its subtle blend of haunting spices, but light and extremely easy to prepare. Studded with tomatoes and rice and sprinkled with fresh parsley, it's a classic of colorful Mediterranean cuisine.

Meatballs:

¼ pound lean ground beef

2 tbsp. minced parsley

salt

black pepper

¼ tsp. allspice

2 tbsp. olive oil

½ small onion, minced

8 cups water

¼ cup uncooked rice, or:

⅓ cup **fideo** vermicelli

4 tsp. beef bouillon

¼ tsp. salt

1 stick cinnamon

½ tsp. Middle Eastern red pepper

1 rounded tbsp. tomato paste

1 ripe tomato, peeled and chopped

1 tbsp. lemon juice, or wine vinegar, or **hamod er rummaan** pomegranate syrup

Garnish:

minced parsley

1. Briefly combine the meatball ingredients in a food processor. Shape the mixture into small meatballs the size of olives.

2. In a skillet, brown the meatballs. Drain on a paper towel. (Some cooks omit this step.)

3. In the same oil, sauté the onion until softened and transparent.

4. Place the meatballs, the onion, and the remaining ingredients (except for the garnish) in a large pot and bring to a boil. Cover and simmer until the rice is tender, 20–30 minutes. (If using vermicelli, let the meatballs simmer for 15 minutes before adding the noodles, then cook for about 10 more minutes, or until noodles are done.) Taste and adjust seasoning.

5. Serve the soup garnished with parsley.

Variations

Palestine: Add 1 tbsp. rice flour to the meat mixture.

Jordan: Omit the rice or vermicelli noodles and lemon juice; remove the finished soup from the heat and stir in 2 eggs beaten with the juice of 1 lemon to produce an avgolemono egg-drop texture.

Andalusia: Omit the rice, noodles, and tomato.

almonds
pistachios, peanuts

Vendor of Nuts and Seeds in Damascus

Vegetables

Wandering the labryinth of Middle Eastern bazaars, I found it difficult to resist the colorful, farm-fresh produce arranged in pyramids of red, green, and yellow designed to tempt every dedicated shopper. When we were staying in our city apartment in Damascus, Mother would sometimes send me across the street to buy a few cucumbers and squash from an open-air market built around the green domed mausoleum of a Muslim saint. In the Gulf, I would throw on my black *abaya* before walking over to the well-lit and air-conditioned vegetable shops, where rosy strawberries and velvety mushrooms flown in that morning from Europe nestled between local melons and Central American bananas.

On Saudi weekends, we would head toward the mammoth wholesale souk on the outskirts of town, where the sun filtered gently through the cotton fabric stretched like butterflies over the brightly laden counters. While the children sucked on chunks of juicy sugarcane pressed into their hands by a portly stallkeeper, we ambled through the crowded aisles, happily sampling honeyed Iraqi dates at one stall, pinching leaves of cilantro to release its aromatic freshness at another booth. I watched with fascination as shoppers bargained before gesturing for wiry Yemenis wrapped in plaid skirts to load their overflowing cases of ripe vegetables and fruit into their cars.

In front of schools and government office buildings in North Africa and throughout the region, farmers and tribal women illegally spread cotton cloths on which they display their produce. And for traditional housewives who preferred to shop in the comfort of their walled front yards, we had Gulam the Pakistani street vendor, who pushed his old-fashioned vegetable cart through the dusty streets of our neighborhood, shouting poetic proclamations about his apples and cucumbers, offering everything needed for our noonday meal.

Nor was it uncommon to see a well-dressed businessman pull off to the side of a highway where a watermelon vendor had stacked several hundred large fruits. The merchant would tap and balance the melons at leisure before selecting six or seven of the largest ones to take home. In the Arab world, vegetables and fruits are attentively selected at the peak of fragrant ripeness and are purchased in huge quantities for the traditional extended families. Although many of these Mediterranean vegetables may be less commonly cooked in the United States, all are readily available year-round, in contrast to the feasts of seasonal abundance.

Most of us were conditioned in our youth to believe that meat and dairy products are our best sources of protein, but today's interest in cooking with vegetables has led us to look eastward for inspiration. The various interrelated culinary traditions of the Middle East provide an extensive list of exciting vegetable combinations, while numerous other recipes dictate only a few ounces of meat. Many of these vegetarian recipes originated in Christian Orthodox communities, principally among Egypt's Copts, Armenians scattered by the diaspora all over the region, and small Christian minorities from Lebanon and throughout the Fertile Crescent. From the arduous Lenten and Advent fasts during which all animal food and milk products are prohibited, we inherit an extensive family of splendid vegetable dishes.

Fresh from the fields and steamed in their own liquid, vegetables retain their full nutritive value. Tomatoes, onions, and garlic add zest to the chosen vegetable, while olive oil supplies full, smooth body. Lighter but more intense than French ratatouille, many of these tangy vegetarian combinations can also be prepared in advance and served at room temperature.

Stuffed squash, tomatoes, and eggplant, delightful packages with exotic fillings, originated in the kitchens of the Ottoman and Abbasid caliphs. Court dishes invented to entertain the extravagant tastes of affluent nobility are today a measure of a woman's technical skill and a customary manner of demonstrating hospitality to a notable visitor. (Or are these elaborate and time-consuming specialties retained by a patriarchal male-dominated society because they occupy a woman's time with domestic affairs and keep her from misadventures outside the home?)

Nearly every vegetable and leaf can be stuffed: in Iraq and the Gulf States even tiny crisp cucumbers are hollowed out and filled, and Syrians roll Swiss chard leaves around a similar filling. The most common stuffing is a combination of rice and fresh herbs blended with a bit of meat, tomatoes, and/or currants. With the large number of women in the Middle East forced by economic necessity to work outside the home, the time and effort required to prepare *dolma* and *mahshi* mean that what was once a daily treat is now increasingly reserved for major social and family events.

Middle Eastern cuisine is built on modest combinations of crisp, colorful vegetables that are prepared with lavish creativity and great attention to detail. Nevertheless, their significance is often overlooked by my talented Arab friends. Arabic language cookbooks also underplay the splendid local vegetable entrées and simpler side dishes, which are just not considered prestige foods. Although often scarce and infrequently served, meat is still the "president" of foods, but vegetables will always remain the "mother."

Artichoke Mélange in Olive Oil

Artichokes are one of my favorite vegetables but were not available in local markets during our years in Saudi Arabia. My husband's Syrian relatives, always overwhelmingly hospitable, lavished us with thoughtfulness during every holiday visit to the village, preparing every intricate and time-consuming specialty we dared to mention. My comment about not finding fresh artichokes in the Kingdom to the south brought instant response.

The following day, Uncle Nadir walked into the kitchen where we sat on sheepskin rugs on the floor, busily coring a monstrous pile of 100 green *koosa* squash. "Mother of Said," (the proper form of address by a man who is not a blood relative, denoting a respectable woman who is the mother of a male child), "I brought you artichokes!" Over Nadir's impressive shoulder, only surpassed by his well-endowed waistline, hung a plastic sack the size of Santa's bag.

How could I complain, especially when the 52 artichokes cost the grand total of 50 Syrian pounds, only one dollar?

"Put them over there, under the bench," ordered Mother imperiously. "We'll take care of those this afternoon."

"My husband only brings *me* artichokes that have already been cleaned," whispered one of the cousins, a new bride, and I began to look at the scratchy, tough bulbs from a new perspective. Until that moment, preparing huge mounds of *koosa* squash had been my least favorite culinary activity, but I could see that it would soon be supplanted by another chore, that of cutting off the dry, leathery artichoke leaves and scraping out the choke.

This recipe is for the tasty dish Mother prepared the next day, but in all honesty I must mention that we only attacked half of the 52 adversaries. I subsequently introduced the family to the Western manner of eating artichokes, and children and adults alike thoroughly enjoyed tearing off the steamed leaves to dip in a lemon-olive oil marinade. (Butter, being an imported black-market item in Syria, isn't readily available.) Now when I make Mother's artichoke recipe, I use canned artichoke bottoms, which in America is a more practical and economical alternative.

1 can (14 or 16 oz.) artichoke bottoms, or frozen artichoke bottoms (10 oz. package), prepared according to package instructions
1/4 cup minced onion
2 tbsp. olive oil
1/2 cup carrots, cut into tiny dice
1/2 cup water (divided use)
    salt
1/2 tsp. cornstarch
    juice of 1/2 lemon
1/2 cup cooked peas

1. Arrange the artichoke bottoms in an oven-safe serving dish.

2. Lightly sauté the onion in the olive oil until soft and transparent.

3. Add the diced carrot and sauté for another minute. Stir in half of the water and the salt. Bring to a boil and simmer, covered, for about 5 minutes.

4. Beat the cornstarch into the remaining ¼ cup water. Add, along with the lemon juice and peas, and simmer for 5 additional minutes.

5. Pour the vegetables and their sauce over the artichokes. Bake at 350 degrees for 15 minutes. Serve warm or at room temperature.

Variations

Lebanon: Substitute green (fava) beans for the carrot and peas.

Turkey: Add 2 small minced potatoes to the carrots and peas, and garnish with fresh dill.

Egypt: Use artichoke hearts and simmer the ingredients together rather than baking.

Artichoke Appetizer

Al Khurshoof (MOROCCO, ANDALUSIA)

It was in the cultured land of Arab Spain that table etiquette and the consumption of cooked vegetables and refined and distinctive spices first appeared in Europe. The Spanish word for artichoke—*alcachofa*—is without doubt of Arab origin (*al-khurshuf*), as is the delicious tart sumac (*el zumaque* or *al summaq*), used in this recipe's dressing. Serve this as a vegetable side dish or as a *mezzeh* appetizer in the manner of Spanish tapas.

2 cans (14 or 16 oz. each) artichoke hearts, or 2 packages (10 oz. each) frozen artichoke hearts

Dressing:

1 clove garlic, crushed with
  salt
¼ cup olive oil
2 tbsp. lemon juice
1 tsp. sumac
¼ tsp. tarragon, or: Middle Eastern red pepper
¼ cup minced cilantro

1. Drain and quarter the canned artichokes. Or, prepare the frozen artichokes according to package instructions, and quarter.

2. Combine the dressing ingredients and pour over the artichoke hearts. Marinate for at least 1 hour. Serve at room temperature.

Black-Eyed Peas in Tomato Broth

Loobia (KURDISTAN)

Black-eyed peas appear often in Iraqi, Kurdish, and Kuwaiti cuisine. One of the most appealing combinations is the following Kurdish tomato-based broth, which is served over white rice. Rich with onions, garlic, and the celery that is characteristic of Iraqi food, it reminds me of some of the soups my Italian aunts used to prepare.

Although this recipe specifies a small amount of lamb, it is equally tasty when prepared as a meatless dish using beef broth.

- 1 large onion, chopped
- 3 tbsp. olive oil
- 2 cloves garlic, minced
- 1/2 pound lamb, cut into small cubes
- salt
- pepper
- 1 cup dried black-eyed peas
- 4 ribs celery, sliced crosswise
- 2 ripe tomatoes, chopped
- 6 cups water
- 1 rounded tsp. tomato paste
- 1 tsp. **kebsa** spice mixture, or: **garam masala**, or curry powder
- 1/2 tsp. Middle Eastern red pepper
- salt
- black pepper

1. Sauté the onion in the olive oil until soft and transparent. Add the garlic and cook for an additional minute.

2. Increase the heat and add the lamb, seasoning with salt and pepper. Toss and cook until browned. Add the remaining ingredients and bring to a boil. Cover and simmer for 1^1/$_2$ hours, until the meat and the peas are tender. The sauce will reduce but still be brothy. Taste and adjust seasoning. Serve over rice.

Variation

Egypt: Omit the celery, red pepper, and **spices.**

Spiced Chickpeas with Fresh Herbs

Tajeen el Hummos (MOROCCO)

For centuries Middle Easterners have believed that dishes like this flavorful Moroccan chickpea stew, when served with bread or over *burghol* wheat or rice, give extra energy. Legumes like chickpeas, beans, and lentils do contain larger amounts of protein than other plant foods, and when eaten together with a grain, the proteins are better utilized by the body.

1^1/$_2$ cups dried chickpeas, soaked overnight

  6 cups water

    salt

  1 tsp. baking soda (optional)

  1 onion, slivered

  2 tbsp. olive oil

  1 large ripe tomato, peeled, seeded, and chopped

  1 stick cinnamon

  ^{1}/$_8$ tsp. Middle Eastern red pepper

  ^{1}/$_8$ tsp. ground ginger

  ^{1}/$_8$ tsp. cumin

  ^{1}/$_8$ tsp. sweet paprika

⅛ tsp. **asfor**, or: pinch saffron

½ cup minced parsley

½ cup minced cilantro

   salt

   black pepper

1. Drain and rinse the soaked chickpeas. Cover with 6 cups water. Add the salt and optional baking soda and bring to a boil. Cover and simmer until tender, about 1½ hours or longer. If less than 1 cup of cooking liquid remains, add water.

2. In another saucepan, sauté the onion in the olive oil until softened. Add the chickpeas and their broth, along with the tomato and all the spices. Cover and simmer for 15 minutes.

3. Stir in the parsley and cilantro and taste to adjust seasoning, adding salt and black pepper as necessary.

Cauliflower with Cilantro

Qarnabeed bil Kuzbara (SAUDI ARABIA)

Ground beef or cubes of lamb are sometimes added to this tasty combination of cauliflower tossed with fresh herbs and two types of chilis.

1 head cauliflower, cut into florets

¼ cup olive oil

6 green onions

3 cloves garlic, minced

1 serrano chili, seeded and minced (optional)

½ cup minced cilantro

1 tsp. Middle Eastern red pepper

  salt

  black pepper

1. Steam the cauliflower in a bit of salted water for 6 minutes. Drain.

2. Heat the olive oil and add the cauliflower, onions, garlic, and chili. Stir-fry for 2 minutes. Add the remaining ingredients, taste to adjust seasoning, and toss to blend flavors.

Poblano Chilis with Cilantro Cheese Stuffing

Filfil Mahshi bil Kuzbara (SAUDI ARABIA)

This is yet another uncommon combination curiously similar to Mexico's extraordinary chiles rellenos, but lower in fat because it is baked rather than fried.

 8 small poblano or Anaheim chilis
 1/2 cup white cheese (feta or similar type)
 1/2 cup Monterey Jack cheese, grated
 1/2 cup minced cilantro

Tomato Sauce:
 1/2 onion, chopped
 1 tbsp. olive oil
 1 can (16 oz.) tomatoes, with juice
 salt
 2 tbsp. minced cilantro

1. Roast the chilis under the broiler as described on p. 73. (Anaheim chilis are milder than poblanos, but are more delicate and harder to handle, especially if roasted directly over the burner of a stove.) Peel the chilis as you run them under cold water. Make a slit in each and remove the seeds, leaving the stem connected.

2. Combine the cheeses and the 1/2 cup cilantro, and fill each chili with this mixture. Place in a baking dish.

3. Sauté the onion in the olive oil until soft and transparent.

4. Whirl the tomatoes and their juice in a blender or food processor until nearly smooth. Pour over the onions and stir to blend. Add salt, taste and adjust seasoning.

5. Pour the sauce over the peppers and sprinkle the 2 tbsp. cilantro over the dish. Bake at 350 degrees for about 20 minutes.

Grilled Eggplant with Apricot Pomegranate Sauce

Beitinjan bil Hamod (IRAQ)

~~~~~~

Here, the Middle Eastern favorite is flavored with the exotic sweetness of pomegranates and apricots, and a touch of tartness. Iraqi cuisine, a remarkably rich blending of Syrian-Turkish influences from the west, Gulf flavors, and Persian cookery from the northeast, frequently includes touches of natural fruity sweetness in its dishes.

  6 small Japanese eggplants, or 1 large eggplant, peeled
     olive oil
     salt

Pomegranate sauce:
  1 piece (about 1 inch square) **amradeen** (sun-dried apricot sheet), or:
 ½ dried apricot, minced
 ¼ cup hot water
  1 tsp. lemon juice
  2 tbsp. **hamod er rummaan** pomegranate syrup
     pinch Middle Eastern red pepper

Garnish:
     minced parsley
     pomegranate seeds (optional)

1. Soak the *amradeen* or dried apricot in the hot water to which you have added the lemon juice.

2. The small eggplants should be cut lengthwise into slices $1/2$ inch thick. A large eggplant should be cut crosswise to the same dimension. Brush each slice on both sides with olive oil, sprinkle lightly with salt, and grill or broil until golden.

3. When the *amradeen* is very soft, stir in the remaining sauce ingredients. (The dried apricot may need to be pressed through a mesh sieve.) The fruit will disintegrate into a syrupy sauce.

4. Arrange the eggplant slices in an attractive pattern on a serving platter and drizzle with the pomegranate sauce. Garnish with parsley and (optional) pomegranate seeds.

Baked Eggplant Slices with Tomato

Beitinjan bil Furan (JORDAN)

This colorful recipe is perfect for a buffet dinner, an especially easy way to prepare eggplant. The first two steps can be done in advance, leaving the tray of vegetables to be slipped into the oven at the last minute.

1 eggplant, peeled and cut into slices $2/3$ inch thick
  salt
  olive oil
$1/2$ small onion, chopped
2 tbsp. olive oil
3 oz. ground beef
$1/2$ tsp. allspice
  salt
  black pepper
2 ripe tomatoes, sliced medium thin

1. Sprinkle the eggplant slices lightly with salt and brush with olive oil. Place broiler rack in the second position and broil the eggplant until soft and a light golden color. Turn, brush the other side with oil, and broil.

2. Meanwhile, sauté the onion in 2 tbsp. olive oil until soft and transparent. Add the ground beef, sprinkling with allspice, salt, and pepper, and cook until all traces of pink disappear. Drain the fat.

3. Press a little of the meat mixture into the center of each softened slice of eggplant. Place in an oven-safe dish and cover with slices of tomato. Season with salt and pepper, and bake at 350 degrees until done, about 15 minutes.

Variations

Saudi Arabia: Use slightly smaller whole eggplants (not Japanese eggplants) sliced in half lengthwise, substituting *kebsa* spice for the allspice, and basting with tomato sauce.

Armenia: Add 1 chopped green pepper to the meat.

Eggplants Stuffed with Burghol

Beitinjan Mahshi (SYRIA)

Although rice is the grain Arabs usually select today for stuffing vegetables, it is pricey in comparison to the wheat for which the Fertile Crescent was invaded countless times. *Burghol* wheat's earthy taste and unique texture are a perfect foil for the smooth cream of cooked eggplant.

Born, according to Arab folklore, in the Garden of Eden, *burghol* rapidly spread to India, China, and Japan. Steamed and sun-dried with minimal processing, a great part of its appeal is that it's an excellent source of vitamins and energy.

2 medium eggplants

1/2 cup olive oil (divided use)

Stuffing:

- 1 onion, chopped
- 2 cloves garlic, minced
- 3 ounces ground beef
- salt
- black pepper
- ³/₄ cup coarse **burghol** wheat, rinsed
- 1 ¹/₂ cups water

1. Cut the eggplants in half lengthwise and remove the green stems. Scoop out the flesh, scraping the inside of the vegetable until a shell about ¹/₃ inch thick remains. Reserve the pulp.

2. Gently sauté the four shells in ¹/₄ cup of the olive oil, turning until all surfaces are softened. Remove and drain on paper towels.

3. Sauté the onion in the same olive oil until soft and transparent. Add the garlic and the meat and sprinkle with salt and pepper. Cook until no traces of pink remain, breaking up all lumps. Remove with a slotted spoon and set aside.

4. Chop about ¹/₄ of the eggplant pulp and stir-fry it in the same oil for about 5 minutes.

5. In a nonstick saucepan, slowly brown the *burghol* in the remaining ¹/₄ cup olive oil until each grain glistens. Stir in the meat mixture, the eggplant pulp, the water, and additional salt and pepper. Cover and simmer until done, about 30 minutes. Taste and adjust seasoning.

6. Place eggplant shells in an oven-safe dish. Mound the cooked filling into the shells, cover with foil, and bake at 350 degrees for 30 minutes.

Variation

Add 1 chopped ripe tomato and 1 round tbsp. tomato paste to the *burghol*.

Green Beans in Light Olive Oil Sauce

Fassooleehah bi Zeit (LEBANON)

~~~~~~

This classic Levantine recipe is rather like a Mediterranean green bean salad, with tomato paste added in place of the vinegar. Across the Fertile Crescent and into the Arabian Gulf States, this is the most popular method of preparing green beans. Its mild garlicky flavor appeals to every nationality, and it's a personal favorite of mine because the frozen beans are always tender and ready to serve in an instant. A perfect component in a large buffet dinner because it is served at room temperature, **Green Beans in Light Olive Oil Sauce** is even more tasty when prepared a day in advance.

1	large onion, slivered
⅓	cup olive oil
8	cloves garlic
1	pound green beans, fresh or frozen (cut into pieces)
1	rounded tbsp. tomato paste
1	large tomato, chopped
	salt
⅓	cup water
1	bunch cilantro, chopped
	generous pinch Middle Eastern red pepper

1. Lightly sauté the onion in the olive oil until softened. Add the garlic and cook for another minute.

2. Add the remaining ingredients except for the cilantro and red pepper. Bring to a boil. Cover, reduce heat, and simmer until the beans have absorbed the tomatoey sauce and are very soft—about 30 minutes, or longer. (Fresh beans may take up to 1 hour, and may require the addition of more water.)

3. Add the cilantro and red pepper and cook 5 more minutes. Taste and adjust seasoning. The sauce should be thick and each bean glistening and coated.

4. Serve chilled or at room temperature.

Variations

Turkey: Add 1 tsp. sugar.

Saudi Arabia: Add a serrano or jalapeño chili, seeded and minced.

Egypt: Add allspice.

Andalusia: Substitute 2 tsp. wine vinegar for the cilantro.

Red Pepper Green Beans

El Loobia Khadra il Mubahira (MOROCCO)

In Morocco, sweet yet sultry red peppers are used in this dish. You may be able to find a similar vegetable in a Mexican market. Or, you can do as I suggest in the following recipe and substitute a fresh red pimento for color and texture and fresh jalapeño chilis for a piquant tang.

- 1 small onion, slivered
- 3 tbsp. olive oil
- 3 cloves garlic, minced
- 1 or 2 jalapeño chilis, seeded and chopped
- 1 small sweet red pimento, seeded, and slivered
- 1 pound green beans fresh or frozen (whole)
- 1 large ripe tomato, peeled, seeded, and chopped

1. Sauté the onion in the olive oil until slightly softened. Add the garlic and chilis and cook for another minute.

2. If you are using frozen beans, cook them according to package instructions and drain. If you are using fresh beans, steam them until tender.

3. Add the drained beans and the tomato to the onion and toss to mix well. Cover and steam for about 3 minutes, until the flavors blend.

Variation

Andalusia: Substitute julienned green peppers for the green beans.

Lentils with Swiss Chard and Cilantro

Adas bi Sili' (SYRIA)

~~~~~~

Syria's fertile Golan Heights farmlands, where a variety of fresh vegetables and fruits grew at varying altitudes nearly all year round, used to supply the vegetable markets of nearby Damascus with fresh produce on into the chilly fall months. The natural growing season of each vegetable was thus lengthened, an essential feature in a traditional economy.

Now, local families prepare for the harsh winters, when blasts of frigid gales rattle the windowpanes and little is available in local vegetable souks, by drying vegetables and by stocking up on legumes. But as soon as the first spring greens poke their heads through the soil, a prayer of thanks is murmured and the leaves are added to the diet as in the following recipe.

Swiss chard is actually a kind of beet that does not develop the usual bulbous root. A favorite of the ancient Romans and Greeks, its flavor, when cooked, is delicate and spinach-like.

1 cup green or brown lentils, rinsed

2 quarts water

   salt

1 onion, chopped

1/4 cup olive oil

3 cloves garlic, minced

4 cups shredded Swiss chard leaves, or flat-leaf spinach

3/4 cup minced cilantro

   juice of 1 lemon

Garnish:

   lemon wedges

1. Add the lentils to the water and bring to a boil. Add the salt, cover, and simmer until tender, 1 to 1 1/2 hours. Drain.

2. In a deep nonstick pan, sauté the onion in the olive oil until soft and transparent. Stir in the garlic and cook for another minute.

3. Add the Swiss chard or spinach and the cilantro, and simmer over very low heat, covered, for 10–15 minutes. Stir occasionally. Add the lemon juice, taste, and adjust seasoning.

4. Serve with lemon wedges.

Variation

Palestine: Add cumin.

Baby Okra in Olive Oil

Bamia bi Zeit (LEBANON)

In Lebanon and Syria, only the tiniest baby okra are used in this dish, none more than 1¹/₂ inches in length. It's one of the most strikingly tasty of a large repertoire of delicious Levantine dishes prepared with olive oil, garlic, and cilantro.

    1 quart okra, as fresh and small as you can find
  ¹/₂ cup olive oil
    2 onions, slivered
   10 cloves garlic
    3 ripe tomatoes, chopped
  ¹/₂ cup water
       salt
       pinch Middle Eastern red pepper (optional)
       pinch sugar (optional)
    1 small bunch cilantro, chopped
       juice of 1 lemon

1. The secret to a proper okra dish is to remove the stem without cutting completely through to expose the sticky central core of the okra pod. Hold the okra in your left hand, with its stem facing your right hand. Using a sharp, short-bladed paring knife, peel off only the outer layer of the cone-shaped tip. One deft twist of each okra, and a thin curl of hard

stem falls off. While this is a time-consuming chore in the Middle East, where okra averages a tiny 1 inch to 1^3/4 inches in length, it only takes a few minutes here because our smallest okra are nearly double that size. Rinse and drain.

2. Sauté the okra in two batches in the olive oil, until it just begins to color. Remove with a slotted spoon. In the same oil, sauté the onions until soft and transparent. Add the whole cloves of garlic and cook for another minute.

3. Stir in the tomatoes, water, salt, red pepper, and optional sugar, and bring to a boil. Cover and simmer for about ^{1}/2 hour. Check frequently, gently moving the okra to keep them from sticking.

4. Sprinkle with cilantro and lemon juice, cover, and simmer for 2 or 3 more minutes. The okra should be soft but not mushy and overdone. Serve at room temperature.

Variations

Iraq: Substitute fresh mint, parsley, and celery leaves for the cilantro; add chopped celery.

Armenia: Add a fresh hot red pepper and substitute fresh basil for the cilantro.

Kuwait: Add *kebsa* spices and *loomi*.

Braised Onions and Celery with Cinnamon

El Basal el Matbooh (MOROCCO)

The onion was a sacred symbol for the ancient peoples of North Africa, who saw in its unique layer-on-layer structure a symbol of eternity. The slaves who constructed the great pyramids of Egypt are said to have subsisted mainly on a diet of garlic and onions, and sacred oaths were taken with the right hand resting on an onion.

 2 large sweet onions, sliced
 2 ribs celery, cut into 3-inch lengths

1 1/2 cups water
  2 tbsp. olive oil
  1 stick cinnamon
1/2 tsp. sugar
1/4 tsp. ground ginger
    pinch saffron
    pinch black pepper

Place all the ingredients in a saucepan and bring to a boil. Cover, reduce heat, and simmer for about 25 minutes, until the vegetables are tender.

Vegetable Omelette

Juz Muz (KURDISTAN)

My half-Kurdish mother-in-law frequently whips up the following delicious and quick Mediterranean vegetable omelette for the evening meal. In the affluent West, the egg has been much maligned because of its high cholesterol content and has been branded as a menace to health. But in the Middle East, healthy nutrition rather than dietary excess is still the guiding factor. Mother never takes eggs for granted, because they're a rich source of protein in a society where meat is expensive and scarce. "It's better an egg today than a chicken tomorrow," she says, a lesson taught by the uncertainties of life in the turbulent Arab world.

  1 large onion, chopped
  2 tbsp. olive oil
1/3 pound ground beef
    salt
    black pepper
  3 ripe tomatoes, coarsely chopped
1/2 cup chopped parsley
  4 eggs
1/2 tsp. allspice
    pinch Middle Eastern red pepper

1. Sauté the onion in the olive oil until soft and transparent.

2. Add the meat and season with salt and black pepper to taste. Sauté until the meat has lost all traces of pink.

3. Stir in the tomatoes and parsley, and cook for 2 minutes.

4. Beat the eggs with the allspice and the red pepper.

5. Pour the beaten eggs over the meat and vegetables, stirring rapidly to combine the ingredients thoroughly.

6. Cook the omelette until dry, turning once.

Parsley Puffs

Ajeja (LIBYA, ANDALUSIA, ARAB STATES)

Across the Arab world a large variety of vegetables are minced and combined with eggs and fresh herbs to form a fluffy sautéed pancake known in most regions as *ijjah*. Although the names differ, this Libyan omelette is no more than the North African cousin of the preceding Kurdish omelette. It's made at home but is also a favorite fast-food choice of laborers during their lunch break.

  3 eggs, beaten
$^1/_4$ cup low-fat milk
  1 tbsp. olive oil
$^1/_4$ cup flour
  1 tsp. baking powder
  2 cups minced parsley
$^1/_2$ cup minced cilantro
  2 green onions, chopped
  1 clove garlic, minced
$^1/_2$ tsp. cumin
     generous pinch Middle Eastern red pepper
     salt
$^1/_4$ cup olive oil for sautéing

1. Combine the eggs with the milk, 1 tbsp. oil, flour, and baking powder. Stir in the herbs and spices.

2. Heat $1/4$ cup olive oil and drop in large spoonfuls of the parsley batter. Sauté until golden, turning once.

Variations

Libya: Use equal amounts of chopped parsley, cilantro, and spinach or Swiss chard.

Lebanon: Add 2 tbsp. minced fresh mint.

Saudi Arabia: Substitute leeks or spinach for the parsley and cilantro.

Safiyya's Potato Surprise

Batata Mbatana (LIBYA)

"I was named for one of the Prophet Muhammad's wives," Safiyya reminded me proudly. "She was a beautiful Jewish lady from Mecca who converted to Islam." The prophet certainly had an eye for attractive women, I recalled, my eyes focused on the silver tray of Libyan specialties that were to accompany our mint tea. Could those be chicken fillets artfully arranged between sprigs of parsley and an assortment of pink and green homemade pickles?

No, not at all. With a thousand opportunities I would never have ventured to guess that they were potatoes, thinly sliced lengthwise, dipped in batter, with a surprise filling of spiced ground meat. The proverb says that "the long arm reaches the cluster of grapes," and I'll admit that my arm stretched out toward the **Safiyya's Potato Surprise** too many times that evening!

2 large potatoes, peeled

Filling:

   3 ounces ground beef

   1 green onion, minced

   1 tbsp. minced parsley

    pinch cinnamon

pinch cloves

pinch cumin

pinch Middle Eastern red pepper

salt

Batter:

1 cup flour

2 eggs

1 egg white

¼ cup water

¼ tsp. salt

olive oil for sautéing

1. Slice the potatoes lengthwise as thinly as possible. Lay out the slices in pairs that are of similar shape and size.

2. Combine the filling ingredients. Divide the filling into small portions, one for each pair of potatoes. Press the meat onto a slice of potato, spreading it into an even, thin layer. Top with the matching slice, to create a thin potato "sandwich" filled with meat.

3. When all the sandwiches are ready, beat together the batter ingredients. Dip each potato sandwich in the thick batter to coat, and sauté in hot olive oil until golden brown. The potatoes will be tender and the meat filling thoroughly cooked.

Preparing Arabian Gulf Coffee

Grandmother's Spicy Sautéed Potatoes

Batata Mi'leeyeh (SYRIA, ANDALUSIA, ARAB STATES)

Small wonder this spicy recipe of sautéed potatoes has so many regional variations! It's simply the finest flavor combination in its category, and easy to prepare as well. The response to this dish is so emphatic that one potato per person is not really sufficient: I've listed 5 large potatoes as required to serve 4 individuals.

5 large potatoes, peeled and cut into bite-sized chunks
4 tbsp. olive oil
2 cloves garlic, minced
1/2 tsp. Middle Eastern red pepper
  salt
  black pepper
1/2 cup chopped cilantro

1. In a nonstick pan (a wok is perfect) sauté the potatoes in the olive oil for 5 minutes. Toss frequently to keep from sticking. Cover the pan and cook on medium heat for 15 more minutes. Uncover and sauté until the potatoes begin to color.

2. Add the garlic and stir-fry over lower heat (so the garlic will not burn) for 3–5 more minutes, until crispy but tender on the inside.

3. Sprinkle with spices, toss in the cilantro, and taste to adjust seasoning.

Variations

Kuwait: Add *kebsa* spices.

Syria: Sprinkle the cooked potatoes with a generous squeeze of lemon juice.

Lebanon: Sprinkle with 1 tbsp. *hamod er rummaan* pomegranate syrup or 1 tbsp. ground sumac soaked in 1 tbsp. hot water.

Andalusia: Add 1 rounded tsp. tomato paste and a dash of wine vinegar, or substitute 1 tsp. sweet paprika for the cilantro.

Libyan Potatoes with Bzar

Batatis bi Bzar (LIBYA)

~~~~~~

Libya is especially proud of its superior varieties of potatoes, and of all the Arab countries, it is Libya that produces so many remarkably unusual potato dishes. New potatoes are especially tasty when seasoned with this recipe's aromatic blend of spices known as *bzar*. Some of Libya's new potatoes are so firm and juicy that they can be eaten without cooking!

    4 large new potatoes (about 1³/₄ pounds), peeled and cut into ¹/₂ inch cubes
    5 tbsp. olive oil (divided use)
1 ¹/₂ cups water
       salt
    1 large onion, chopped
    1 tsp. Middle Eastern red pepper
  ¹/₂ tsp. turmeric
  ¹/₂ tsp. ground coriander
  ¹/₄ tsp. cumin
       pinch cloves
       pinch cinnamon
       pinch black pepper
       pinch ground ginger
       juice of 1 lemon
    1 or 2 tbsp. water
       butter (optional)

1. Lightly sauté the potatoes in 3 tbsp. of the olive oil until golden. Add the 1¹/₂ cups water and the salt and bring to a boil. Cover and simmer for about 10 minutes, until potatoes are partially cooked but still slightly firm. Drain any water that remains in the pan.

2. Meanwhile, sauté the onion in the remaining 2 tbsp. olive oil until soft and transparent. Add the spices and stir to coat the onion with the spices. Simmer, uncovered, for 1 minute to blend flavors.

3. Add the drained potatoes and toss until they are glistening with spices. Sprinkle with lemon juice and 1 or 2 tbsp. water; many Libyan cooks add a bit of butter at this point for sweetness. Cover and simmer 3–5 minutes, or until tender.

Saudi Potato Pancakes

Keftit Batata (SAUDI ARABIA)

~~~~~~

This is probably a regional variation of a very intricate Iraqi stuffed potato delicacy known as *batata chap*. In the following Saudi version mashed potatoes are kneaded together with a bit of well-seasoned ground meat, onions, and cilantro. The technique doesn't require the elaborate and delicate handiwork of similar northern dishes born in the courts of the Abbasids and the Ottomans, yet it is a sure crowd-pleaser.

  4 potatoes, peeled
 ½ onion, chopped
  2 tbsp. olive oil
  3 ounces ground beef
     salt
     black pepper
 ½ tsp. **kebsa** spices
  2 tbsp. minced cilantro
  2 eggs, beaten with
  1 tbsp. water
  1 cup seasoned bread crumbs
     olive oil for sautéing

1. Steam the potatoes in salted water until tender. Drain, and mash until smooth.

2. Sauté the onion in olive oil until soft and transparent. Add the meat, season with salt and spices, and cook until no traces of pink remain. Drain in a colander. Taste and adjust the seasoning, keeping in mind that the meat will be mixed with the mildly flavored potato dough.

3. When the potatoes and meat are cool enough to handle, mix them together, adding the cilantro. Form into balls the size of large walnuts and flatten between the palms of your hands.

4. Dip first into beaten egg and then into seasoned crumbs. Lightly sauté in olive oil until a pale golden brown.

Stewed Potatoes with Chickpeas and Tomatoes

Msa'it Batata (LEBANON)

A classic Mediterranean combination, this dish is known in every country of the region, although the name frequently is modified and another vegetable sometimes replaces the potatoes.

 2 large onions, slivered

 ¹⁄₄ cup olive oil

 2 cloves garlic, minced

 4 large potatoes, peeled and sliced medium thick

  salt

  black pepper

2–3 cups cooked chickpeas

 3 large ripe tomatoes, cut into wedges

1. Sauté the onions in the olive oil until soft but not yet transparent. Add the garlic and cook for another minute. Remove from the oil with a slotted spoon.

2. Add the potatoes to the same pan and sauté over medium to high heat until golden. They will be seared on the outside but not completely cooked or tender. Season with salt and pepper. Return the onions to the pan, cover, and simmer for 2 or 3 minutes to blend the flavors. Transfer the vegetables and the olive oil to a shallow baking dish.

3. Distribute the cooked chickpeas over the potatoes. Top with tomato wedges and sprinkle with salt and pepper. Cover with foil and bake at 350 degrees for 30–40 minutes, or until the potatoes are tender. Serve warm or at room temperature.

Variations

Lebanon: Cook on top of the stove.

Syria: Use 1 large cubed eggplant in place of the potatoes.

Palestine: Add 1 rounded tsp. tomato paste.

Fresh Spinach with Onion Crisp

Sabanigh ma Basal (SYRIA)

~~~~~~

This wholesome village dish is straightforward and direct: nothing but the nutritious goodness of steamed spinach, served with a refreshing squeeze of lemon juice and the sweet, nutty crunch of a toasted onion garnish.

Spinach originated in Persia, where it is creatively combined with pilafs and with dried fruits. Not until the 19th century did it reach the shores of America.

- 1 onion, chopped
- 2 tbsp. olive oil
- 2 bunches spinach, cut into ribbons
- 2 tbsp. water
- salt
- juice of 1 lemon

Garnish:

- 2 onions, slivered
- 3 tbsp. olive oil
- 1 lemon, cut into wedges

1. Sauté the chopped onions in the 2 tbsp. olive oil until soft and transparent. Add the spinach, water, and salt, and simmer, covered, until wilted (about 10 minutes). Stir occasionally. Raise the heat a bit, if necessary, to dry up the liquid by the end of the cooking time.

2. Meanwhile, slowly sauté the slivered onions in the 3 tbsp. oil until dark golden brown and crispy.

3. Stir the lemon juice into the cooked spinach and transfer to a serving tray. Top with the crisped onions and their cooking oil.

4. Decorate the serving tray with the lemon wedges, to be squeezed over the spinach as desired.

Shepherd's Pie with White Beans

Tajeen (TUNISIA)

~~~~~~

In North Africa, the word *tajeen* indicates a meat and vegetable stew that is scooped up with bread. In the following Tunisian version, white beans are simmered until tender with bits of lamb and the trusted Mediterranean flavors of tomato, garlic, and onion. Then beaten eggs and white cheese are added and the casserole is baked.

1/4 pound lamb, cubed

  6 tbsp. olive oil (divided use)

    salt

    black pepper

  1 large onion, chopped

  2 cloves garlic, minced

  1 serrano chili, seeded and minced

1/2 cup large white beans, soaked overnight and drained

  4 cups water

  2 rounded tbsp. tomato paste

1/2 tsp. oregano

1/2 tsp. cumin

    salt

1/2 bunch spinach, cut into ribbons

  2 eggs, beaten with

  1 egg white

1/2 cup feta or similar white cheese

1/4 cup bread crumbs

1. Brown the lamb in 2 tbsp. olive oil, sprinkling with salt and pepper. Remove with a slotted spoon.

2. Add 2 tbsp. more oil and sauté the onion until soft and transparent. Add the garlic and chili and cook for another minute. Stir in the beans, water, tomato paste, and spices, and bring to a boil. Cover and simmer until both the beans and the meat are tender, about 1 hour or longer. The broth will reduce and nearly dry up, but take care that the beans do not stick and burn. Add a few spoonfuls of water if necessary.

3. When the contents of the pot are dry and tender, stir-fry the spinach until wilted in the remaining oil. Add to the meat and beans, simmering for 5 minutes.

4. Combine the eggs with the cheese and bread crumbs and stir into the pot. Transfer to a casserole and bake at 350 degrees for 30–40 minutes.

Variations

Libya: Substitute chickpeas for the white beans.

Andalusia: Use chickpeas and prepare through step 3, then sprinkle with crumbled hard-boiled eggs.

Spinach and Black-Eyed Peas or Fava Beans

Sabanigh bi Loobia (KUWAIT)

Black-eyed peas, a favorite in the Fertile Crescent and Gulf States, are here tossed with fresh spinach, garlic, and lemon juice. Large brown fava beans are an equally delicious choice for this healthy combination.

$3/4$ cup dried black-eyed peas or brown fava beans (soaked overnight)
  1 bunch spinach, cut into ribbons
  2 cloves garlic, minced
$1/4$ cup olive oil
    juice of 1 lemon
  1 tsp. cumin
$1/2$ tsp. cinnamon
$1/4$ tsp. cloves
$1/4$ tsp. ground coriander
$1/2$ tsp. Middle Eastern red pepper
    salt
    black pepper

1. Boil the black-eyed peas or the presoaked fava beans in a large quantity of water. Cook the peas for $1/2$ hour or the fava beans for 1 hour. Stir in the spinach and steam for another $1/2$ hour, watching carefully to see that the vegetables do not stick to the bottom of the pan. The amount of liquid in the pan should reduce and evaporate, but spoonfuls of water may be added, if necessary, to prevent burning.

2. In a small pan, sauté the garlic in the olive oil until it begins to color, and add the lemon juice. Stir in the spices, mix well, and add to the peas or beans and spinach. Taste and adjust seasoning.

Spinach Kefta

Kofta al Sabanigh (SAUDI ARABIA)

I was startled when a vegetarian Saudi friend introduced me to this dish, whose fragrant taste and light texture reminded me of the wonderful vegetable dishes of Turkey and Greece. Most likely adopted during the Kingdom's long years of Ottoman colonization and influence, this type of Mediterranean dish is common in the Arabian peninsula, and balances the heavier meat and rice pilafs that are a part of the bedouin cultural heritage.

2 bunches spinach, chopped

2 tbsp. water

2 to 3 ounces ground beef (optional)

1 clove garlic, crushed with salt

1 cup minced cilantro

4 green onions, minced

$1/4$ cup minced fresh mint, or:

2 tsp. dried mint

$1/2$ tsp. Middle Eastern red pepper

1 egg, separated

flour or bread crumbs

olive oil for sautéing

1. Steam the spinach in the water, covered, for 5 minutes. Add the ground beef, garlic, cilantro, green onions, and mint. Cover and simmer for 5 more minutes. Remove the cover and allow the liquid to dry up.

2. Transfer to a colander and squeeze most of the liquid out of the mixture.

3. When the vegetables are cool, use your hands to mix in the red pepper and the egg yolk. Squeeze the mixture into croquettes the size of small rounded hamburgers. Dip the croquettes into the egg white and then into the flour or bread crumbs.

4. Lightly sauté in the olive oil.

Variation

Add 1/4 cup cooked rice and 1 rounded tsp. tomato paste.

Herbed Spinach with Tomatoes and a Touch of Meat

Sabanigh bil Lahm al Mafroom (SAUDI ARABIA)

Just 4 ounces of meat turn this plate of fresh vegetables into a substantial main dish. Serve it with a mildly flavored rice such as **Trablosi Red Rice** or **Bahraini Green Rice**.

    1 large onion, chopped
    4 tbsp. olive oil (divided use)
    2 ripe tomatoes, chopped
    4 ounces ground beef
       salt
       black pepper
       pinch cumin
    2 bunches spinach, cut into ribbons
 1/4 cup minced parsley
 1/4 cup minced cilantro
       juice of 1/2 lemon

1. Sauté the onion in 2 tbsp. of the olive oil until soft and transparent. Add the tomatoes and cook for 5 minutes.

2. In a large, deep pan, sauté the ground beef in the remaining 2 tbsp. olive oil, sprinkling with salt, pepper, and cumin. Add the cooked tomatoes and onions and simmer to blend flavors for 5 more minutes.

3. Stir in the remaining ingredients and mix well. Cover and simmer for about 10 minutes.

Variations

Egypt: Omit the meat and add 3/4 cup cooked white rice.

Lebanon: Omit the cumin, stir 2 tbsp. sautéed pine nuts into the meat and use the meat as a garnish.

Turkey: Add 1 tsp. sugar.

Green Squash Stuffed with Saffron Rice

Koosa Mahshi (SYRIA)

In the long hot days of July and August, when my dear Syrian mother-in-law places her order for *koosa* with one of the men of our family, we know that the following famous recipe is on the menu. Immediately after the dawn prayer, Mother arranges her sheepskin and cushion on the spotless kitchen floor "so that the cold from the floor will not damage one's bones and female parts" and eases herself down next to a towering pile of 80 or 100 slender pale green squash. Patiently and deftly, she inserts a tool called a *mahfara* into each vegetable and twists to remove its core. When all the vegetables are reduced to thin shells through which Mother can view the warm Syrian sunlight, she stuffs them with aromatic saffron rice.

Sometimes she varies the dish by serving it with **Yoghurt Sauce** (p. 238) or by stuffing tiny purple "Japanese" eggplants rather than squash.

The *koosa* squash characteristic of the region is the length of a zucchini but pale hued and more sensually rounded. Occasionally they can be found in America in farmers' markets, perhaps wearing the label "Lebanese squash." You can try substituting fat zucchini.

8 green **koosa** squash (about 2 pounds)

Stuffing:

1/2 cup short-grained fat Egyptian rice, or other white rice

1/4 pound ground beef

2 tbsp. minced onion (reserve the rest of the onion for the broth)

3 cloves garlic, crushed with salt

1/2 tsp. cumin

1/2 tsp. **asfor**, or:

 generous pinch saffron

 generous pinch Middle Eastern red pepper

 black pepper

Broth:

 remaining part of 1 onion, chopped

2 tbsp. olive oil

1 to 2 cloves garlic, minced

4 cups water

1 rounded tbsp. tomato paste

1/2 tsp. Middle Eastern red pepper, or:

1 tbsp. **hamod er rummaan** pomegranate syrup

1/2 tsp. dried mint

 salt

1. Remove the stem end of the squash and use the special tool called the *mahfara* to remove as much as possible of the pulp of the vegetable. (Reserve the pulp for the following dish or for a dip.) The walls should remain of equal thickness and must not be pierced. Holding the hollow squash up to a bright light will help determine where too much flesh remains inside.

2. Combine the stuffing ingredients and knead to mix well.

3. Fill each squash only 2/3 to 3/4 full to allow for expansion of the rice.

4. For the broth, sauté the onion in the olive oil in a large saucepan until soft and transparent. Add the garlic and cook for another minute. Stir in the remaining ingredients and drop in the squash. Bring to a boil, reduce heat, and simmer gently, covered, for about 50 minutes. The shells should be tender and the rice completely cooked. Immediately remove the squash from the pan as they may split open if allowed to sit in the broth.

5. Serve the broth in a separate bowl. Each guest should cut his or her squash in half lengthwise to expose the mildly flavored rice stuffing and spoon the rich, tomatoey broth over the vegetables.

Steamed Squash with Chermoola Sauce

Shara'eh il Koosa bi Chermoola (MOROCCO)

~~~~~~

Moroccan dishes frequently depart from the norm of Levantine and eastern Mediterranean cuisines with their traditions of vegetables stuffed with rice and meat and their tomato-based flavors reminiscent of the Italian peninsula. Not only are the North African combinations of fresh vegetables and spices startling, but the cooking techniques are often similar to those used for generations in Spain.

In the following squash dish, the herbed vegetables are steamed in a lemon and olive oil marinade, an unusual and lavishly flavored alliance.

    1 pound zucchini or other green squash, cut lengthwise into 6 or 8
       slender wedges
  1/4 cup minced parsley
  1/4 cup minced cilantro
       juice of 1 lemon

Chermoola sauce:
  1/2 small onion, grated
    1 clove garlic, minced
    3 tbsp. olive oil
    3 tbsp. water

1/2 tsp. cumin

1/4 tsp. sweet paprika

1/4 tsp. Middle Eastern red pepper
   black pepper
   salt

1. Combine the sauce ingredients.

2. Place the zucchini or squash in a frying pan and pour on the sauce. Simmer, covered, for 10 minutes, tossing occasionally. Remove the cover and increase the heat, until the vegetables are tender and the sauce has reduced. (Moroccans like them well done.)

3. Toss in the remaining ingredients and serve, warm or at room temperature.

Stir-Fried Zucchini and Carrots

Koosa ma Djezar (ARMENIA)

Striking in its brilliant hues of orange and green, this beautiful combination brightens a plate of pale chicken or fish.

1/4 cup olive oil

2 carrots, julienned

1/2 pound (about 3 small) zucchini, julienned

4 cloves garlic, crushed with salt
   black pepper or Middle Eastern red pepper

1. Heat the oil and add the carrots. Sauté, tossing, for 2 minutes. Cover and simmer for 3 additional minutes.

2. Increase the heat and add the zucchini and the garlic. Stir-fry for about 4 minutes, until the vegetables are crispy-tender. Transfer to a serving dish and sprinkle with pepper.

Stuffed Tomatoes

Tamatum Mahshi (SAUDI ARABIA)

~~~~~~

Vegetables from the New World, such as tomatoes and potatoes, have been so fully assimilated into the various Mediterranean cuisines, that is hard to imagine a kitchen in which they are not continually on hand. When soft vegetables like tomatoes are stuffed, I prefer a precooked rice filling so that the fragile skin doesn't disintegrate during the hour required to steam the rice stuffing.

> 8 medium firm, ripe tomatoes
>
> 1 onion, chopped
>
> 2 tbsp. olive oil
>
> 1 clove garlic, minced
>
> 3 ounces ground beef
>
> salt
>
> black pepper
>
> 3 tbsp. short-grained fat Egyptian rice, or other white rice
>
> 1/3 cup water
>
> 1/4 cup minced fresh mint
>
> 1/2 cup tomato juice, or:
>
> 1 tbsp. tomato paste, dissolved in:
>
> 1/2 cup hot water

1. Cut off the tops of the tomatoes and keep them to use as covers. Use a spoon to remove the pulp, which should be reserved. Place the tomatoes upside down on paper towels to drain.

2. In a small nonstick saucepan, sauté the onion in the olive oil until soft and transparent. Add the garlic and the ground beef, sprinkling with salt and pepper, and sauté until the meat is no longer pink. Add the reserved tomato pulp, rice, water, and a pinch of salt. Cover and simmer for 15 minutes.

3. Stir in the mint leaves.

4. Sprinkle the inside of the tomatoes lightly with salt and pepper, and fill with the rice mixture. Spoon the tomato juice or tomato paste dissolved in hot water into each vegetable, cover with the reserved tops, and place in a baking dish.

5. Place a few tbsp. of water in the bottom of the baking dish and cover with foil. Bake at 350 degrees for ½ hour.

Variations

Palestine: Season the rice filling with allspice and cinnamon.

Egypt: Add 2 tbsp. sautéed pine nuts to the filling.

Turkey: Add pine nuts and currants to the filling and season with allspice and cinnamon.

Quick Vegetables a la Cairo

Khodra bi Benadora (EGYPT)

Nevine, a young Egyptian mother and self-professed kitchen neophyte I met in Jeddah, was ardently trying to learn some impressive Arab dishes with which to entertain her husband's friends. After working for several years as a manager in a Saudi firm, she had decided to stay home with her new daughter and dedicate herself for a period to the domestic tasks of a more traditional Arab woman. The following recipe is Nevine's standby, a basic Mediterranean way of enhancing the flavor of frozen vegetables with tomato paste and onion. "Highly recommended for noncooks or for novices," she suggests.

1 onion, slivered
1 tbsp. olive oil
1 rounded tbsp. tomato paste
1 package (10 oz.) frozen green beans, spinach, peas, or lima beans
¼ cup water
   salt
   black pepper

1. Sauté the onion in the oil until it is softened. Add the tomato paste and cook for 1 or 2 minutes, stirring occasionally.

2. Add the frozen vegetables, water, and salt and pepper. Cover and simmer until flavors are blended and the vegetables are tender. Do not overcook.

Variation

If it's appropriate with the vegetable of choice, I like to add garlic and/or red pepper

Mixed Vegetables with Tarator Sauce

Khodra bil Tarator (LEBANON)

Although I've listed a combination of vegetables for this dish, for a simple family meal you may want to use only one or two. Whatever the choice, the creamy **Tarator Sauce,** prepared from sesame seed tahini, fresh lemon juice, and yoghurt, is a healthy addition. Try this dish with a hearty grain-based soup like **Sun-Dried Meat Soup with Couscous and Rice**.

- 1 small eggplant, peeled
   olive oil for brushing
- 1 large zucchini
- 1/2 small head cauliflower, broken into florets
- 1 large potato, peeled

Tarator sauce: prepared with added:
1/3 cup low-fat yoghurt

Garnish:
   minced parsley

1. Slice the eggplant into cubes about ³/₄ to 1 inch square. Brush with olive oil on both sides and broil until golden on both sides.

2. Slice the zucchini ¹/₂ inch thick. Steam in a small amount of water until tender but still crunchy.

3. Steam the cauliflower until crispy-tender.

4. Cut the potato into bite-sized pieces and boil until tender.

5. Prepare the **Tarator Sauce** and beat in the yoghurt. Combine the cooked vegetables and pour the sauce on top. (Or use the sauce as a dip.) Garnish with parsley.

Lebanese Village Home

Pilafs and Pastas

Grains play an essential role in the healthful Middle Eastern diet, with light, fluffy kernels of rice, *burghol*, or couscous present in some form at every meal. They appear most frequently as flavorful, economical pilafs accompanying richly flavored meat or vegetable stews. Pilafs may also steam with fragrant herbs and seasonings, and tasty decorative bits of vegetables and meats, producing elaborate creations in which each beautifully distinct particle glistens with exotic spices. These life-sustaining grains are also enjoyed as the principal ingredient in stuffings for *dolmas* and fresh vegetables, in soups, and in desserts.

Burghol (sometimes referred to in the West as bulgur, or incorrectly called cracked wheat) is an inexpensive Middle Eastern food product that has survived the passage of centuries virtually unchanged. This ancient food is prepared from whole wheat that is parboiled before being cracked into smaller pieces which retain the complex carbohydrates that are efficiently converted into energy. The millstone does not remove the cellulose skin (bran) or the germ, which is a rich source of vitamins and protein. In this process, wheat germ and bran diffuse into the starchy center of the wheat, conserving the nutritious goodness of the whole grain. (Cracked wheat, on the other hand, is uncooked wheat that has been cracked apart by milling, and it requires extensive cooking before it can be digested.)

Finely ground and medium-grain *burghol* are reserved for *tabbooleh* and *kibbeh*, while coarsely ground *burghol* is cooked like rice, its unique processing method lending a nutty flavor and fluffy texture. Lentils and beans combine well with *burghol* to produce a variety of high-protein, high-fiber meatless meals, such as **Mujeddara with Burghol**.

Up to 80% of daily calories in the Middle Eastern diet are provided in the forms of cereals and olive oil, but while *burghol* may be increasingly recognized in the West, it is not the only Middle Eastern wheat product. Armenian communities rely on natural wheat kernels for their earthy peasant dishes, which physicians credit with reducing rates of osteoporosis and other degenerative diseases. North Africans process the wheat into delicate, velvety-textured couscous, a type of fine semolina that Westerners find easy to cook. In the Gulf States and across the Arabian peninsula, where wheat was a traditional agricultural product of the desert oases, bedouins and villagers alike are fond of pasta products, which can be stored and transported easily.

Rice is a relative newcomer to the Middle Eastern kitchen, most likely carried to Greater Syria and Egypt by the spice traders whose camel caravans traversed the deserts between India and Mesopotamia. First introduced in Europe in the eighth century by the Arab tribes who colonized Al Andaluz in Spain, it is now the core of nearly every meal. Rice has become the beloved favorite, the preferred grain praised in the proverb "Glory to rice, and death to *burghol!*"

Kurds call this staple food *birinj*, while it is *pilav* to the Turks and *yeghintz* to the Armenians. In Saudi Arabia and the Gulf States, huge trays of steaming *ruz*, tossed with roasted nuts and freshly ground spices, hold an entire baked lamb. In Iraq, *timman* is delicately flavored with saffron and a hint of sweetness from raisins or other dried fruits, while an extensive repertoire of dishes incorporates traditional Turkish and Persian cooking techniques. Some Kuwaiti rice dishes, on the other hand, so strongly resemble spicy Indian *biryanis* that they are known by the same term.

Rice recipes in this part of the world seem to be of three general types. Most of those known in the West are simple dishes like the first ones described in this chapter. These are not highly flavored because they are intended, as in Chinese cuisine, to accompany and extend a nearly unlimited variety of vegetable and meat stews. Broth or yoghurt sauces containing a small amount of meat are also served over this modest type of rice.

Pilafs embellished with spices, nuts, and tiny bits of meat are a common accompaniment to shish kebab and other grilled meats. Dishes like **Festive Spiced Rice** and **Saffron Rainbow Rice**, beautifully garnished with almonds and raisins, are sometimes used to line a tray on which is displayed a whole roast baby camel or lamb, or a dozen chickens.

A third type is a substantial dish like **Upside-Down Pilaf with Potatoes and Meat**, a complete meal in itself, usually containing some meat or seafood and a healthy combination of vegetables. Recipes that call for rice as an integral part of the dish, cooked together with fish, meat, or chicken, are especially popular in Saudi Arabia and the Gulf. They may be layered in one pot and cooked on top of the stove, or spread in casseroles for the oven.

When dealing with a grain-based cuisine in which the indispensable pilaf may be prepared separately or with the other ingredients, some recipes are difficult for the Western reader to categorize. Is a certain combination more appropriately labeled "Chicken with Rice" or "Rice with Chicken"? Consequently, several other dishes of this type, which seemed to me more substantially "meaty," can be found in the Meat and Poultry chapter of this book, while a few other rice combinations are listed under the Seafood heading.

Around the world some 7,000 varieties of rice are known, but many Arab governments limit their imports to a fat grain known as "Egyptian" rice and a medium grain of inferior quality, often broken pieces, that requires at least half an hour of soaking to remove the starch. Iraq produces a number of superb rices, the finest of which is called *ambar*, but these are not always available in other Arab countries. An abundance of rices are conveniently sold, of course, in the wealthy states of the Arabian Gulf, where imports are almost unlimited.

Although each variety of rice has its own flavor and cooking characteristics and therefore is more suited to some dishes than to others, the talented Middle Eastern housewife has learned to adapt her techniques to the grain that is available. The rice used in traditional Gulf recipes, for example, can be either basmati, medium-grain, or the highly esteemed converted type called "American rice." Nor are the cooking methods exclusive. Basmati can be prepared in the traditional three steps or can be used like converted rice, while converted rice is sometimes soaked and steamed in the Persian manner usually reserved for basmati.

Personally, I recommend the glutinuous short- or medium-grained "Egyptian" rice only for stuffing vegetables, and prefer the converted type for most pilafs, unless another variety is specifically called for. The finest pilafs, however, extraordinarily light and aromatically fragrant, are those basmati dishes prepared in three time-consuming but easy steps.

All of these wondrous white grains, fortunately, are available from import food stores, whether they be labeled as "Greek," "Italian," or "Middle Eastern" establishments. Brown rice is neither known nor appreciated in this region of the world.

Middle Eastern cooks rinse the rice before cooking and soak it to prevent sticking and clumping during cooking. I find that while "American" (converted or parboiled) rice does not require these additional steps, it is advisable to rinse and soak other types, such as the fat-grained "Egyptian" rice. Basmati rice and its somewhat similar American hybrid labeled Texmati should be soaked in a large quantity of heavily salted water for a period of 30 minutes to overnight, depending on the cook's preference and the specific preparation technique. The salt is then rinsed away before beginning the cooking process.

Total cooking time for the converted rice I recommend for most of the following dishes is about 25 minutes. If the rice is still too firm when the water has been completely absorbed, an additional 2–4 tbsp. of water may be added. The pot is then covered, and steaming continues for a few more minutes. If the rice is too soft and water still remains in the pot, remove the cover and increase the heat for a minute or two.

You'll have greater success if you use a nonstick pan for your pilafs and reserve it solely for these dishes.

Clarified butter, called *semne* (ghee in the Indian subcontinent and in most import food shops), has always been used in the Middle East for preparing pilafs, because it stores well without refrigeration and has a high burning point. Today, a few Arab friends are experimenting and substituting margarine or a low-cholesterol oil for *semne* or butter. The majority of them use corn oil, marketed as a healthier alternative in the Middle East under the brand name Mazola, while a few have tried olive oil. But all agree that the flavor of the dish is detrimentally affected unless the oil is mixed with at least an equal amount of butter.

As for myself, I usually try to limit the amount of butter used in pilafs dishes, but I am unwilling to sacrifice its wonderful flavor. The amount of fat (butter or oil) specified in the recipes is my suggested minimum for a tasty yet authentic dish. The final decision is up to the reader, who should not find it difficult to make minor modifications to suit personal requirements for well being and delicious taste.

Plain White Rice

Ruz (ARAB STATES)

~~~~~~

There's nothing mystifying about preparing converted rice, as this recipe will demonstrate. My general rule is to boil the grain with about twice as much liquid for about 10 or 12 minutes, until the water level is about equal to that of the rice and little bubbly holes have appeared. Then I reduce the heat to the lowest level, cover, and simmer until tender.

Converted rice, my choice for most pilafs, has been parboiled or steamed before being milled into white rice. This process drives most of the nutrients into the rice kernel, making it the healthiest of the white rices. The grains remain fluffy and separate during cooking and don't become gummy. Converted rice takes a few minutes longer to cook than other types and requires a bit more water. Unlike some other grains, it need not be set aside after cooking to reach maximum fluffiness.

1 1/4 cups converted rice

2 1/2 cups water

   2 tbsp. butter or olive oil

     salt

1. Place all ingredients in a nonstick saucepan and bring to a boil. Stir, and let the mixture cook uncovered over medium heat.

2. When the water level is equal to that of the rice, and little bubbly holes have appeared in the rice, cover and reduce the heat. Simmer until done. The total cooking time is about 25 minutes. If the water has evaporated but the rice still seems a bit hard, sprinkle with a few spoonfuls of water and simmer for 5 more minutes.

Vermicelli Rice

Ruz ma Shayreeyeh (SYRIA, LEBANON, JORDAN, PALESTINE, EGYPT)

Syrians love this handsome rice dish with its tiny golden brown noodles that usually accompanies the wide variety of Levantine tomato-based vegetable stews. In Egypt, it's the rice served with **Mlookheeyeh Soup**, the national broth thick with fresh greens and herbs.

Across the Arab world, vermicelli rice is a simple favorite usually prepared with fat-grained Egyptian rice or whatever medium-grained rice is available. Tossing the grain in a little butter or oil before adding the liquid helps to keep the kernels from sticking together.

When chicken broth or bouillon is used instead of water, you have the original Middle Eastern specialty that inspired the packaged mix known as Rice-A-Roni.

1 ¼ cups rice, either short-grained, fat Egyptian rice or long-grained
      converted rice
 ½ cups **fideo** vermicelli, or more to taste
 2 tbsp. butter or olive oil
2 ⅔ cups water or chicken broth
      salt

1. Egyptian short-grained rice requires at least ½ hour of presoaking. Some cooks rinse it until the water runs relatively clear, soak it for up to 2 hours, and rinse it again several times before cooking. Converted rice is ready to use.

2. Crush the noodles between your hands to break them into pieces about ½ to ¾ inch long. Sauté them in the butter or oil over medium heat, stirring frequently, until they are evenly golden brown. Add the rice and stir-fry until the grains are all coated and glistening.

3. Pour on the water or broth, add the salt, and stir. Bring to a boil.

4. When the water level is equal to that of the rice, and little bubbly holes have appeared in the rice, cover and reduce the heat. Simmer until done. The total cooking time is about 25 minutes.

Trablosi Red Rice
or Bahraini Green Rice

Ruz Ahmar (LEBANON) ◆ *Ruz Bahreyni* (BAHRAIN)

~~~~~~

These two simple variations on the basic rice dish are finely tinted with a blush of pink and a mellow green hue.

   2 tbsp. butter or olive oil

  1/4 small onion, minced (optional)

1 1/4 cups rice

2 1/2 cups water

   1 slightly rounded tbsp. tomato paste (for Red Rice), or:

  1/2 bunch cilantro, minced (for Green Rice)

      salt

Garnish:

      toasted pine nuts (for Red Rice)

      cilantro leaves and pistachios (for Green Rice)

1. Heat the butter or oil and lightly sauté the onion until softened and transparent. Add the remaining ingredients (except garnish) and bring to a boil. Stir to mix well.

2. When the water level is equal to that of the rice, and little bubbly holes have appeared in the rice, cover and reduce the heat. Steam until done. The total cooking time is about 25 minutes. If the water has evaporated but the rice still seems a bit hard, sprinkle with a few spoonfuls of water and simmer for a bit longer.

3. Garnish with toasted pine nuts or cilantro leaves and pistachios.

Pilaf of Rice with Peas

Ruz bi Bizalia (SYRIA)

Served with a large bowl of yoghurt and a favorite soup or salad, **Pilaf of Rice with Peas** is a quick and easy family meal that's elegant enough to honor a guest.

  2 tbsp. butter or olive oil

1 ²/₃ cups
    rice
    salt

3 ¹/₃ cups chicken broth

  ²/₃ cup frozen peas

Garnish (optional)

  ¹/₃ pound lean ground beef

  2 tbsp. olive oil

  ¹/₄ tsp. allspice
    salt
    black pepper

1. In a nonstick coated saucepan, heat the butter or oil over low heat and add the rice, tossing to coat each grain.

2. Add the salt and broth, stir to blend, and bring to a boil over medium heat. Continue to cook until much of the water has been absorbed and little holes begin to form across the surface of the rice: about 10 minutes. Stir in the peas, reduce the heat, and cover.

3. Meanwhile, sauté the ground beef in 2 tbsp. olive oil, sprinkling with the spices. Remove with a slotted spoon.

4. The rice will be ready to serve after about 15 additional minutes of steaming. Transfer it to a platter and top it with the ground beef.

Variations

Lebanon: Prepare the garnish ingredients and stir most of them into the rice.

Syria: Substitute frozen or canned green fava beans for the peas and add ³/₄ cup chopped cilantro.

Spiced Rice from Saudi Arabia

Kebsit Ruz (SAUDI ARABIA)

~~~~~~

Kebsit Ruz, or as it is commonly known, *Kebsa*, is the most famous example of Saudi Arabian cuisine. This savory rice dish, flavored with tomatoes, mild green chilis, and exotic spices, is similiar to a paella, but with all the passion and mystery of the East. Like paella, its exciting variations may include tender chunks of lamb, baby camel, or chicken, or even potatoes, eggplant, or other vegetables.

When we returned to the States after 11 years in the Middle East, my supply of *kebsa* spices, an essential combination added to nearly every Gulf dish, dwindled quickly. So when Saudi friends planning an extended visit with us asked what we needed from their region, I begged for *kebsa* spices. My friend Leila, a teacher who prepares this dish every evening, pulled out of her suitcase what she considered a year's supply: 2 quarts of freshly ground spices from the old spice market in the Eastern Province port of Dammam.

In the following *kebsa*, I've used slightly fewer spices than Leila would recommend, but if you're adventuresome, you might try adding more.

> 1 large onion, chopped
> 2 tbsp. olive oil
> 2 cloves garlic, minced
>   salt
> 1 tsp. **kebsa** spices
>   pinch ground **loomi**, or:
> 1 whole **loomi**, pierced
> 1 serrano or jalapeño chili
> 1 carrot, pared and minced
> 1 can (14–16 oz.) tomatoes, with liquid
> 1 ¼ cups rice
> 2 ½ cups water

1. Sauté the onion in the oil until softened. Toss in the garlic, spices, chili, and carrot, and cook for another minute. Whirl the canned tomatoes in a blender or food processor, add, and simmer a bit longer.

2. Add the rice and water and bring to a boil. Cover and simmer until done, about 25 minutes. Serve with **Saudi Herbed Salsa** (p. 42).

Festive Spiced Rice

Al Koozy (SAUDI ARABIA)

~~~~~~

More mildly seasoned than many Gulf pilafs, this spiced rice is a famous bedouin favorite reserved for festive occasions. The moment honored guests appear at the encampment of black tents, the sheikh or patriarch gives the order to kill one or more sheep or a young camel. The men ceremoniously share ritual green coffee, reclining on red cushions and carpets until the feast is carried in on an immense tray: a whole roast animal splendidly arrayed on a mountain of savory buttered rice, luxuriously garnished with a bounty of golden brown nuts.

This rice, richly adorned with allspice, cinnamon, and almonds, is a reflection on the prosperity and generosity of the host family. Like baklava and roast meats, it's an extravagant and delightful interruption in the usual routine of vegetables and grains.

The following side dish of fragrant rice is still suitable for a feast, but with the butter/oil and nuts reduced by 50%.

- 1 recipe **Plain White Rice** (p. 167)
- 2 tbsp. blanched almonds, halved or slivered
- 2 tbsp. olive oil
- 2 tbsp. pine nuts
- 1/2 pound ground beef
- salt
- black pepper
- 1 tsp. allspice (divided use)
- 1/4 cup butter or olive oil
- 1/2 tsp. cinnamon
- 1/4 tsp. nutmeg

1. Prepare the **Plain White Rice** in advance. Fluff the cooked grains and let cool to room temperature.

2. Slowly sauté the almonds in the olive oil, stirring frequently. When the almonds are beginning to brown, stir in the pine nuts and continue to cook until all the nuts are golden. Remove with a slotted spoon.

3. Brown the ground beef in the same oil, sprinkling with the salt, pepper, and half the allspice. Remove from the pan and drain in a sieve.

4. In a large nonstick pan, heat the 1/4 cup butter or olive oil. Stir in the rice and sprinkle with cinnamon, nutmeg, and the remaining allspice. As the rice heats, continue to toss until it is hot and coated with spices. Taste and adjust seasoning.

Saffron Rice Supreme

Timman Azz'affaran (IRAQ)

Richly exotic with spices and a hint of sweetness, this is a splendid and evocative dish that dates back to the extravagant Baghdad court of the Abbasid caliph Harun al Rasheed. It's ideal for your feast, too, because the rice can be prepared in advance and tossed with the spices just before serving.

Saffron is a common addition to Iraqi rice dishes. It can be utilized in several different ways that reflect Iraq's location at the crossroads of civilizations. In the following recipe it is tossed with the cooked rice to add tiny flecks of brilliant color. Other cooks may tint the rice a canary shade by adding the prized spice to the boiling water. A third technique popular in the Gulf is to soak the fragile threads in a bit of warm or room-temperature water to release its color and perfume before sprinkling it over the nearly tender rice. (Hot water is believed to destroy the spice's distinct aroma.)

1 recipe **Plain White Rice** (p. 167)
1/3 to 1/2 cup yellow raisins
1/3 cup blanched almonds, halved or slivered
1 tsp. ground coriander seeds
1 tsp. ground cumin

⅓ cup butter or olive oil

½ tsp. saffron threads, slightly crushed

salt

pepper

1. Prepare the **Plain White Rice** in advance. Fluff the cooked grains and let cool to room temperature.

2. Soak the raisins in hot water for about 10 minutes; drain.

3. Sauté the almonds and spices in the butter or oil over low heat for about 2 minutes. Add the raisins and saffron and toss together for 1 minute, taking care that the raisins do not burn.

4. Add the cooked rice and toss to color each grain and coat it with spices. Sprinkle with salt and freshly ground pepper to taste.

Variations

Morocco: Omit the coriander, cumin, and almonds; cook the saffron and raisins in the rice.

Iraq: Omit the coriander and cumin; sauté ⅓ cup minced dates along with the almonds and ⅓ cup raisins.

Basmati Rice with Crisped Onion

Al Mashkool (KUWAIT AND THE GULF STATES)

This simple onion-flavored rice recipe is a classic of Gulf cuisine prepared from long, thin strands of basmati rice grown in the Punjab foothills of the Himalayas. Basmati kernels have been aged to decrease their moisture content and increase their extraordinary bouquet. They are soaked before cooking and boiled for only 10 minutes in a large quantity of furiously bubbling water. Drained of the cooking liquid, they then steam with the onions over low flame, without the addition of more broth. These light, fluffy grains taste as if you were eating in your dreams.

Many families in Kuwait and the Emirates enjoy this famous dish several times a week, as its uncomplicated flavor complements the highly spiced fish, meat, and vegetable stews of the region. Serve it with a side dish of **Saudi Herbed Salsa**.

1 ¼ cups basmati rice

   2 tbsp. salt (for soaking)

   2 onions, minced

   2 tbsp. butter or olive oil

1. At least 2 hours before you begin to cook, cover the basmati rice with 6 cups of water (or more) and add the salt. Set aside to soak.

2. Bring 6 cups or more fresh water to a boil. Drain and rinse the rice and add to the boiling water. Cook 10 minutes.

3. Meanwhile, in a deep pan, sauté the onions slowly in the butter or oil until crisp and light golden brown.

4. Drain the rice and add to the onions, stirring to mix well. Arrange the rice so that it covers the bottom of the pan and is piled into a cone shape. Lower the heat to the minimum. Cover the pot with a clean dish towel and put on the lid, flipping the ends of the towel over the top. Steam for 30–40 minutes without stirring or opening the pot.

Variation

Saudi Arabia: Add precooked cubed lamb, chicory, generous pinches of cloves, cinnamon, cardamom, and (optional) tomatoes.

Pilaf with Carrots and Sun-Dried Lemon

Timman Djezar (IRAQ)

~~~~~~

This simple and tasty rice pilaf can be prepared as described below or in the Gulf fashion using basmati rice (see previous recipe).

2 tbsp. butter or olive oil
1 onion, chopped
4 large carrots, pared and diced
6 ounces beef sirloin, diced
  salt
  black pepper
1 2/3 cups rice
3 1/3 cups water
  salt
1 tsp. turmeric
1/2 tsp. ground **loomi**

Garnish:
1 medium carrot, julienned

1. In a nonstick saucepan, heat the butter or oil over low heat and sauté the onion until soft and transparent. Add the carrots and cook for another 2 minutes. Add the meat, sprinkle with salt and pepper, and stir-fry for a few minutes, until browned. Add the rice and stir to coat each grain.

2. Add the water and spices, stir to blend, and bring to a boil over medium heat. Continue to cook until much of the water has been absorbed and little holes begin to form across the surface of the rice: about 10 minutes. Reduce the heat and cover.

3. Steam the carrot garnish in a bit of water until tender. When the rice is done, after about 25 minutes total cooking time, transfer to a serving platter, garnish with the steamed julienned carrot.

Variation

Substitute cinnamon, red pepper, and allspice for the turmeric and *loomi*.

Saffron Rainbow Rice

Aish Azz'afaran (BAHRAIN AND THE ARABIAN GULF)

Many of the rice dishes from the subcontinent are stunningly elegant, as beautiful and artistic as the pastry confections of Vienna, with some grains stained a brilliant scarlet while others are yellow or pure white. The secret lies in an Eastern technique that is amazingly easy: when threads of saffron are soaked in a small amount of liquid and sprinkled over the semicooked grain, the colored broth stains the spots it touches, while the threads themselves dye other portions of the rice a more brilliant shade.

Saffron Rainbow Rice is a quick and easy recipe lightly scented with the fragrance of raisins and rosewater. Although "American rice" is usually preferred (the term in Arabic refers to long-grain converted rice), the three-step cooking method is one ordinarily reserved for Indian and Iranian (basmati) rice.

Aish Azz'afaran symbolizes for me the crossroads of cultures that is the tiny Arabian Gulf island of Bahrain. A major stopping point of graceful dhows sailing the spice route from India to Europe, Bahrain is a fascinating cultural mix of Persians, Arabs, Indians, and (during the past 150 years), British and American expatriates. Lacking petrodollars, it has learned to rely on an educated, open-minded population that has transformed its traditional trading ventures into multinational firms.

1 ¼ cups basmati rice
  2 tbsp. salt (for soaking)
 ½ tsp. saffron threads
 ¼ cup rosewater
  3 tbsp. raisins
  1 onion, slivered
  4 tbsp. butter or olive oil
  3 tbsp. slivered almonds
    salt

1. At least 2 hours before you begin to cook, cover the basmati rice with 6 cups of water (or more) and add the salt. Set aside to soak.

2. Place the saffron threads (do not use ground saffron, as it will not stain the rice properly) in a small bowl and pour on the rosewater.

3. Soak the raisins in hot water.

4. Bring 6 cups or more fresh water to a boil. Drain and rinse the rice and add to the boiling water. Cook 10 minutes.

5. Meanwhile, cook the slivered onion in a nonstick saucepan with the butter or oil until soft and transparent. Add the almonds and sauté them, stirring frequently, until at least half of them have turned a light golden shade. Drain the liquid from the raisins and stir them into the mixture along with the salt.

6. Strain the partially cooked rice in a colander, shaking it to remove all the water. Stir the drained rice into the onion/nut mixture until every grain is coated and glistening. Smooth out the surface of the rice and dribble the reserved saffron rosewater over the rice. Do not stir. Cover the pot with a clean dish towel and put on the lid, flipping the ends of the towel over the top. Simmer gently on the lowest heat for 30–40 minutes.

Pilaf with Lemon Garlic Chicken

Ruz ma Dajaaj (LEBANON)

This delicious combination was invented by my friend Jan Andary, who is married to a Lebanese Druze. Frustrated with some of the time-consuming traditional Lebanese chicken and rice dishes that call for stuffing a tough old bird with an elaborate spiced rice mixture, with additional rice on the side, Jan created this uncomplicated pilaf.

The chicken can be prepared at your leisure a day or two in advance, making it ideal for a celebration or special event. Steam the rice at the last minute, pop the chicken topping in the microwave to heat, and this elegant dish is ready to go!

Jan's chicken pilaf is one of the few Arab dishes my Syrian mother-in-law requests that I make for her. She is quite certain that it is authentically Arabian, but she can't quite remember which region it represents!

Chicken:

- 2 whole breasts of chicken with bone (or 4–5 thighs)
- 4 cups water
- salt
- 1 carrot, pared and coarsely chopped (optional)
- ½ small onion, chopped (optional)
- 1 rib celery, coarsely chopped (optional)
- 1 stick cinnamon (optional)

Marinade:

- 3 cloves garlic, crushed with salt
- 4 tbsp. melted butter or olive oil
- juice of 1 lemon

1 ½ cups rice

2 tbsp. butter or olive oil

Garnish:

- toasted pine nuts
- minced parsley

1. Boil the chicken pieces in salted water, adding the optional flavoring ingredients if you wish. Cook until the meat is well done and falling off the bones. Using a slotted spoon, remove the chicken from the cooking liquid and set aside to cool. Reserve the broth until you prepare the rice. If you've enriched its flavor by adding the optional vegetables, you may wish to remove them by straining the broth; or you may leave them undisturbed and add their little bits of goodness to the rice pilaf.

2. Combine the marinade ingredients. Strip the chicken from the bones and toss it with the marinade mixture. Marinate for at least 2 hours. (Overnight is better, but please do refrigerate.)

3. To prepare the rice, measure the reserved liquid and add water, if necessary, to make 3 cups. Heat the broth in a nonstick pot and taste to adjust seasoning. If it is weak you may wish to add a bit of real chicken bouillon. Stir in the rice and 2 tbsp. butter or oil.

4. Boil the rice about 10 minutes, until the water level is just above that of the rice. Cover and reduce the heat to low. Steam until tender, about another 15 minutes.

5. Heat the chicken and its marinade in the microwave or on the stove.

6. To serve, heap the rice on a platter and top with the chicken and its marinade. Garnish with pine nuts or parsley.

Upside-Down Pilaf with Eggplant

Ma'loobeh (SYRIA)

~~~~~~

Ma'loobeh means "upside down," a marvelous layered mold of juicy bits of meat and pine nuts topping a middle of eggplant slices and a base of spiced rice. In the mountain villages of Syria, the eggplant layer is always fried, but I prefer to broil it. *Ma'loobeh* is another one-pot main dish that is a complete meal when served with traditional **Cucumber Yoghurt Salad** (p. 75)

  1 large eggplant, peeled
     olive oil

1 ³/₄ cups rice

3 ¹/₂ cups beef broth or water with beef bouillon (divided use)

  3 tbsp. butter
     salt

Meat layer:

  2 tbsp. olive oil

  ¹/₃ cup pine nuts

  ¹/₂ pound beef sirloin or fillet, cut into very small cubes
     salt
     black pepper

1. Slice the eggplant ¹/₃ inch thick and arrange in a single layer on a cookie sheet. Brush the surface of each slice lightly with olive oil. Turn and oil the other side. Broil until tinged with brown, then turn, to cook the other side.

2. Place the rice, all but about ¹/₃ cup of the broth or water with bouillon, butter, and salt in a nonstick saucepan. Bring to a boil. When the water is about level with the rice, reduce the heat and cover for about 13 more minutes. The rice will be dry but still slightly firm.

3. Meanwhile, heat 2 tbsp. olive oil almost to smoking. Toss in the pine nuts, shake to distribute evenly in the hot oil, and remove the pan from the heat. When the nuts are a dark golden brown, remove with a slotted spoon to a dish lined with a paper towel.

4. Reheat the same oil almost to smoking. Add the meat and immediately sprinkle generously with salt and pepper. Brown the meat until just barely done. As this will provide the most flavorful portion of the dish, be certain to season generously. Remove the beef to a large nonstick pot or deep nonstick fryer. Add the reserved pine nuts and distribute evenly over the bottom of the pan.

5. Arrange the broiled eggplant slices in one even layer over the meat. Spread the rice on top, pressing down slightly to fill in all crevices. Sprinkle with the remaining ¹/₃ cup broth and steam over very low heat for about 10 minutes. If you hear the layer of meat and nuts pop, it is an indication that it is beginning to dry out. To avoid burning the bottom layer, sprinkle a few additional spoonfuls of water over the rice. When the rice is tender and steaming hot, remove the pot from the heat and set aside for about 10 minutes.

6. Place a large, round serving platter over the pot and flip to unmold the pilaf. Serve accompanied by **Cucumber Yoghurt Salad** (p. 75) to spoon over each serving.

Variations

Saudi Arabia: Substitute cooked chickpeas for the eggplant.

Lebanon: Flavor with cinnamon.

Palestine: Substitute cauliflower florets for the eggplant (they are traditionally fried, but you can steam them) and cooked deboned chicken for the beef; use chicken rather than beef broth.

Iraq: Add cauliflower and zucchini to the eggplant and substitute cooked deboned chicken for the beef; use chicken rather than beef broth and flavor with *garam masala* or curry powder.

Upside-Down Pilaf with Potatoes and Meat

Al Ruz al Kabli (SAUDI ARABIA AND THE GULF STATES)

~~~~~~

The southern Arabian cousin of the previous *Ma'loobeh* recipe, this *Kabli* layered rice is topped with a bit of meat and wedges of potatoes. The numerous fragrant Eastern spices—dried roses, orange peel, saffron, and cardamom—distinguish it from a similar dish popular in Syria, although the method of layering various precooked ingredients is the same.

Meat and potato layer:

- 2 onions, chopped
- 4 tbsp. olive oil (divided use)
- 1 clove garlic, minced
- 1/2 pound beef sirloin, cut into very small cubes
- salt
- black pepper
- 5 medium potatoes, cut into 4 or 5 pieces lengthwise
- 1 cup water
- 1 cup low-fat yoghurt
- 1 tbsp. tomato paste (optional)
- 1/2 tsp. freshly grated orange peel
- 1/2 tsp. freshly grated lemon peel
- pinch cinnamon

Rice layer:

- 1 3/4 cups rice
- 2 tbsp. butter or olive oil
- 3 1/2 cups water
- 1 dried rosebud (optional)
- 6 whole cloves
- 4 pods cardamom
- 1 tsp. **asfor** or turmeric, or:
- generous pinch saffron
- salt

Garnish:

> sprigs of fresh parsley

1. Sauté the onions in 2 tbsp. olive oil until soft and transparent. Add the garlic and the meat and sprinkle with salt and pepper, and stir-fry until slightly browned. Remove from the pan.

2. Add the remaining 2 tbsp. oil along with the potatoes. Lightly sauté to hold their shape during the remainder of the cooking. Sprinkle with salt and pepper.

3. Return the meat and onions to the pan and add the remaining ingredients for the meat and potato layer. Cover and simmer for about 20 minutes, until the potatoes are tender. Taste and adjust seasoning. The liquid will reduce into a thick sauce.

4. While the potatoes are steaming, place the rice and 2 tbsp. butter or olive oil in a nonstick pan and toss over medium heat to coat the rice evenly. Add the remaining ingredients for the rice layer and bring to a boil. Cover and simmer until tender, about 25 minutes.

5. Transfer the meat and potatoes to the bottom of a large nonstick pot and top with the rice. Cover and steam for about 10 minutes, or until well heated. Remove from the heat and let sit for about 10 minutes.

6. Place a large round serving platter over the pot and flip to unmold the pilaf. Garnish with sprigs of fresh parsley.

Variation

Use basmati rice and cook the layers as in **Saffron Rainbow Rice** (p. 177), sprinkling with saffron water, garnishing with toasted almonds and raisins.

Pilaf with Lentils and Chili Garlic Shrimp Garnish

Machboos er Rubiyaan (KUWAIT)

This striking main dish offers a basic grain flavored with colorful vegetables and a pale yellow shrimp garnish, a whole meal on one beautiful platter.

Meatless lentil dishes from the Arab Mediterranean, especially combined with rice or *burghol*, are traditionally prepared with a substantial amount of olive oil to improve the flavor. The olive oil is also good for your health because it sweeps the circulatory system clean of dangerous LDL cholesterol while leaving the essential HDL cholesterol untouched.

$^1\!/_3$ cup brown or green lentils

4 cups water

1 large onion, chopped

2 tbsp. olive oil

1 clove garlic, minced

1 large serrano chili, seeded and minced

1 large ripe tomato, chopped

1 tsp. turmeric

2 pods cardamom (optional)

1 stick cinnamon

2 tbsp. butter or olive oil

1 $^1\!/_2$ cups rice

3 cups water

salt

Shrimp garnish:

1 tbsp. olive oil

$^1\!/_2$ pound shrimp, shelled

1 clove garlic, minced

1 small serrano chili, seeded and minced

$^1\!/_4$ tsp. turmeric

salt

minced parsley

black pepper

1. Boil the lentils in the 4 cups water for $^1\!/_2$ hour. Drain.

2. Sauté the onion in 2 tablespoons olive oil until soft and transparent. Add the garlic, chili, tomato, spices, and butter and toss for another minute. Stir in the rice and toss until every grain is glistening with spices.

3. Add the 3 cups water, salt, and reserved precooked lentils. Mix well and bring to a boil. Cover and simmer until tender, about 25 minutes.

4. To prepare the garnish, heat 1 tbsp. olive oil and toss the shrimp, garlic, chili, turmeric, and salt until the shrimp is pink and flavored with spices.

5. Arrange the rice on a serving platter and top with the spiced shrimp. Garnish with parsley and sprinkle with black pepper. Serve with **Saudi Herbed Salsa** (p. 42).

Koshari

Koshari (EGYPT)

~~~~~~

Al Bagdhadi, the famous culinary historian of ancient Bagdhad, described this combination of lentils and rice as including meat, and it is sometimes still prepared as he reported. But today olive oil is more frequently added in place of lamb.

In the countries that formed the historical land of Syria (which include today's Lebanon, Israel, and Jordan) the dish is prepared with brown or green lentils and is usually called *Mujeddara*. Lots of crispy onions browned in olive oil garnish the dish and complement the mild flavor. For Kurdish *Adas Pilaw*, red lentils are cooked and smashed before being added to the rice, while in the Gulf States the red lentils disintegrate as they are being cooked together with the rice.

But the prize for creativity goes to Egypt, where the traditional dish is served with a mandatory **Spicy Tomato Sauce** and an optional **Green Chili Vinaigrette**. Never have lentils and rice been transformed into such an irresistible delicacy as in this regional adaptation, called *Koshari*.

3/4 cup brown or green lentils, rinsed
5 cups water or chicken broth
   salt
1/2 cup **fideo** vermicelli
2 tbsp. olive oil
1 cup rice
1 3/4 cups water or chicken broth
   salt

Garnish:
2 onions, slivered
2 to 4 tbsp. olive oil

Spicy Tomato Sauce:

- 1 small onion, chopped
- 2 tbsp. olive oil
- 1 clove garlic, minced
- 1 can (14–16 oz.) whole tomatoes
- 1 tsp. wine vinegar (optional)
- $1/2$ tsp. cumin
- salt

Green Chili Vinaigrette:

- 3 cloves garlic, crushed with salt
- $1/4$ tsp. cumin
- $1/3$ cup wine vinegar
- $1/2$ cup olive oil
- 2 serrano chilis, seeded and minced

1. Boil the lentils, covered, in the salted water or broth until tender but not sticky, about $1^{1}/4$ hours. Drain any excess water.

2. Brown the vermicelli in 2 tbsp. olive oil and add the rice, stirring to coat every grain. Pour on the $1^{3}/4$ cups water with added salt (or the chicken broth), cover, and simmer until tender, about 22 minutes.

3. Meanwhile, slowly cook the slivered onions for the garnish in the 2–4 tbsp. olive oil until dark golden brown and crisp. Remove from the heat and set aside.

4. For the **Spicy Tomato Sauce**, lightly sauté the chopped onion in 2 tbsp. olive oil. Add the garlic and cook for another minute. Whirl the tomatoes and vinegar in a blender or food processor and add to the garlic and onions. Stir to mix well, add cumin, season to taste with salt, and simmer covered, about 10–15 minutes.

5. Combine the vinaigrette ingredients.

6. Turn the cooked rice into the drained lentils. If you feel that a few more minutes cooking are necessary, sprinkle with a few spoonfuls of water, cover, and simmer until both rice and lentils are tender.

7. To serve, mound the pilaf on a large round platter and top with the crisped onions with their olive oil. Transfer the tomato sauce and the

vinaigrette to small bowls, to be spooned over each dish of pilaf as desired. Arabs enjoy this dish served warm or at room temperature.

Shalimar Pilaf

Moghazleyat al Lahm (SAUDI ARABIA, GULF STATES)

~~~~~~

An Eastern connection, strikingly obvious to aficionados of Indian cuisine, lies in the technique used to prepare the meat portion of this delicious dish: it's slowly simmered in yoghurt and spices, a cooking method common in the subcontinent.

1 3/4 cups basmati rice
   2 tbsp. salt (for soaking)
     large pinch saffron
   2 tbsp. warm water
   2 onions, chopped
   2 tbsp. olive oil
 1/2 cup low-fat yoghurt
   1 cup water
 3/4 pound beef sirloin, cut into small cubes
     salt
   3 cloves garlic, minced
     black pepper
     generous pinch ground cardamom
     generous pinch Middle Eastern red pepper
 1/2 tsp. cinnamon
 1/4 tsp. ground cloves
   1 tomato, chopped

1. At least 2 hours before you begin to cook, cover the basmati rice with 6 cups of water (or more) and add 2 tbsp. salt. Set aside to soak.

2. Combine the saffron with the warm water and set aside for 1/2 hour.

3. Sauté the onions in the olive oil until golden brown. Remove with a slotted spoon to a food processor or blender. Stir in the yoghurt and 1 cup water and whirl until smooth.

4. Brown the sirloin in the oil that remains in the frying pan, sprinkling with salt. Add the garlic and the spices except for the saffron. Add the tomato and the onion/yoghurt mixture, cover, and simmer until tender, 1½ hours or longer. As the sauce reduces you will probably want to add small amounts of water to keep it from burning. Taste and adjust seasoning. (The meat and sauce should be highly spiced, to balance the mild flavor and delicate texture of the rice.)

5. While the meat is cooking, bring 6 cups or more fresh water to a boil. Drain and rinse the rice and add to the water. Boil 10 minutes and pour into a colander.

6. Transfer half of the rice to a 9 x 12-inch baking dish and arrange the meat mixture on top. Cover with the remaining rice. Sprinkle the saffron water over the rice, cover with aluminum foil, and bake at 350 degrees for 30–40 minutes. Serve with **Saudi Herbed Salsa** (p. 42).

Vegetarian Wheat Pilaf

Burghol (SYRIA, LEBANON, JORDAN, PALESTINE)

~~~~~~

Burghol is commonly served like rice, with a meat or vegetarian stew spooned over the grain. The following tasty meatless version is especially popular during Orthodox fasting days. Today imported rice is supplanting *burghol* in the northern Arabian countries, and these dishes are rarely seen outside of private homes.

> 2 tbsp. butter or olive oil
> 1 onion, chopped (optional)
> 1½ cups coarse **burghol** wheat, rinsed
> 3 cups chicken, beef, or vegetable broth, or water
> salt
> black pepper

1. Heat the butter or oil. Over medium heat, sauté the onion until softened and transparent.

2. Add the *burghol* wheat and toss it until glistening in the butter or oil. Pour on the liquid and bring to a boil. Cover and simmer until light and fluffy, about 30–35 minutes. (A few tbsp. more water may be added if necessary.)

3. Sprinkle with freshly ground black pepper.

Mujeddara with Burghol

Mujeddara (SYRIA)

~~~~~~

This lentil and *burghol* pilaf, when served with the usual accompanying yoghurt and salad, is a complete hearty meal without meat. High in protein and fiber, it's popular during the cold winter months, when fresh vegetables may be unavailable. In Egypt, Lebanon, and Jordan, *Mujeddara* is frequently prepared with lentils and rice, but I prefer the contrast of nutty, full-bodied wheat with the creamy texture of lentils.

Many villagers would add 2 or 3 times the quantity of olive oil suggested below, and across the Mediterranean total dietary fat is often as high as 35–40% of calories. Research proves this to be healthy as long as the amounts of saturated fat from meat sources (only 7–8% of this total) and polyunsaturated fat (only 3–6%) are low, with the remainder from healthy olive oil.

    1 cup brown or green lentils
       salt
    8 cups water
    2 tsp. beef bouillon (optional)
    1 cup coarse **burghol** wheat, rinsed
   1/2 cup olive oil (divided use)
    2 large onions, slivered
       salt
       black pepper

1. Place lentils, salt, water, and bouillon in a deep nonstick pan and simmer, covered, for about 45 minutes. The lentils should be nearly tender.

2. Sauté the *burghol* in half the olive oil until each grain is coated, about 3 minutes.

3. Strain the lentils, reserving the broth. It is difficult to estimate how much water the lentils will have absorbed, but you need about 2 1/2 cups for the remainder of the cooking. Add water if necessary to make this amount. Stir the liquid and the lentils into the *burghol*. Bring to a boil, reduce heat, and simmer, covered.

4. Sauté the onions in the remaining olive oil until transparent. Transfer half of them and their oil to the *burghol* mixture. Continue cooking the remaining onions until they are a dark golden color and nearly crispy. (This may require an additional 5 or 10 minutes.) Remove the pan from the heat and set aside.

5. As the *Mujeddara* simmers, taste for seasoning and add salt and black pepper as necessary. The cooking time for the *burghol* and lentil combination should be about 35 minutes. Keep the heat low to avoid burning the bottom of the dish, and add small amounts of water if the pilaf is drying up too quickly.

6. Mound the *Mujeddara* onto a serving dish and top with the crispy onions and their cooking oil. Serve with generous amounts of yoghurt, which each person spoons on top of his or her dish.

Variations

Egypt, Lebanon, and Jordan: Substitute rice for the *burghol*.

Saudi Arabia: Substitute rice for the *burghol*, use red lentils, and flavor with cinnamon and *kebsa* spices.

Traveling Jew

Yahoodi Mnsaafir (SYRIA, IRAQ)

Yahoodi Mnsaafir is yet another example of wholesome Arab one-pot cookery: a tiny bit of meat, healthy fresh vegetables, and lots of hearty grain. With a side dish of yoghurt and fresh bread, it's a complete and well-balanced meal.

Urban Arabs may not have heard of this village dish, but **Traveling Jew** blends the flavors of crushed wheat and eggplant so well that it has been an instant favorite with family and friends for years. My mother-in-law swears that it is popular among Syrian Jews, too, who refer to it as *Runaway Muslim*, and I have recently discovered it in two books of Sephardic Jewish cookery, described as being of Yemeni and Iraqi origin.

   1 onion, chopped

  1/3 cup olive oil (divided use)

   1 clove garlic, minced

  1/2 pound beef sirloin, coarsely chopped

     salt

     black pepper

   1 medium eggplant, diced but not peeled

1 1/4 cups coarse **burghol** wheat, rinsed

2 1/2 cups water

1. Sauté the onion in 2 tbsp. of the oil until softened and transparent. Add the garlic and the sirloin and season with salt and pepper. Stir-fry over high heat until the meat has lost all traces of pink. Remove from the pan with a slotted spoon.

2. Add the eggplant and the remaining oil and sauté about 5 minutes, tossing frequently, until it becomes slightly opaque.

3. Stir in the *burghol* wheat and toss to coat each grain with the oil. Add the meat and water and bring to a boil. Cover, reduce heat, and simmer for about 40 minutes, until the wheat is tender and fluffy. Taste and adjust seasonings. Serve with yoghurt.

Variations

Yemen: Add red pepper, and substitute meat broth for the sirloin and water.

Iraq: Substitute 1/2 cup minced parsley for the garlic.

Syria: Substitute chopped zucchini or green *foul* beans for the eggplant and add 1/2 cup minced cilantro.

Libyan Pasta with Orange-Blossom Chicken and Raisins

Rashda (LIBYA, MOROCCO)

~~~~~~

In the original Libyan version of this exotic dish, the pasta is made by hand. After the dough is rolled out and cut into strips, it is pressed several times through a metal sieve, until tiny irregular lumps form. Then the cook rubs the bits of dough between the palms of her hands to produce tiny balls of somewhat standard size. If this sounds strangely Italian, it's interesting to note that Italy for many years included its southern neighbor in its colonial empire.

A dried pasta labeled Moughrabiye Toasted Couscous, available in import food stores, is close to the authentic home product, or you can use pearl pasta, sometimes labeled *acini di pepe*. There is also a frozen Moughrabiye, but I find its texture unappealing. Or you can prepare this dish with **Couscous** (p. 197), which is preferred in neighboring Morocco.

In Jordan and Lebanon a similar version of this North African dish is enjoyed, flavored with cinnamon and allspice, the usual spices of the Levant. Called *Magrabeeya*, or *The Moroccan One*, it's a perfect example of how people of one region borrow elements of neighboring cuisines, while incorporating local vegetables and spices.

- 2 medium onions, chopped
- 2 tbsp. olive oil
- 1/2 tsp. **Harissa Red Chili** Paste (p. 41)
- 1/4 tsp. Middle Eastern red pepper

1 stick cinnamon

¼ tsp. ground ginger

¼ tsp. nutmeg

⅛ tsp. ground cloves

   black pepper

   salt

1 tsp. tomato paste

4 cups water

6 pieces chicken

   salt

¼ to ⅓ cup raisins

2 cups cooked chickpeas

1 package (14 oz.) Moughrabiye Toasted Couscous, or:

1 package (12 oz.) pearl pasta (**acini di pepe**)

2 tbsp. melted butter or olive oil

2 tbsp. orange-blossom water (divided use) (optional)

Garnish:

   sprigs of parsley

1. Sauté the onions in 2 tbsp. olive oil until soft and transparent. Add the spices and tomato paste and toss for 1 minute. Pour on the water, add the chicken, and bring to a boil.

2. Meanwhile, soak the raisins in very hot water and set aside. When the chicken has been cooking for about 30 minutes, add the drained raisins and the chickpeas.

3. Cook until the meat is very well done and falling off the bones, about 10–20 minutes longer. (White meat will require less cooking.) Taste and adjust seasoning. Using a slotted spoon, remove the chicken from the cooking liquid and set aside to cool. Reserve the broth until you prepare the pasta.

4. Cook the Moughrabiye or pearl pasta in boiling salted water until tender, according to package instructions. Drain.

5. Toss the cooked pasta with 2 tbsp. melted butter or olive oil, sprinkling with half of the orange-blossom water. Arrange on a serving platter.

6. Separate the warm broth from the vegetables by passing it through a colander, and serve in small bowls. Reheat in the microwave if it cools before mealtime.

7. Strip the chicken from the bone and shred or tear into large pieces. Combine the chicken with the onions, chickpeas, and raisins that have been removed from the broth. Sprinkle with the remaining half of orange-blossom water and toss. Arrange the mixture over the pasta and garnish with parsley. The broth is poured as desired over each bowl of pasta and vegetables.

Spaghetti with Yoghurt Sauce

Macarona bil Leban (SAUDI ARABIA)

From Egypt to the Gulf, spaghetti or macaroni is most commonly served with a simple yoghurt sauce. Pasta is an easily stored staple, always on hand, and yoghurt is consistently available from a neighbor who owns a cow. Not subject to seasonal harvests, economic conditions, or governmental import policies, yoghurt and pasta are a familiar standby.

In this Saudi version the garnish of minced meat and boiled eggs adds protein, but in the northern Arabian states it is usually omitted.

Spaghetti layer:
- 12 ounces spaghetti
- salt
- 2 cups low-fat yoghurt
- 1 clove garlic, crushed with salt
- 2 tbsp. olive oil

Meat layer:
- 1/4 pound lean ground beef
- 1/4 onion, minced
- 2 tbsp. olive oil
- salt
- black pepper
- 1/4 cup minced parsley
- 1 or 2 hard-boiled eggs, peeled and sliced

1. Cook the spaghetti in boiling salted water. While the pasta is cooking, combine the yoghurt and garlic.

2. Meanwhile, sauté the ground beef and minced onion in 2 tbsp. olive oil, seasoning with salt and pepper. Transfer to a sieve and set aside.

3. Drain the cooked pasta thoroughly and immediately toss with 2 tbsp. olive oil. Combine the spaghetti with the yoghurt and spread on a serving tray.

4. Top with the meat and parsley, and garnish with boiled eggs. At this point, some cooks transfer the tray to the oven and bake it for 5 minutes, but I prefer to omit this.

Variation

Syria: Omit the meat and eggs, and add 1 1/2 cups crumbled white Middle Eastern cheese (Haloomi, feta, Akawi, Nabulsi, or other) to the yoghurt, garnishing with parsley.

Dumplings in Yoghurt Sauce

Sheeshbarak bil Leban (SYRIA)

I remember the days in the Middle East when I used to make these little meat-filled dumplings from scratch. No need now to spend hours rolling and stuffing pastry: frozen and dried tortellini filled with meat (or only beef for Muslim guests) are nearly indistinguishable from the original item, while fresh tortellini from your supermarket's deli section are superb.

6 ounces fresh tortellini, filled with beef

Yoghurt sauce:
   3 cloves garlic, minced
   2 tbsp. butter or olive oil
   2 rounded tbsp. cornstarch, dissolved in:
1 1/2 cups water
   2 cups low-fat yoghurt
   salt

Garnish:
   minced cilantro

1. Sauté the garlic in the butter or olive oil for 2 minutes. Stir in the water in which you have dissolved the cornstarch. Add the yoghurt and whisk, stirring in one direction only, until the sauce begins to thicken and comes to a boil. Lower the heat and simmer for 2 or 3 minutes, continuing to stir in the same direction. Add salt and taste to adjust seasoning. (If the yoghurt sauce curdles, you may be able to salvage it by pureeing in a blender.)

2. Boil the tortellini according to package directions, and drain.

3. Drop the tortellini into the yoghurt sauce, garnish with cilantro, and serve immediately, with rice.

Mother of the Chunks

Um Kutah (LIBYA)

From a fresh cuisine completely unknown in the West comes this stunning recipe, one of the most exciting new dishes I've discovered. Its unpresuming provincial name, **Mother of the Chunks**, refers to the dark slices of sun-dried beef that adorn each serving, sitting like queens atop the white pasta and its thick tomato broth rich with onions, garlic, and whole serrano peppers.

In Libya, the stewed tomato sauce is served over spaghetti, *acini di pepe* pearl pasta, couscous, lentils, thin egg noodles, lentils, or rice. Our family favorite is *fusilli*, a spiral spaghetti that promises fun as well as great flavor.

After the wonderful exhilaration of this hot dish, I like to serve a North African **cooked carrot salad** (p. 79), whose natural sweetness balances the tangy red pepper dressing just as the pasta was a foil for its blazing chunky broth.

12 oz. your favorite pasta

Meat Sauce:
   2 onions, chopped
   3 tbsp. olive oil
   3 cloves garlic, minced
   4 serrano or jalapeño chilis, whole
   4 cups water
   2 rounded tbsp. tomato paste

2 ripe tomatoes, minced

4 ounces beef jerky (from a health food store), cut into bite-sized pieces

1/2 tsp. sweet paprika

1/4 tsp. cumin

    pinch nutmeg

    pinch cinnamon

    pinch ground cloves

    black pepper

    salt

    Middle Eastern red pepper (to taste)

1. Sauté the onions in the olive oil until soft and transparent. Stir in the garlic and chilis and stir-fry for 3–5 minutes.

2. Add the water, tomato paste, minced tomatoes, beef jerky, and spices, and bring to a boil. Reduce the heat and simmer for 2 or 3 hours, until the beef is softened. Cooking time depends on the age and type of jerky; the superior thin product sold by the ounce in the meat department of health food stores requires a shorter cooking time. The sauce should be liquidy, like a thick broth. Add more water as necessary. The dish should be pleasantly spicy. Little or no additional spice may be needed if the jerky is well seasoned, but taste and add salt and red pepper if needed.

3. Prepare the pasta according to package instructions.

4. Serve the pasta in bowls and fill with the brothy sauce just to cover.

Couscous

Cooscoos (MOROCCO AND NORTH AFRICA)

Although packaged couscous is now available in most American supermarkets, in North Africa it is still a home product. Two sizes of crushed semolina grains, the roughly milled endosperm or nutritive tissue of durum wheat, are sprinkled with water and are slowly stirred together with a circular motion. More water and semolina are added until the grains agglomerate to the desired size. Passing the couscous through a sieve assures even-sized particles. After steaming, the grains are sun-dried for 3 to 4 days.

In North Africa, couscous is incredibly light and fluffy, steamed to perfection in a special cooking pot called a *keskes* or *couscousiere*, which is rather like a large double boiler or vegetable steamer. Boiling water or broth is placed in the bottom cooking pan, and the couscous is steamed in the upper pan for 30 to 40 minutes. From time to time the cook sprinkles the grains with fresh water and stirs them with a large wooden spoon to break up lumps.

Unfortunately, the directions offered on most commercial couscous packages recommend preparing the grain in boiling water, just as rice and *burghol* are cooked. This results in a gooey, heavy product. It's better to improvise a *keskes*: line a vegetable steamer or very fine metal strainer with cheesecloth (to keep the tiny grains from falling into the boiling water) and set in a large pot.

The following directions are for the couscous pilaf that accompanies North African meat, chicken, and vegetable stews (these stews are also called couscous) that appear elsewhere in this book.

1 package (1 pound) couscous

1. Rinse the couscous and immediately drain it, breaking up all lumps.

2. Fill the bottom part of your improvised couscous pot with water and bring to a boil.

3. Arrange the upper part of your pot (perhaps a vegetable steamer or pasta sieve with cheesecloth) above the water. Transfer the moistened grain to the upper pot, cover, and steam, fluffing with a fork every 5 minutes. The pot should be covered to trap the steam, but if you cannot fit the cover over the improvised steamer, you may wish to try steaming the grain in 2 batches, so that more steam will reach all the grain. Commercial couscous usually needs only about 15 minutes to be light and evenly steamed.

4. When the couscous is done, many North Africans toss it with a few spoons of melted butter before transferring it to a platter and arranging the accompanying stew on top.

Seafood

With large areas of the Arab states stretching along the placid azure peripheries of the Mediterranean, the Red Sea, and the Arabian Gulf, even desert countries like Kuwait boast a lavish array of seafood recipes. Most of these are amazingly simple, yet intensely bright with flavor.

After a long day out at sea, fishermen along the Arabian Gulf (the geographic term the Arab world prefers for the body of water labeled the "Persian Gulf" by the Western powers) used to steam their catch over charcoal in a hole dug deep in the sand. The most common technique today is to rub a combination of spices, often with garlic and lemon juice, into the freshly caught fish several hours before it is grilled. *Masgoof*, the famous national dish of Iraq that is the specialty of the open-air restaurants lining the Euphrates, is whitefish broiled over a brushwood fire. Red mullet is similarly roasted along the sea coasts of Cyprus, Lebanon, and Egypt, with rice traditionally accompanying all these seafood specialties.

Mildly flavored dishes of baked fish are popular in the Levant as well as across the southern Mediterranean coast. In Tunisia, baked fish is lightly brushed with cumin and olive oil. Egyptian *plaki* dishes, in which a whole *bolti* or *morgaan* is baked in a bed of tomatoes and other fresh vegetables, are dramatic and elegant presentations for a festive occasion. In Lebanon, *Sayadeeyeh's* dark color develops from slow braising of onions, which subtly flavor the rice and the fish stock.

Istanbul, built on the cross flow between the cool waters of the Black Sea and the warmer Sea of Marmara, boasts that it has the tastiest and most varied seafood of the region. Fish restaurants and street vendors seem to be found everywhere: on obscure side streets close to the fish market, in the floating markets at the edge of the Galata Bridge, and—best of all—in Kumkapi, an unpretentious earthy old neighborhood.

Fish may also be poached in an intricately spiced broth. Curries popular in the Gulf States and Arabian peninsula call for cardamom, curry powder, and dried limes (*loomi*), and rice can be prepared in the same luxuriously seasoned liquid.

In 1976, when I arrived in Jeddah on the Red Sea coast, I had absolutely no experience preparing fish. In the American Midwest of those days, unless one spent the weekend down at the river, the only fish available was either mushy or freezer-burned. Like many Americans, my family handled all seafood in one manner: they rolled it in cornmeal and heated up the frying oil. Little wonder that many Americans are still reluctant to cook fish!

Nor did my Syrian husband, usually so creative in the kitchen but inexperienced with techniques of preparing fish, think beyond frying the bounty he brought home from weekend snorkeling outings in Jeddah's crystal coastal waters. Even in the Middle East countries bordered by the Mediterranean, the Red Sea, and the Arabian Gulf, population centers more than a few hours inland usually were not supplied with a reliable stock of seafood. While Beirutis enjoy fresh red mullet (*sultan ibraheem*) and bass (*lu'us*), and the Istanbuli swordfish (*kilich*), mussel (*midya*), and bluefish (*lufer*) dishes are famous, the culinary artists of landlocked Damascus are unaccustomed to seafood and have failed to develop a significant cuisine built on the sea's resources.

Our house in Jeddah was situated at the side of a huge rocky field on which a Saudi army battalion had pitched its white tents, and from my flat roof I could see the graceful sails of Saudi fishing dhows nestling in a tiny sheltering cove just a few blocks to the west. But for years lack of roads between my neighborhood and the sea disallowed fanciful seaside walks. Nor was it culturally acceptable in those days for a young woman to wander along the beach peering into nets and talking to fishermen, or even to visit the invitingly colorful and smelly fish market in the old Jeddah port downtown.

In that astonishing place where the twentieth century pounded at the door of a medieval society, surprises became the norm, as long hours and weeks of boredom alternated with events of unexpected clarity. With public entertainment forbidden in the Kingdom there were no cinemas or concert halls or musical presentations to break the monotony. But on Friday (the Muslim sabbath) evenings thousands of families escaped in a northerly stream toward the pounding surf of the Red Sea, to spread woven mats on the sand and relax in the cool of the late afternoon.

One sabbath evening, as we joined the caravan of cars heading homeward along the primitive asphalt track along the sea, the flaming rays of a brilliant red sunset illuminated one solitary dark figure squatting in the sand beside some small gray bundles at the edge of the road. To catch the twilight sea breezes, the man had twisted the ends of his red and white *kaffeeyah* up over his head and tucked them into his black *agal* (a double cord securing the headdress). Instead of the elegant white *thobs* of my urban neighbors, he wore a plain white undershirt and a piece of buff plaid fabric wrapped between waist and knees: the traditional costume of Saudi fishermen and pearl divers.

Propriety unfortunately demanded that I remain inside the car, but my husband went to investigate and discovered to our delight that the dark mounds were fish. Bargaining was minimal. The shrewd fisherman was aware that hundreds of cars filled with Arab and expatriate families would pass on their return to the city, and chances were good that he'd sell his small catch easily for the price he requested.

The huge red snapper and *najil* (grouper) that we took home that evening (Arabs usually buy in large quantities, and my husband could never accustom himself to buying just a little bit of any food) were enough for several meals. I froze one and baked the other with onions and fresh vegetables, reserving the tails and gigantic heads for soup.

Middle Eastern methods of cooking seafood are ideal for the health conscious, because animal fats and buttery sauces are not added to counteract the benefits of eating fish. Those on a low-sodium diet will find the highly seasoned Gulf recipes of special interest, as the quantity of salt may be reduced without affecting the flavor.

Many of us unnecessarily shy away from fish because we don't know how to select a variety that suits the recipe we have in mind. Americans living on the east or Gulf coasts will find different varieties of fish in local fish markets than those available on the west coast, while mid-America sometimes faces a limited selection of frozen fish. Often the favorite catch of a seaside vacation, such as a tender and flaky redfish, is not commercially harvested, and will be unavailable back home. Where a type of fish is recommended for one of the following recipes, I suggest you try that particular one first.

However, I have discovered that for most of these mouth-watering traditional recipes the specific type of fish is less important than its size and cut. Flatfish (such as flounder, sole, halibut, plaice), for example, produce thinner fillets than roundfish and require less cooking time, while roundfish (such as trout, mackerel, whitefish, red snapper, salmon), are easier to stuff and bake. In general, any white-fleshed fish is well-suited to Mediterranean cooking techniques.

The spectacular dishes from the Arab Mediterranean, Gulf, and Red Sea are very adaptable, and I have even used them with delicious results with American farm-bred freshwater catfish and trout. So don't be afraid to experiment as I have, using your favorite seafood in a new way, or bringing home a fish that is specially priced and trying your hand at a wonderfully unusual dish. If you'd feel more comfortable with specific information about the fish that is available in your area, ask the advice of the salesperson where you usually purchase seafood.

It is difficult to be specific in recommending cooking times when the same delicious recipe can be prepared with such a variety of types of fish. As a general rule, Arabs tend to cook seafood, as well as other meats for a longer time than we do in the West. Even if a recipe in this chapter suggests a certain length of cooking, a larger (or thicker) fish will always require more than a smaller (or thinner) one. A general principle is to lay the fish (any form) on a counter and stand a ruler perpendicular to it. Cooking time is calculated at 10 minutes per inch, with 5 additional minutes per inch if cooked in a sauce.

Garlicky Grilled Fish

Semak ma Toom (SAUDI ARABIA)

Not even an unpretentious grilled fish escapes the kitchen artist's palette. In this Saudi version of a classic dish found on all coasts of the Mediterranean, the snowy white flakes of fish are seasoned with garlic, mild green chili, and fresh lemon juice.

2 1/2 pounds whole fish, or:

1 1/2 pounds fish fillets, or:

1 1/2 pounds octopus or squid

Marinade:

   juice of 1 lemon

4 cloves garlic, crushed with salt

1 serrano chili, seeded and minced (optional)

1/2 tsp. pepper

1 tsp. cumin, ground coriander, allspice, **kebsa** spices, or curry powder

2 tbsp. olive oil

Garnish:

   chopped parsley

   lemon wedges

1. Make a paste of the lemon juice, garlic, salt, optional chili, pepper, and your spice of preference. Rub it into the flesh and inside of the fish, or into the surface of the fillets. (A large fish may be cut into pieces.) If you are using octopus, cut it into 3-inch sections. If you are using squid, stuff its tentacles into the hollow body cavities. Marinate for at least 2 hours, or cover and refrigerate overnight.

2. Brush seafood on both sides with olive oil.

3. Grill over charcoal or oven broil until done.

4. Garnish with parsley and lemon wedges.

Garlic Saffron Marinated Fish Brochettes

Kebab Assemak el Maghribee (MOROCCO)

Shark's firm, meatlike texture makes it ideal for this grilled dish. Swordfish is the only other fish comparable in texture and flavor. Virtually boneless, the shark's spinal column is long but lacks the fine dorsal bones common to other fish, and it is increasingly available in local supermarkets.

Other possibilities for a fish kebab are mackerel, pike, rockfish, tuna, and monkfish, but shark and swordfish are recommended because they are also low in fat. Don't use a tender fish that might flake off the skewers. Add mushrooms, green peppers, and tomatoes to the skewers, if you like, and serve with rice.

1 1/2 pounds thick fish fillets

Marinade:

> juice of 1 large lemon
> 2 tbsp. olive oil
> 2 cloves garlic, crushed with
> salt
> 1/2 tsp. red pepper
> 1/2 tsp. sweet paprika
> 1/8 tsp. saffron
> 2 green onions, minced
> 1/4 cup minced parsley
> 2 tbsp. minced cilantro

1. Rinse the fish and dry it completely with paper towels. Cut the fillets into cubes about 1 inch thick.

2. Mix the marinade ingredients thoroughly.

3. Marinate the fish for at least 2 hours, turning occasionally, or cover and refrigerate overnight.

4. Thread fish cubes onto skewers. Grill for just a few minutes over charcoal, or oven broil.

Grilled Fish with Cumin

Hoot Mishwee bil Kamoon (LIBYA)

In Libya, fish is often served as a first course, and as cumin is considered an appetite stimulator, the combination is culturally appropriate. Moreover, while cumin may seem strong and intense when tasted alone, it mellows when used with fish, complementing rather than dominating. In fact, in Libya the spice is so valued as a fish seasoning and so rarely used with other foods that it is often referred to as *kamoon il hoot*, "cumin of the fish." Whether the fish is boiled, simmered, stewed, fried, or baked, and whether the spice is used alone or blended with several other spices, cumin is essential to every Libyan fish dinner.

2 ½ pounds whole fish

Marinade:
   ⅓ cup olive oil
      salt
      black pepper
   1 tsp. cumin
   1 tsp. red pepper

1. Wash and dry the fish. Cut 3 or 4 deep diagonal slits on each side of the fish.

2. Combine the marinade ingredients and rub them into the skin, slits, and belly of the fish. Marinate for at least 2 hours, or cover and refrigerate overnight.

3. Grill over charcoal or oven broil.

Fragrant Trout, Basra Style

Semak bil Tamer (IRAQ, GULF STATES, SAUDI ARABIA)

In Iraq one might prepare this with a whitefish called *shaboot*, freshly caught in the waters of the Tigris or the Euphrates. Now that commercial fish production in this country has made trout easily available and affordable for all of us, I find that its delicate flesh is perfect for the traditional technique of grilling fish flavored with dates.

This is another fine example of the exquisite combinations that have been created when an ingenious cook makes use of local ingredients. The first time I prepared it, a strange musky perfume began to fill the house, and my teenage son strode into the kitchen in unrestrained protest. "Mom! Are you burning that darn incense again?" Not only is this delicious dish of the "quick and easy" variety, but when the date marinade is placed near a flame, it releases a heavenly perfume worthy of a caliph's pleasure.

3 whole trout (about 2 1/2 pounds total)
salt
black pepper

Marinade:

6 large moist dates, pits removed
2 tbsp. hot water

1. Chop the dates and soak them in the hot water until they disintegrate when stirred. Or whirl them in a food processor.

2. Wash and dry the trout and sprinkle with salt and pepper.

3. Rub the date paste into the cavity and skin of the fish. Grill or oven broil until tender, about 5 minutes on each side.

Curried Fish with Dried Lime

Semak bi Salsit al Karry (BAHRAIN, GULF STATES, SAUDI ARABIA)

Curries are very popular in the Arabian Gulf and the Eastern Province of Saudi Arabia. The tiny island of Bahrain was for centuries a commercial center where dhows plying the spice trade from India to Europe settled in for a few days' rest and provisions. Approximately 20% of Bahrain's population is of Indian/Pakistani origin, and this cultural influence is conspicuous in this dish. Ten or twenty spices are frequently combined in Gulf dishes to flavor one principal ingredient, but in this recipe I suggest a commercial curry powder for ease of preparation.

2 onions, chopped
2 tbsp. olive oil
2 cloves garlic, minced
salt

1 tsp. curry powder

½ cinnamon stick

3 tomatoes, peeled and chopped

2 cups water or chicken stock

1 **loomi**

1 ¼ pounds fish fillets, or:

2 ½ pounds whole fish

1. Sauté the onions in the olive oil until softened. Add the garlic, salt, and curry powder and cook for another minute. Stir in the cinnamon stick, tomatoes, and water. Cover and simmer for 5 minutes.

2. Drop the *loomi* into the pot and lower the fish into the sauce. Cover the pot and poach the fish over low heat until it is tender and flaky.

3. Serve over rice.

Saffron Seafood Stew

Yaknit Semak (SYRIA, LEBANON)

This famous Mediterranean stew is related to Italian cioppino and French bouillabaisse, which were built on whatever seafood the fishermen happened to catch, plus a few seasonal vegetables. A variety of seafood will provide an interesting texture, but you needn't be bound by the ones listed below. Do try a bit of tender squid cut into small rings, but remember to add the seafood gradually, according to the relative amount of time it will need to cook.

You might try adding diced potatoes to this dish. Or serve it with boiled new potatoes or rice.

¼ pound octopus

2 onions, chopped

2 tbsp. olive oil

3 cloves garlic, minced
   generous pinch red pepper
   pinch saffron, or:

¼ tsp. **asfor**

1 can (16 oz.) tomatoes, with liquid

salt

pinch black pepper

1/2 tsp. basil

2 tsp. minced parsley

2 tsp. minced cilantro

1/4 cup fish stock

3/4 pound thick fish fillets

1/2 pound squid, with tentacles

1/3 pound shrimp, shelled

1/4 pound crabmeat, real or imitation

Garnish:

minced parsley

lemon wedges

1. Cut the octopus into 3-inch lengths. Because it requires so much more cooking than the rest of the fish, I suggest that you precook it for about 1 hour in boiling salted water, or until nearly tender. Then drain in a colander.

2. Meanwhile, sauté the onions in the olive oil until soft and transparent. Stir in the garlic, red pepper, and saffron or *asfor* and cook for another minute.

3. Chop the tomatoes and add them, with their juice, to the onions. Add the remaining seasonings and the fish stock and bring to a boil.

4. Reduce the heat and drop in the precooked octopus. Cover and simmer for 10 minutes.

5. Rinse the squid and cut it into little rings. Remove the "eye" at the center of the tentacles and section them into 2 or 3 lengths. Stir the squid and the fish into the liquid, cover, and cook for 5–7 minutes.

6. Add the shrimp and the crabmeat. (If you are using imitation crabmeat, which is ready to eat, add it only when all the seafood is done.) Taste and adjust seasoning. Cover and simmer for about 5–10 minutes, until all the seafood is tender.

7. Garnish with parsley. Serve with lemon wedges.

Spicy Octopus or Squid in Pomegranate Sauce

Akhdaboot bi Salsit il Filful (ARAB STATES)

The development of the consumer sector in Saudi Arabia was as sudden and astonishing as growth in industry, medicine, and education. When we arrived in 1976, Jeddah's population of nearly one million was served by three tiny supermarkets, each the size of a quick shop back home. But within a few years of booming economic development, Jeddah was selected by a European travel magazine as the most beautiful city in the world!

One day in 1982 I found in the local Safeway no less than six different types of squid. I could choose between Spanish, Chinese (the most economical), Moroccan, and Japanese (which cost three times more than the Chinese). Stores also stocked canned calamari "en su tinta" from both Spain and China.

Both the old fish market and the spotless fish shops that soon sprouted around the Kingdom were filled with an exciting variety of seafood. Crab, lobster, and baby shark were normal fare. One British couple were stunned to discover a live turtle in the fish souk, which they subsequently purchased and set free on the seashore.

- 1 onion, slivered
- 2 tbsp. olive oil
- 2 cloves garlic, minced
- 1/2 to 1 serrano chili, seeded and minced
- 1/4 tsp. sweet paprika
- 1 1/2 pounds octopus or squid
- 1 can (16 oz.) tomatoes, with liquid
- salt
- 1 tsp. wine vinegar
- 1/4 cup water
- 1 tsp. **hamod er rummaan** pomegranate syrup

1. Sauté the onion in the olive oil until soft and transparent. Stir in the garlic, chili, and paprika and cook for another minute.

2. Cut the tips of octopus tentacles into 2- or 3-inch lengths and the upper portions of the tentacles diagonally to produce long, thin slices; slice the squid into rings. Add to the onion and lightly sauté.

3. Whirl the tomatoes in a food processor until broken up but not smooth. Pour tomatoes over the fish. Add the salt, vinegar, and water. Bring to a boil, reduce the heat, and simmer until tender. As the sauce reduces, stir frequently to avoid sticking. Squid will require about 10 minutes cooking, while octopus may take up to 1 hour.

4. When the fish is tender and the sauce is thick and rich, stir in the *hamod*. Taste and adjust seasoning.

5. This dish can be served warm or at room temperature. You can use it in a creative seafood *fetteh* (p. 21), serving the stew over crisped bread and topping it with yoghurt sauce. It is also great with pasta or rice.

Simmered Fish Tajine

Tajeen (MOROCCO)

In this recipe, the mild flavor of fish is accented with the earnest sunny flavors typical of North Africa's Mediterranean coast: garlic and fresh tomatoes, aromatic cumin and cilantro, lemon and red peppers. Tuna is ideal for this steamed dish, which can be prepared with a whole fish that will fit in your largest skillet, or with thick fish steaks. Thin fillets will cook too quickly, not allowing enough time for the sauce to cook down.

2 1/2 pounds whole fish, or:
1 1/2 pounds fish steaks
   2 cloves garlic, crushed with
     salt
   1 tsp. sweet paprika
   1 tsp. red pepper
     black pepper
1 1/2 tsp. cumin
   2 tbsp. olive oil

2 tomatoes, sliced

1 lemon, sliced

1/2 cup minced cilantro

1. If the fish is whole, cut 3 or 4 deep diagonal slits on each side. Combine the spices and rub the fish with the mixture. Set aside for at least 2 hours, or cover and refrigerate overnight.

2. Heat the oil in a large skillet and arrange the fish over its surface in one layer. Top with the tomatoes, lemon, and cilantro. Cover and steam over very low heat until tender. (Steaks or thick fillets will require less than 1/2 hour, while whole fish may take twice as long.)

Fish in Aromatic Tomato Sauce

Semak bil Tomatum (SAUDI ARABIA, GULF STATES, NORTH AFRICA)

For years one of our favorite fish dishes has been **Huachinango a la Veracruzana**, from the seacoast state of Veracruz in Mexico. We love the fragrance of the cinnamoned tomato sauce flavored with lime and hot chilis in which the red snapper is served. It's not at all difficult to trace this Mexican jewel's culinary heritage back to Andalusian Spain and North Africa (see the preceding recipe) and even to the Arabian peninsula, the original homeland of the Arab peoples often referred to as Moors.

The following recipe is prepared all over the Arab world. Amazingly, the Moroccan variation features the same cinnamon and piquant fresh chili found in Veracruz's famous dish. But as the tomatoes and chilis found in all these recipes are of New World origin and were brought back to Europe by the Spanish conquistadors, one can only speculate about this strikingly memorable dish enjoyed by the peoples of three very different remote regions.

1 large onion, chopped

2 tbsp. olive oil

3 cloves garlic, minced

1 serrano chili, seeded and minced

1   can (16 oz.) tomatoes, with liquid
½   cup minced cilantro
    salt
    black pepper
    juice of ½ lemon
1 ½ pounds fish fillets

1. Sauté the onion in the olive oil until transparent and softened. Add the garlic and chili and cook for another minute.

2. Whirl the canned tomatoes and their juices in a food processor until broken up but not entirely pureed. Little bits of tomatoes should still be visible.

3. Add the tomatoes, cilantro, salt, black pepper, and lemon to the onions, and bring to a boil. Lower the fish fillets into the sauce. Reduce the heat and cover. Simmer until the fish is tender, about 5–15 minutes. Taste and adjust seasoning.

4. Serve with rice or pasta.

Variations

Morocco: Add a half a cinnamon stick, allspice, and cumin.

Libya: Add tarragon, cumin, and red pepper.

Stuffed Fish
with Sun-Dried Lime

Semak ma Loomi (GULF STATES)

A specialty of the Gulf States and the Arabian peninsula, *loomi* is an odd-looking, hard, shriveled citrus that one would expect to uncover in a Chinese apothecary's shop rather than in the spice market. Also referred to as "Omani limes," "Basra lemons," or "black limes," *loomi* is harvested and dried in the intense sun of Iraq's fertile Basra region, in Oman, and the citrus orchards of

Shiraz (Iran). When a dish requires long simmering, *loomi* is usually pierced in one or two places to permit the cooking liquid to pass through and absorb its pungent, fruity bouquet. But when cooking time is short or when the dish is relatively dry, *loomi* is crushed and ground in a spice mill or blender before it is added.

In the following recipe, ground spice flavors the stuffing that is tied into the fish's cavity, while a whole dried lime is dropped into the broth.

2 ½ pounds whole fish

Stuffing:

  1 large onion, chopped
  ¼ tsp. ground **loomi**
  1 tsp. **kebsa** spices
  ¼ tsp. turmeric
     salt

Seasoned broth:

  1 **loomi**, pierced
  ½ tsp. turmeric
  4 sticks cinnamon
  3 pods cardamom
     salt
  1 tsp. **kebsa** spices
  3 whole cloves
  4 cups water

1. Combine the stuffing ingredients and pack them into the fish cavity. Tie closed with a cord.

2. Place the broth ingredients in a large, deep skillet that will hold the fish. Bring to a boil.

3. Lower the fish into the broth. Cover, reduce heat, and simmer until done, about 20 to 30 minutes or longer, depending on the type and size of fish.

Cumin Poached Fish with Potatoes

Haraimy (LIBYA)

~~~~~~

The preferred fish in Libya is the *farooj*, a reddish or yellowish brown grouper with dark patches or orange spots. Known as the *menany ahmar* in neighboring Tunisia, it is a firm white fish with few bones that can be poached, steamed, baked, fried, grilled, or made into soup. (You may substitute red snapper, redfish, bass, or any firm white roundfish).

Although this dish is often prepared without the potatoes and served at room temperature ("cold" in Arabic), it is equally delicious when warm. Along the southern Mediterranean every good housewife would automatically have a simmering cauldron of fish heads on the stove's back burner, and a bit of the broth would be used to poach the fish. Not to worry! Substitute canned clam juice, chicken broth, or water.

- 1 onion, chopped
- 1/4 cup olive oil
- 1 tsp. red pepper
- 4 potatoes, peeled and sliced
- 2 cups **Fish Stock** (p. 101), clam juice, chicken broth, or water
- 2 tbsp. tomato paste
- 2 tsp. cumin
- 3 cloves garlic, crushed with salt
- 1 1/2 pounds thick fish fillets or steaks

Garnish:

lemon wedges

1. Sauté the onion in the olive oil until slightly softened. Add the red pepper and cook for 2 more minutes to release the flavors.

2. Add the potatoes to the onions and stir to coat them with the oil.

3. Add the fish broth, tomato paste, cumin, and garlic. Bring to a boil, then cover, reduce heat, and simmer for 5–10 minutes. (If the fish fillets are thin, cook the potatoes a little longer, so that when the fish is added, both will be tender at the same time.)

4. Gently slip in the fish fillets or steaks. Simmer until both potatoes and fish are tender, about 15 minutes. Serve with fresh lemon wedges to be squeezed over the seafood.

Baked Fish with Cilantro

Al Kuzbarreeyah (KUWAIT AND THE GULF STATES)

Cilantro is a regional favorite of the Arabian peninsula and the Gulf States. The mild flavor of fish readily accepts a sharp accent of cilantro, lemon, or spices.

2 1/2 pounds whole fish

Marinade/Stuffing:

  1 onion, chopped
  4 cloves garlic, crushed with
     salt
  1 tsp. curry powder
 1/4 tsp. red pepper
  3 tomatoes, chopped
  1 bunch cilantro, chopped
 1/2 serrano chili, seeded and minced
     juice of 1 lemon

1. Combine the marinade ingredients and rub into the outside of the fish. Fill the fish cavity with the remaining mixture and tie it closed with a cord. Wrap in foil and refrigerate for at least 6 hours.

2. Bake at 350 degrees for about 30 minutes. Unwrap the fish and brown for about 10 minutes longer. The fish is done when it flakes when pierced with the tines of a fork.

Baked Fish Fillets a l'Orange

Semak Mishwee (EGYPT)

What could be easier than this quick fish dish with a North African touch of citrus?

1½ pounds fish fillets
   salt
   black pepper
2 tbsp. lemon juice
2 tbsp. olive oil
1 or 2 oranges, sliced

1. Season the fish on both sides with salt and pepper and place in a single layer in an oiled baking dish.

2. Combine the oil with the lemon juice and brush onto the fish.

3. Arrange the orange slices over the fish.

4. Cover with foil and bake at 350 degrees until the fish is flaky. Cooking time will vary from 10 to 20 minutes, depending on the thickness of the fillets.

Tamarind Fish

Semak bil Tamarhindee (GULF STATES) ✦ *Semak bil Hamir* (SAUDI ARABIA)

The pods of the tropical tamarind tree (*hamir*) are a popular seasoning agent around the world. In the pediatric hospital where I worked in Mexico, our little patients were served a tan-colored tamarind water, and in Pakistan it flavors lentil dishes. Tamarind sauce, called *tamarhindee* or *humi* in Arabia, adds a sweet and sour touch to fish dishes and to sauces of all types. Tamarind can be found in import food stores in its original light brown pod form or in jars or blocks of bean pulp.

2 ½ pounds whole fish

½ tamarind pod, or:

1 rounded tbsp. tamarind paste

1 ½ cups water

1 tsp. cumin

½ tsp. ground coriander

½ tbsp. black pepper

1 tbsp. olive oil

4 cloves garlic, crushed with
   salt
   juice of 1 lemon

1 onion, chopped
   salt

Garnish:

minced parsley

1. Soak the tamarind pod in the water for at least ½ hour. (Skip this step if using tamarind paste.)

2. Cut 3 or 4 deep diagonal slits into each side of the fish.

3. Combine the cumin, coriander, black pepper, and olive oil.

4. Mix half of the spice mixture with the garlic and the lemon juice and rub it into the outside of the fish.

5. Combine the remaining spice mixture with the onion and additional salt and stuff the fish cavity with it. Place the fish in a baking dish.

6. Rub the tamarind pod or the paste between the fingers to release all its flavor. Strain the tamarind liquid, pushing as much as possible of the solid matter through the strainer, and pour it over the fish. Cover the baking dish with foil and bake at 350 degrees for about 45 minutes, basting occasionally with the tamarind liquid. The fish is done when it flakes easily when gently probed with a fork.

Oven-Steamed Fish, Mediterranean Style

Semak bi Saneeyeh (SAUDI ARABIA, EGYPT, ARAB STATES)

This recipe and the following three are fine examples of Mediterranean *plaki* cooking, in which whole fish or fillets are smothered with a mixture of fresh vegetables and herbs, onions, and garlic. The fish can be steamed in the delicious vegetable juices either in the oven or atop the stove. Simmering the fish together with vegetables locks in nutrients, producing a juicy and delightfully fresh flavor with minimal fat (only about 15 grams per serving.) Serve all *plaki* dishes over rice, which will absorb the mouth-watering sauce.

1 ½   pound fish fillets, or:
2 ½   pounds whole fish
  1   large onion, chopped
  2   tbsp. olive oil
  1   or 2 green peppers, veined, seeded, and chopped
  1   small serrano chili, seeded and chopped
  2   tomatoes, chopped
     salt
     black pepper
  2   small tomatoes, sliced

1. Line a shallow baking dish generously with foil, leaving extra on all sides.

2. If you are using whole fish, it will significantly reduce the total baking time if you lightly sauté it first in a bit of olive oil. Place the browned whole fish or the fillets in the dish.

3. Sauté the onion in the same oil until softened. Add the green peppers and chili and cook for 3 minutes.

4. Add the chopped tomatoes and their juices and simmer for 3 minutes. Season with salt and pepper. Taste and adjust the seasoning. Pour the sauce over the fish, arrange the slices of tomato decoratively on top, and bring the extra foil on the sides together to seal.

5. Bake at 350 degrees until the fish is flaky. Cooking time will vary from 10 to 25 minutes, depending on the thickness of the fillet, and longer if whole fish is used.

Variations

Egypt: Season with oregano, bay leaf, and 2 large ribs celery.

Armenia: Add 1 large diced potato and 2 chopped carrots to the vegetable mixture.

Morocco: Season with saffron and cumin.

Steamed Fish with Double Lemon Saffron Marinade

Assemak el Moobahar el Mishwee bi Tabil el Magribee (MOROCCO)

Lemon and garlic have an affinity for fish's mildness, and both fresh and pungently spiced preserved lemons accent this dish. Moroccans, with their admiration for the exquisite flavor and color imparted by saffron, add it to most fish dishes. Saffron is the most expensive spice, but a tiny amount goes a long way in this sophisticated combination of fragrances and colors.

1 1/2 pound thick fish fillets

Marinade:

  1/4 cup olive oil
      juice of 1/2 lemon
    2 cloves garlic, crushed with
      salt and:
  1/8 tsp. saffron
  1/8 tsp. red pepper
    1 **preserved lemon** (p. 22)
    2 tbsp. minced parsley
    2 tbsp. minced cilantro
    2 green onions, minced
      black pepper

1. Combine the olive oil, lemon juice, garlic, saffron, and red pepper. Cut the preserved lemon in half and remove and discard the fruity pulp. Cut the rind and skin into thin slivers.

2. Place each fillet on a sheet of foil and brush the marinade evenly over the fish. Distribute the sliced preserved lemon evenly over the fillets along with the parsley, cilantro, and green onions. Sprinkle with freshly ground black pepper.

3. Seal each fillet in the foil and bake at 350 degrees for 15–25 minutes, or until the fish flakes when pierced with a fork. Cooking time will vary with the type and thickness of the fish.

Honey Raisin Fish

Semak mal Asal wal Sbeeb (MOROCCO, ANDALUSIA)

If a Moroccan were preparing this recipe, she would simply reach over to her spice jar and toss a generous handful of her own special *ras il hanoot* ("best of the shop") mixture on a fresh *tassargal* fish to enhance its natural goodness. Unless you plan to cook a large number of Moroccan dishes, you will do just as well with the breakdown of sweet spices listed below.

1 ½ pounds fish fillets

Marinade:
- ½ tsp. cinnamon
- ½ tsp. black pepper
- ½ tsp. red pepper
- ¼ tsp. allspice
- pinch nutmeg
- pinch turmeric
- pinch ground cardamom
- pinch ginger
- pinch ground cloves
- salt
- 4 tbsp. olive oil (divided use)

3 tbsp. raisins or currants

1 onion, chopped

4 tbsp. wine vinegar

2 tbsp. minced parsley

4 tbsp. honey

1. Combine all the spices with 2 tbsp. olive oil and brush the fish sparingly with the mixture, reserving the remaining marinade for the sauce. Set the fish aside for 2 hours or longer, or cover and refrigerate overnight.

2. Soak the raisins in hot water.

3. Sauté the onion in the remaining 2 tbsp. olive oil until soft and transparent. Drain the raisins and add them to the onions along with the reserved spice marinade and the remaining ingredients. Reduce the heat and simmer for 10 minutes, to combine flavors and reduce the sauce.

4. Meanwhile, broil the fish until flaky and almost done.

5. Transfer the fish to a baking dish and spoon on the sauce. Cover with aluminum foil and bake at 350 degrees for 10 minutes, or until tender.

Variation

Andalusia: Substitute 1/4 tsp. saffron for the turmeric, cardamom, ginger, and cloves; sauté 1 chopped green pepper with the onion.

Saudi Shrimp in Garlic Chili Salsa

Jamberry bil Deema (SAUDI ARABIA AND EGYPT)

Unfortunately, many Gulf Arabs cook shrimp for 30 minutes to an hour—not quite my style. Countless times we were served chewy pieces of shrimp (in wonderful sauces) as part of an immense banquet over which a devoted cook had labored for days. Cookbooks in Arabic generally recommend an hour of cooking time for shrimp in recipes like the following one! An unpardonable fault in a region where the finely flavored combinations are truly fascinating and the shrimp are inexpensive and of the highest quality.

2 onions, chopped

2 tbsp. olive oil

pinch red pepper

1/2 small serrano chili, seeded and minced

2 cloves garlic, minced

2 carrots, chopped

4 tomatoes, chopped

salt

black pepper

1/2 cinnamon stick

1 pound shrimp, shelled

Yoghurt sauce: (optional)

2/3 cup low-fat yoghurt

1 clove garlic, crushed with
salt

2 tbsp. water

1. Sauté the onions in the olive oil until soft and transparent. Stir in the red pepper, chili, and garlic, and cook for 2 or 3 minutes to release the flavors.

2. Add the vegetables and the remaining seasonings and simmer uncovered for about 10 minutes.

3. Stir in the shrimp and cover. Cook about 5 minutes, just until the shrimp is pink and firm. Taste and adjust seasoning.

4. Combine the yoghurt with the garlic and water. Stir to mix thoroughly.

5. Serve the shrimp on a bed of rice with the optional yoghurt sauce drizzled on top.

The Mother of All Shrimp

Rubiann bi Toom (KUWAIT, GULF STATES, LEBANON, NORTH AFRICA, ANDALUSIA)

Among my collection of Middle Eastern cookbooks is a Kuwaiti one published in Arabic that includes a lobster recipe bearing this ironic name. I've borrowed it for this classic garlic shrimp recipe.

2 pounds giant shrimp with shells

Marinade:

5 cloves garlic, crushed with
   salt

3 tbsp. olive oil
   juice of 1 lemon
   black pepper
   pinch red pepper

1. Combine the marinade ingredients. Add the shrimp and turn to coat each piece with the marinade. Refrigerate for 2 hours or longer, or refrigerate overnight.

2. Thread onto skewers and grill or oven broil, basting with the marinade.

Yoghurt Marinated Shrimp

Awaal Arrubyaan bil Lebaneh (KUWAIT, GULF STATES)

Across the Arab world, the acidic properties of yoghurt are valued for their usefulness in tenderizing meat. This Kuwaiti recipe is a cousin of *Shisk Taook*, the Egyptian/Lebanese specialty of grilled chicken that has been marinated in yoghurt. As this technique is also popular in the Indian subcontinent, where the delicious dish is flavored with identical pungent curry spices, the recipe was probably introduced in the Gulf by spice merchants who traveled back and forth along the ancient trade routes, or by Kuwaitis of Indian origin.

2 pounds shrimp, shelled

Marinade:

1 cup low-fat yoghurt

1/2 tsp. curry powder, cumin, or allspice

1/4 tsp. red pepper

   pinch black pepper

2 cloves garlic, crushed with
   salt

1. Combine the marinade ingredients. Add the shrimp and turn to coat each piece with the marinade. Cover and refrigerate for 2 hours or longer.

2. Thread onto skewers and grill or oven broil, basting with the marinade.

Shrimp Cakes with Fresh Herbs

Koftit Jamberry bil Khodar (SAUDI ARABIA)

This fritter, although referred to as a *kefta* (ground-meat kebab), is actually more like an *ijjah* (fried vegetable omelette seasoned with fresh minced herbs). In Saudi Arabia it is often prepared with frozen mixed vegetables and seasoned with the cumin that many Middle Easterners prefer with fish.

I appreciate the bright color and refreshing flavor that the herbs and vegetables add, but I prefer to add fresh carrots, which I've shredded to a vermicelli consistency in my food processor. You might also enjoy trying this recipe with 1/2 pound of imitation crabmeat (which is a fish/crab product) in combination with an equal amount of shrimp.

Batter:

2 medium eggs, or:

1 egg, plus 1 egg white

5 tbsp. flour

2 tbsp. water

1 pound shrimp, shelled and chopped

2 medium carrots, finely shredded

1/4 cup minced parsley

1/4 cup minced cilantro

5 green onions, minced

1/2 to 1 serrano chili, seeded and minced

10 leaves fresh basil, minced, or:

1 tsp. dried basil

salt

black pepper

oil for sautéing

1. Mix together the batter ingredients. Stir in the shrimp and the remaining ingredients (except oil).

2. Drop a large spoonful of batter into a small amount of hot oil of your preference. Turn once to brown on both sides. Repeat with remaining batter.

Curried Shrimp with Vegetables and Pasta

Salonit Arrubiann (KUWAIT) ◆ *Machboos al Rubiann* (SAUDI ARABIA, GULF STATES)

Cultural exchanges with India were the inevitable result of the Gulf's proximity to the subcontinent and the trade that continues even today. Nowhere is this influence more evident than in this very popular Gulf dish, which was my first experience with Kuwaiti food.

This dish is often prepared precisely like an Indian curry, with up to 20 spices steeped in a thick tomato base with meat, fish, or shrimp. Often one or two vegetables are added: potatoes, green beans, small okra, green *foul* beans or lima beans, and spinach are all quite tasty. Some cooks cook the rice in the curry sauce, while others serve the stew over steamed white rice.

The version presented below is developed from a recipe given me by a charming Italian-Swiss lady married to a high-ranking Saudi diplomat from the holy city of Medina. Instead of serving fish recipes on a traditional bed of rice or *jareesh* (whole-wheat kernels), she prefers pasta, which has long been a favorite in the Kingdom. Creative cooks are always looking for innovations to tempt their dinner guests, and fish on a bed of pasta, I am told, is now the latest fashion in Medina.

Shrimp broth:

- 2 cups water
- 1 cinnamon stick
- 1 **loomi**, pierced
- 3 black peppercorns
- 1 pod cardamom
- 3 whole cloves
  - pinch **kebsa** spices
  - pinch turmeric
- 1 pound shrimp, shelled

- 1 onion, chopped
- 2 tbsp. olive oil
- 3 cloves garlic, minced
- 1 serrano chili, seeded and chopped
- 1 tsp. fresh ginger, minced
- 2 potatoes, peeled and cut lengthwise into 8 wedges
- 1 large tomato, chopped
- 1/4 cup minced parsley
- 1/4 cup minced cilantro
- 1 rounded tsp. tomato paste
  - salt
- 1 (10-oz.) package frozen green beans
- 12 oz. pasta (spaghetti is most commonly used)

Garnish:

slivered almonds, toasted, or:
minced parsley

1. Bring the water to a boil and add the broth seasoning ingredients. Drop in the shrimp and cook until they just begin to turn pink, about 3 minutes. Do not overcook, as they will later be steamed in the curry sauce. Strain the shrimp, reserving the seasoned broth.

2. Sauté the onion in the olive oil until soft and transparent. Stir in the garlic, chili, ginger, and potatoes, and stir-fry for about 5 minutes.

3. Add the fresh tomato, parsley, and cilantro and sauté for 2 more minutes.

4. Stir in the tomato paste and salt along with 1½ cups of the reserved broth. (Transfer the *loomi* and cinnamon stick also, adding water if necessary to make the necessary amount of liquid.) Stir to mix well. Leaving the potatoes in the pot, transfer about ¼ of the sauce to a medium-sized saucepan and set aside.

5. Add the green beans to the potato mixture, cover, and simmer until the vegetables are tender, about 20 minutes.

6. While the curry is cooking, reduce the reserved tomato sauce over medium heat, about 10 minutes. Stir in the reserved shrimp, cover, and simmer for about 5 minutes.

7. Meanwhile, prepare the pasta according to package instructions.

8. To serve, arrange the cooked spaghetti on a large round or oval serving platter. Mound the curried shrimp in the center. Distribute the curried vegetables evenly around the shrimp and garnish with almonds or parsley.

Shrimp with Kebsa-Spiced Rice

Machboos a Rubiann (KUWAIT, GULF STATES)

This is a lighter, simpler version of the previous curry, the Gulf equivalent of Spanish *arroz con pollo*, and every bit as exciting!

The Arabic origin of many Spanish and Latin American seafood dishes is attested to by their Arabic names: Clams are *almejas* (*al-majjah* in Arabic), tuna is *atun* (*al tun* in Arabic), and shad is *sabalo* (*shabil* in Arabic). Shrimp and rice dishes like this one were first prepared by the converted Muslims of eastern Spain to replace the staple couscous (even today the national dish of North Africa) when it was banned by the Spanish Inquisition.

1 pound shrimp, shelled

salt

black pepper

2 tsp. **kebsa** spices (divided use)

3 tbsp. olive oil (divided use)

1 onion, chopped

3 cloves garlic, minced

2 ripe tomatoes, chopped

$^1/_4$ tsp. ground **loomi**

salt

juice of 1 lemon

2 tbsp. butter or olive oil

1 $^3/_4$ cups rice

3 $^1/_4$ cups water

1 rounded tsp. tomato paste

1. Sprinkle the shrimp with salt, pepper, and 1 tsp. of the *kebsa* spices and rub the seasonings into the shrimp. Very lightly sauté in 2 tbsp. hot olive oil in a large nonstick saucepan for 2–3 minutes. Be careful not to completely cook the shrimp. (Alternatively, they can be boiled for approximately the same amount of time, but I find that the spices are absorbed more thoroughly through the searing action of sautéing.)

2. In the same pan, sauté the onion in the remaining 1 tbsp. oil until soft and transparent. Add the garlic, remaining 1 teaspoon *kebsa* spices, tomatoes, *loomi*, salt, lemon juice, and butter. Stir and cook for 2 or 3 minutes.

3. Add the rice and stir to coat each grain with the spice mixture.

4. Pour on the water, stir in the tomato paste, and bring to a boil. Cover, reduce the heat, and simmer for about 25 minutes. (A bit more water may be added if the rice is too dry. If it is too moist, remove the cover and carefully raise the heat for a few minutes.) Extinguish the flame. Gently turn the shrimp into the rice, or simply arrange them on its surface. Replace the cover and steam without additional heat for about 5 minutes longer.

Fish Biryani

Biryani Samak (KUWAIT, BAHRAIN, THE GULF STATES)

Biryani is the pride and glory of the Indian subcontinent, a wondrous mound of light, delicate perfumed grains of basmati rice, splashed with pale gold and deep saffron tints, in which are hidden scented bits of tender meat. This Gulf **Fish Biryani** includes so many spices, herbs, and vegetable seasonings that it's nearly impossible to count them! But it's well worth the time and trouble.

- 1 ¼ pound fish fillets or steaks
- 3 tbsp. olive oil for frying (optional)

Sauce for fish:

- 1 onion, chopped
- 1 potato, peeled and sliced
- 2 tbsp. olive oil
- 2 or 3 ripe tomatoes, chopped
- ½ tsp. ground coriander
- ½ serrano chili, seeded and chopped
  salt
- ½ tsp. **kebsa** spices
- ⅔ cup water
- ⅓ cup chopped cilantro

Fish marinade:

- 1 tsp. **kebsa** spices
- 2 cloves garlic, crushed with salt
- 1 tsp. grated fresh ginger
  juice of ½ lemon

Rice layer:

- 1 ¾ cups basmati rice
- 6 cups or more water (for soaking)
- 1 tbsp. salt (for soaking)
  pinch saffron
- ¼ cup warm water

8 cups water

$^1/_2$ cinnamon stick

2 pods cardamom

3 black peppercorns

2 tsp. **kebsa** spices

$^1/_2$ tsp. rosewater

Garnish:

1 onion, sliced in rings

2 tbsp. olive oil

1 potato, cut into small cubes

3 tbsp. water

salt

black pepper

1 tbsp. minced cilantro

1. Soak the rice in 6 cups water to which you have added 1 tbsp. salt. Set aside for at least 2 hours. Some cooks do this step in the morning, or even the night before the *biryani* is to be prepared.

2. Cover the saffron threads with $^1/_4$ cup warm water and set aside.

3. For the fish layer, sauté the onion and the potato in 2 tbsp. olive oil until the onion is transparent and softened. Add the tomatoes, coriander, chili, salt, $^1/_2$ tsp. *kebsa* spices, and $^2/_3$ cup water, and simmer for 7 or 8 minutes, until the liquid is reduced and the vegetables absorb the seasonings. Stir in the cilantro and remove from the heat.

4. Combine the crushed garlic with the ginger, lemon juice, and remaining 1 tsp. of *kebsa* spices, and rub this seasoning mixture into the fish. If delicate fillets are being used, continue to step 5, but if the fish is firm and thick, you will need to brown it lightly in olive oil.

5. For the rice layer, bring the 8 cups of water to a boil. Drain the water in which the rice has been soaking. Add the rice to the pot, along with the cinnamon, cardamom, peppercorns, and *kebsa* spices. Return to a boil and cook, uncovered, for 10 minutes. Pour into a strainer and drain completely.

6. Heat the oven to 350 degrees. Spread half of the hot steaming rice (with its whole spices) in a 9 x 12-inch baking/serving dish. Place the fish evenly on top of the rice. Cover with the tomato vegetable sauce. Distribute the remaining rice on top of the sauce. Stir the rosewater into the saffron water and sprinkle the liquid over the rice. Cover the dish very tightly with foil and bake for about 35–45 minutes.

7. While the *biryani* is steaming in the oven, prepare the garnish. Lightly sauté the onion rings in the olive oil for about 5 minutes. Add the potato cubes and brown them. Add 3 tbsp. water, cover, and simmer until tender, about 10 more minutes.

8. Top the *biryani* with the onion-potato garnish. Sprinkle with salt and pepper and decorate with cilantro.

Fish with Onioned Rice

Sayadeeyeh (EGYPT, LEBANON, SYRIA)

~~~~~~

To many northern Arabs, this famous dish is the only way to prepare a whole fish.

    2 onions, slivered
    3 tbsp. butter or olive oil
    2 cloves garlic, minced
      pinch saffron
      pinch red pepper
1 1/2 cups rice
2 3/4 cups **Fish Stock** (p. 101), or:
1 3/4 pounds small whole fishes
      olive oil for sautéing
      salt
      black pepper

Garnish:
      lemon wedges
      toasted pine nuts

1. Sauté the onions in the butter or olive oil until soft and transparent. (Some cooks very slowly cook the onions until dark brown but still soft.) Stir in the garlic and spices and cook for another minute.

2. Add the rice and toss until each grain is glistening and coated.

3. Stir in the Fish Stock and bring to a boil. Cover, reduce heat, and cook for about 25 minutes.

4. While the rice is cooking, wash and dry the fishes and sprinkle with salt and pepper.

5. Sauté the fishes in the oil until done, remove, and set aside.

6. Mound the rice on an oval serving platter. Place the fish on top and garnish with lemon wedges and toasted pine nuts.

Zesty Moroccan Vinaigrette for Fish

Chermoola (MOROCCO)

This is a tasty side dish from Morocco used to flavor grilled or baked fish.

- 2 tbsp. wine vinegar
- 2 tbsp. water
- 4 tbsp. olive oil
- 1/2 tsp. cumin
- 1/2 tsp. red pepper
- 2 cloves garlic, crushed with salt

Combine all ingredients. Serve as a side dish to be sprinkled over fish.

Variation

Libya: Sauté red pepper, cumin, and 1 rounded tsp. tomato paste in olive oil; add garlic, vinegar, sugar, 1 cup water, and simmer.

Meat and Poultry

The folk heroes of any culture say much about its values. For the Arabs, for whom the key to honor and manliness is hospitality, Hatim Tai is still the epitome of irreproachable generosity. As a child, Hatim was a source of tribal pride, toddling over to strangers and giving them whatever was in his hands, but as he grew older his behavior became more burdensome.

One day when Hatim was out on the plains of Najd tending his grandfather's small but fine herd of camels, a group of riders passed by, three famous poets heading toward the court at Baghdad. Hatim proudly demanded that they relax and make camp. He then set out to slaughter the choicest animals and lay out a feast of whole roasted camels stuffed with lambs on huge trays of shimmering spiced rice. His eminent guests spread the tale in rhymed couplets at every bedouin campfire and at the caliph's extravagant banquets. Hatim's family was outraged, but his place in history was assured.

Similar tales abound: the destitute widow who slaughtered her only remaining sheep to make a banquet of buttery wheat pilaf crowned by juicy chunks of roast meat for a visitor whose identity was unknown. The gentleman, of course, turned out to be none other than the caliph in disguise, who rewarded her kindness a thousandfold.

The fundamental lesson in these narratives is that the hospitality incumbent on all the numerous cultural and religious groups of the region is expressed principally through extremely generous offerings of food. As a well-known proverb comments with commendation but little surprise, "He doesn't have any money to pay the barber, and yet he invited guests."

Without question, the most prized dish is meat. A visit to any Middle Eastern restaurant is testimony to this fact: other than a long list of *mezzeh* appetizers, the menu may list only a variety of succulent roast meats. For weddings, circumcisions, religious and tribal feasts, the model passed down from Hatim Tai's nomadic heritage still recommends that a young camel or sheep be rubbed with aromatic spices and roasted in the traditional pit dug in the ground, or perhaps in the village oven.

Just before major holidays, and in particular before the *Eid al Adha* "Feast of Sacrifice" marking the end of the pilgrimage to Mecca, most families purchase a live lamb in the marketplace and tether it on the terrace for a few days. Sheep are visible everywhere being carried on men's shoulders, on bicycles, atop bus roofs, in taxis, in carts, in white Toyota trucks, and on donkey back. In Morocco, King Hassan II, symbolic father of his tribe, symbolically slaughters a praiseworthy animal on television. At the same time, men of every Arab family are butchering their sheep in the identical prescribed manner, so that all blood drains away.

Three days of feasting follow, during which no part of this excellent source of essential protein and vitamins is ignored. First, in accordance with Islam's strict precepts, small bundles of meat from the freshly slaughtered animal are delivered to widows and other needy neighbors, with a second third reserved for relatives and friends.

In the shade of Jordanian grape arbors and on Cairo's tiny balconies, men roast and grill the tenderest cuts and choice specialty meats. Across the cities and villages of Syria and Lebanon, aunts, cousins, sisters, and nieces stop by to shape patties of *kibbeh* (meat ground with *burghol* wheat, filled with nuts and tender bits of choice lamb). Inside the tiled courtyards of Marrakesh and Benghazi, ladies hang thin slices of meat (*gadeed*) out in the bright sun to preserve it for later use. Tantalizing aromas drift out of every kitchen as the cooks outdo themselves with regional delicacies such as braised liver with onions and garlic, lamb's feet in broth on a bed of crisped bread, and herbed lamb *tajeens* seasoned with preserved lemons.

For ceremonial occasions when serving a whole animal is inappropriate, shish kebabs of every type have developed. Within the enticing alleys of Morocco's twisting bazaars, the tempting smells of brochettes perfumed with cumin, cinnamon, and coriander guide you to little braziers of glowing charcoal. Istanbul is full of kebab houses whose massive charcoal grills fronting the sidewalk are impossible to resist.

Only the cook's creativity limits the combinations of finely textured Arab meatballs known as *kefta*: snakes of minty *kefta* filled with rice or pine nuts; *kefta* sausages steamed in broth on a bed of potatoes; small round *kefta* topped with a thick blanket of tomatoes and onions; *kefta* kebab grilled over a glowing ruby fire.

Yet, in spite of all this, meat actually plays a modest role in the total Middle Eastern diet. It has taken the affluent West generations to reach the economic power that allows us to derive almost two-thirds of our daily calories from animal fats and meat protein (a proportion now known to be unhealthy). The vast majority of Middle Easterners still live a simple traditional lifestyle short on materialism and waste, long on thrift.

It is the amazing array of vegetables and grains, rather than the bedouin's animal protein, that shaped the Middle East into the Roman Empire's breadbasket, and that still forms the backbone of this cuisine. Traditional family meals from Morocco to the Gulf have always called for only minimal amounts of lean meat, slowly cooked over low heat until tender, to intensify the taste of substantial dishes. For economic reasons, an individual meat portion may be no more than an ounce, two or three bites, with rich olive oil substituting when meat is unobtainable or proscribed by religious codes.

In contrast to the feast of holiday meat dishes that also typify restaurant cuisine, lamb is most frequently utilized on a daily basis merely as a flavoring ingredient in a variety of Mediterranean-style stews: fresh seasonal vegetables subtly seasoned with herbs and spices and gently simmered in a broth that reduces to form a velvety sauce. These earthy meals, called *yakney* (Lebanon), *tajeen* (North Africa), or *mnehzele* (Syria), are rich with crisp green beans or okra, cauliflower or squash, or leafy spinach. The traditional Armenian *misov* and Saudi *makhtoom* blend flavors so well that the label "stew" seems undeserving. Surely it is more appropriate to christen them cassoulets or ragouts or some similarly lyrical epithet.

Luckily, it is possible for those of us living in the West to enjoy these delicious dishes all year round. But along the Arab Mediterranean during winter when vegetables are expensive or unobtainable, lentils or beans with sun-dried tomatoes or tomato paste are substituted. The dried legumes absorb the lovely flavor of the sauce as they enrich and thicken it.

Lamb is the favored meat of the region, and I do prefer it for stews and similar dishes that require long cooking because it becomes meltingly tender. However, beef and veal are acceptable substitutes and are becoming more popular in the Middle East as their availability increases. Beef is an excellent choice for grilling, and I recommend it for the great variety of *keftas* and kebabs made from ground meat.

For centuries, some nomadic Middle Eastern peoples kept chickens only for their eggs, preferring to consume the meat of freshly slaughtered sheep. Others considered poultry to be a rare and expensive delicacy. Chickens were usually large, flavorful birds of considerable age that had survived a life of egg-laying to finally end up in the pot. Like local lamb, they usually required extended slow cooking and marinating to flavor and tenderize the meat, and one bird prepared with vegetables or pilaf produced a dish adequate for a very large family.

In the past few years, modern poultry farms have made chicken available to all, and ingenious cooks continue to transform simple ingredients into subtly flavored delicacies. At home or in restaurants, chicken is marinated in yoghurt or lemon juice and grilled over charcoal, allowing the fat to drip away. For many, "fast food" can mean nothing but a roast chicken flavored with fresh garlic, hot off the rotisserie next to one's office or bus stop.

Imaginative and refined preparations by the royal cooks of the great caliphs have given us vibrantly flavored poultry dishes such as **Saffron Chicken with Chickpeas and Almonds**. From the Saudi oases we have tasty chicken and vegetable combos, which were originally baked on trays in the village oven or clay tannours built into the ground. Throughout the eastern Mediterranean, chicken stuffed with rice, meat, and pine nuts is a popular festive meal.

Most cooks, however, prefer the lighter and quicker family dishes of poultry simmered in a richly, seasoned broth. Saffron, turmeric, or tomato paste flavor combinations of chicken and rice to which are added red pepper and garlic or cinnamon and nutmeg. When a vegetable like peas, cauliflower, or chickpeas is available, the result is another easy and healthy meal, cooked in one pot. One piece of well-seasoned chicken, with its own stewed vegetables and a pilaf, makes a wholesome Mediterranean entrée that delights family as well as guests.

Braised Lamb in Gulf Tomato Sauce

Makhtoom al Lahm (SAUDI ARABIA AND THE GULF STATES)

~~~~~~

At first glance, this looks like an Italian pasta sauce with chunks of meat, the kind of dish my Italian aunts loved to serve up on Wednesday nights. But one whiff of the Oriental spices and there's no doubt of its Indian heritage. The dab of yoghurt added to the tomato sauce confirms that detail.

A dish like this would have entered the Gulf culinary repertoire when an expatriate trader or pilgrim to Mecca set up residence in Saudi Arabia, or perhaps when a bright young son of a Bahraini trading family was sent to an Indian coastal state to open a branch office. Never heavy or overpowering like some of the subcontinent curries, these new scents fragrantly overlay familiar Mediterranean flavor combinations.

3 tbsp. olive oil

1 onion, chopped

1 clove garlic, minced (optional)

1 pod cardamom

1 cinnamon stick

1/4 tsp. cumin

1 1/4 pounds lamb, cubed

   salt

1 can (16 oz.) tomatoes, with juices, or:

1 pound ripe tomatoes

1 cup water

1/4 cup low-fat yoghurt

Garnish:

   minced parsley

1. Sauté the onion in the olive oil until soft and transparent. Add the optional garlic (some cooks believe garlic interferes with the sweet spice mixture) and cook for another minute.

2. Stir the spices into the oil to release the flavors. Cook for a minute or two.

3. Raise the heat and add the lamb, sprinkling with salt. Sauté until browned on all sides.

4. Whirl the canned or fresh tomatoes in a food processor or blender until nearly smooth, and add to the meat. Stir in the water and yoghurt. Taste and adjust the seasoning.

5. Cover and simmer about 2 hours, until the meat is tender. The tomato sauce will reduce somewhat; you may add water if you prefer a thinner sauce.

6. Traditionally this dish is served over white rice, but I think it is even more delicious over spaghetti. Garnish with parsley.

Lamb in Minty Yoghurt Sauce

Shakreeyeh (SYRIA, LEBANON)

This particular lamb dish, cooked in a rich yoghurt sauce and served with rice or *burghol*, is a Ramadan favorite. During the Muslim month of daytime fasting, yoghurt is thought to "cool" a thirsty stomach and is consumed in every possible delicious manner: in salads and soups, as sauces for meat-filled pasta and meatballs, and as an ever-present accompaniment to the main dish.

2 tbsp. olive oil
1 ¼ pounds lamb, cubed
    salt
    black pepper
2 cups water
    salt

Yoghurt sauce:
1 tbsp. olive oil
¼ onion, minced
1 clove garlic, minced
1 cup water
2 tbsp. cornstarch
3 cups low-fat yoghurt

1 cup cooked chickpeas (optional)
   salt

Garnish:
   fresh minced mint or cilantro

1. Lightly sauté the lamb in 2 tbsp. olive oil, sprinkling with salt and pepper. Add 2 cups water and salt and bring to a boil. Cover and simmer for 2 hours, skimming the foam. The liquid will reduce considerably.

2. For the sauce, sauté the onion in the remaining 1 tbsp. olive oil until soft and transparent. Add the garlic and cook for another minute.

3. Add 1 cup water to the onion and immediately whisk in the cornstarch, stirring until it is dissolved completely. Beat in the yoghurt, whisking in one direction only. Slowly bring the yoghurt sauce to a boil as you continue to stir. Remove from the heat.

4. Pour the meat, the cooking liquid that remains, and the optional chickpeas into the yoghurt and gently return to a boil. Simmer for 2 or 3 minutes to blend flavors. Taste and adjust seasoning.

5. Serve over **Vermicelli Rice** (p. 168) or **Vegetarian Wheat Pilaf** (p. 188), generously garnishing with mint or cilantro.

Variation

Sauté the mint and garlic in a bit of olive oil and drizzle over the cooked dish.

Tajeen of Marrakesh Lamb with Preserved Lemon

Tabah Moostafah (MOROCCO)

This spectacular recipe embodies all the exotic flavors of North Africa, an easy way to infuse lamb with the spirit of the Arab Mediterranean.

Nearly any braised or stewed North African dish can be called a *tajeen*, actually a term derived from the beautiful unglazed earthenware casserole with its graceful cone-shaped cover, placed over a second large clay vessel containing a charcoal fire, in which the meal is slowly simmered. In Morocco this customarily refers to a combination of meltingly tender meat and vegetables served with a velvety rich sauce, which is scooped up with thick pieces of whole-wheat bread.

In neighboring Tunisia the ingredients are transferred to a baking dish, while the liquid is reduced and several eggs beaten into it. The resulting sauce is poured over the *tajeen* and the dish is then baked until firm. Cut into wedges, it's rather like a *tortilla española*, Spain's cakelike potato omelette.

The authentic recipe calls for a fascinating Moroccan spice mixture known as *ras il hanoot*, which means "best of the shop." This essential combination contains 10 or more ingredients, which I've attempted to approximate below.

1½ pounds lamb, cubed

2 cups water

3 tbsp. olive oil

2 large ripe tomatoes, peeled, seeded, and chopped

1 small onion, grated

1 preserved lemon (or less, to taste)

3 tbsp. minced cilantro

3 tbsp. minced parsley

1 clove garlic, minced

1 dried rosebud

½ tsp. cumin

¼ tsp. ground ginger

pinch allspice

pinch black pepper

pinch cardamom

pinch cinnamon

pinch cloves

pinch ground coriander

pinch nutmeg

pinch turmeric

salt

Garnish:

minced parsley or cilantro

1. Combine all the ingredients (except garnish) in a large saucepan and bring to a boil. Cover and simmer for about 2 hours, until the meat is tender.

2. Traditionally, *tajeens* are served with bread. In Morocco only the more brothy couscous stews are served over a wheat pilaf, but I think that this dish is wonderful with rice or *burghol*, too.

Variation

Add vegetables (potatoes, turnips, carrots, green beans, etc.) to the *tajeen*.

Kurdish Green Bean Cassoulet

Loobia (KURDISTAN)

Most Kurdish cooking, like this dish of lamb and green beans, is straightforward and unassuming. Their meat and vegetable stews are similar to the Syrian and Lebanese tomato-flavored *mnehzele* and *yakney* but are more brothy, and are presented with plain white rice rather than vermicelli rice.

You could substitute almost any other vegetable or legume for the green beans specified in the following recipe. Or try a combination, like chunks of cabbage with potatoes.

1 large onion, chopped

2 tbsp. olive oil

3 cloves garlic, minced (optional)

³/₄ pound lamb or beef, cubed

   salt

   black pepper

3 cups water

2 tbsp. (rounded) tomato paste, or:

2 large ripe tomatoes, peeled and chopped

2 carrots, pared and sliced

1 pound green beans (fresh or frozen), cut up

¹/₂ tsp. cinnamon

¹/₂ tsp. cumin

$^1/_2$ tsp. (or more to taste) red pepper

$^1/_8$ tsp. black pepper

pinch ground cardamom

pinch nutmeg

salt

1. Sauté the onion in the oil until softened. Add the garlic and cook for another minute. Stir in the meat, sprinkle with salt and pepper, and sauté until browned.

2. Stir in the water and tomato paste or tomatoes and bring to a boil. Reduce heat, cover, and simmer for about 1$^1/_4$ hours.

3. Stir in the carrots and fresh green beans (if you are using them) and cook for 30 more minutes. If you are using frozen green beans, simmer the carrots only 10 minutes, then add the green beans and cook for 20 minutes. More water may be added if necessary.

4. Stir in the remaining flavoring ingredients and cook for 10–15 minutes more.

5. Taste and adjust seasoning. Serve with **Plain White Rice** (p. 167).

Variations

Saudi Arabia: Omit the carrots and flavor only with cumin and cinnamon.

Armenia: Omit the carrots and flavor only with chopped dill.

Iraq: Omit the carrots and flavor only with turmeric and cinnamon.

Syria: Omit the carrots and flavor as in the following recipe.

Damascan Ratatouille with Lamb

Kawaaj (SYRIA)

A basic meat and vegetable stew, *Kawaaj* was one of my husband's favorite dishes. Naturally, it was one of the first Arab recipes I learned, and since it is so easy to prepare, I fixed it often.

Two months after our arrival in Saudi Arabia, our son was born. My husband surprised me by bringing his mother for an extended stay, to help me with my new responsibilities. Hoping to impress her with my culinary skills and erase her suspicions that an American Christian daughter-in-law was a hopeless handicap for her son, I set a plate of *Kawaaj* before her.

Mother examined it carefully from all angles, and a minute later I heard her comment to my husband with typical Syrian directness, "Hmmm. Son, if I'd known you had brought these ingredients, I would have made some *Kawaaj* for you."

- 1 large onion, slivered
- 2 tbsp. olive oil
- 2 cloves garlic, minced (optional)
- 3/4 pound lamb, cubed
  salt
  black pepper
- 3 cups water
- 1/4 tsp. red pepper (optional)
- 2 large potatoes, peeled and sliced into wedges
  salt
- 2 tbsp. fresh lemon juice or **hamod er rummaan** pomegranate syrup
- 3 zucchini or koosa squash, sliced into 1/2-inch pieces
- 2 large ripe tomatoes, peeled and cut into wedges

1. Sauté the onions in the olive oil until softened. Add the garlic and cook for another minute. Push to one side of the pan.

2. Stir in the meat, sprinkle with salt and pepper, and sauté until browned.

3. Add the water, additional salt, black pepper, and red pepper, and bring to a boil. Reduce heat, cover, and simmer for about 1 1/2 hours.

4. Add the potatoes and simmer for about 8 minutes. Additional water may be added if necessary. Add the lemon juice or *hamod*, taste, and adjust seasoning.

5. Arrange the sliced zucchini over the potatoes and top with the tomatoes. Cover and steam until tender, about 10 minutes. Serve over **Vermicelli Rice** (p. 168).

Couscous with Lamb and Vegetables

Cooscoos (MOROCCO)

The national dish of the Maghreb countries (Morocco, Libya, Algeria, and Tunisia), Couscous is prepared for feast days or as a special family meal, much as chicken was in the United States until recently. Both chicken and lamb can be the basis for a great Couscous—in fact, sometimes both are combined in one dish—and the vegetables vary with the season. In the fall or winter, pumpkin, potatoes, and chickpeas or turnips might grace the platter, while in the summer, zucchini and other squash are popular.

Couscous stew is usually presented on a tray, over a glistening mound of light semolina wheat pilaf. The reserved broth is flavored with *harissa*, a flaming red chili paste, and served in small bowls so that each guest may spoon the desired amount over the finished dish.

    1 pound lamb, cubed
    2 tbsp. olive oil
       salt
       black pepper
    2 onions, sliced
    1 tsp. ground ginger
  1/4 tsp. saffron
  1/4 tsp. allspice
    1 tbsp. minced parsley
    2 cups water
    5 carrots, peeled and cut into 2-inch lengths
    2 turnips, peeled and cut into large wedges
    2 small zucchini, cut into 1-inch wedges
    2 tbsp. raisins, soaked in hot water
       (to taste) **Harissa Red Chili Paste** (p. 41), red pepper, or Tabasco sauce

1. Sauté the lamb in the olive oil, sprinkling with salt and pepper. Remove with a slotted spoon and set aside.

2. Add the onions to the same pot and cook until softened. Reduce the heat, return the lamb to the pan, and stir in the ginger, saffron, and allspice, cooking for about 2 minutes to release the flavors.

3. Add the parsley, the water, and additional salt as desired, and bring to a boil. Cover and simmer for 1 1/2 hours. Taste and adjust seasoning.

4. Add the carrots and turnips and simmer for 20 minutes. (Additional water may be added if necessary.)

5. Stir in the zucchini and the drained raisins and cook for another 10 minutes.

6. Use a slotted spoon to lift the vegetables and meat from the cooking broth and transfer them to a tray of prepared couscous grain (p. 197).

7. Flavor the broth to taste with **Harissa Red Chili Paste**, red pepper, or Tabasco sauce, and pour into small bowls.

Lamb with Fresh Spinach in Red Lentil Sauce

Adas bil Lahme (SUDAN)

If you've never before tried Sudanese cooking, this appetizing combination is a good place to begin. The red lentils disintegrate with extended cooking, forming the base of a fragrant sauce flavored with cumin, coriander, cinnamon, and hot pepper. Not only do the crisp shreds of spinach add a mildly crunchy texture, but they are filled with nutrients, extremely high in beta carotene and potassium. Like most Arab vegetable/meat combinations, **Lamb with Fresh Spinach in Red Lentil Sauce** is served with rice.

2 onions, sliced
2 tbsp. olive oil
1 pound lamb, cubed
  salt
  black pepper

6 cups water

½ tsp. red pepper

1 cup red lentils, rinsed

2 rounded tsp. tomato paste

1 tsp. cumin

1 tsp. ground coriander

½ tsp. cinnamon

2 bunches fresh spinach, sliced into wide threads

1. Sauté the onions in the olive oil until softened. Push to one side of the pan.

2. Stir in the meat, sprinkle with salt and pepper, and sauté until browned.

3. Add the water, additional salt, and bring to a boil. Reduce heat, cover and simmer for about 1½ hours.

4. Stir in the remaining ingredients, except for the spinach. Bring to a boil, then cover and simmer for 1½ hours. Stir occasionally to keep the softened lentils from sticking to the bottom of the pot. Add more water as necessary to maintain the preferred consistency. The liquid should be about as thick as a cream sauce.

5. Add the spinach, mixing thoroughly, and simmer for 15–20 more minutes. Taste and adjust seasoning.

6. Serve with **Plain White Rice** (p. 167).

Lamb with Fresh Okra

Bamia (SYRIA, LEBANON)

This delicious stew is flavored with the typical Mediterranean combination of tomatoes, onion, garlic, and olive oil. In winter, when fresh okra is unavailable, dried okra strung on long knotted strings is used, along with pieces of sun-dried tomatoes stored in the same manner, or homemade tomato paste that was dried in the bright August sun.

1 large onion, chopped

2 tbsp. olive oil

3/4 pound lamb, cubed

   salt

   black pepper

3 cups water

10 cloves garlic

2 rounded tbsp. tomato paste, or:

2 large ripe tomatoes, peeled and chopped

1 quart okra, the smallest ones available

2 tbsp. lemon juice or **hamod er rummaan** pomegranate syrup

1. Sauté the onion in the olive oil until softened. Push to one side of the pan.

2. Stir in the meat, sprinkle with salt and pepper, and sauté until browned.

3. Add the water, garlic, tomato paste or tomatoes, additional salt and pepper and bring to a boil. Reduce heat, cover, and simmer for about 1 1/4 hours.

4. Meanwhile, remove the stem ends from the okra in the following manner: hold the okra in your left hand, with its stem facing your right hand. Grasping a sharp, short-bladed paring knife at an angle, peel off only the outer layer of the cone-shaped tip. One deft twist of each okra, and a thin curl of hard stem falls off. Rinse and drain.

5. At this point it is possible to add the okra to the semicooked meat, but the vegetable will maintain its shape and be less mushy if it is first lightly sautéed in a bit of olive oil. Do this in 2 batches and cook it just until it begins to color. Drain on paper towels and add to the stew.

6. Stir in the lemon juice or *hamod* and cook for about 20 minutes, until the okra is tender. Taste and adjust seasoning.

7. Serve with **Vermicelli Rice** (p. 168)

Variations

Egypt: Substitute ground beef for the lamb, reducing the cooking time, and substitute cumin for the lemon juice or *hamod*.

Sudan: Substitute fresh dill or cinnamon, cumin, and ground coriander for the lemon juice or *hamod*.

Lamb in Tomato Broth with Peas and Carrots

Mnazelit Bazalia (SYRIA, LEBANON)

~~~~~~

Healthy and simple, this basic lamb stew is enjoyed around the world in one guise or another. The brothy Syrian version, lightly flavored with the tartness of lemon juice or sour pomegranate syrup, is ladled over rice or *burghol*.

- 1 large onion, chopped
- 2 tbsp. olive oil
- 1 pound lamb, diced or coarsely chopped
  salt
  black pepper
- 4 cups water
- 2 rounded tbsp. tomato paste
- 3 carrots, pared and sliced
- 8 ounces (or more) frozen or fresh peas
- 2 tbsp. lemon juice or **hamod er rummaan** pomegranate syrup

1. Sauté the onion in the olive oil until softened. Push to one side of the pan.

2. Stir in the meat, sprinkle with salt and pepper, and sauté until browned.

3. Add the water, tomato paste, and additional salt, and bring to a boil. Cover and simmer about 20 minutes.

4. Stir in the carrots and fresh peas (if you are using them) and cook for 25 more minutes.

5. If you are using frozen peas, cook the carrots only 15 minutes. Then add the peas and the lemon juice or *hamod* pomegranate syrup, and cook for 10 minutes longer. Taste and adjust seasoning.

6. Serve with **Vermicelli Rice** (p. 168) or *burghol*.

Double Herbed Lamb with Saffron Potatoes and Green Olives

Tabah il Lahm bil Batata waz Zeitoon (MOROCCO)

Although several hundred varieties of olives are cultivated, only about 20 are used for table olives, the others being a source of olive oil. Morocco is a proud producer of 10% of the world's crop.

From late September until early November, the fields of rippling silver-green leaves explode into activity. Families extend bed sheets under one side of the tree while a strong young person knocks at the branches with a long stick to loosen the olives from the boughs. Women and children scamper to catch each fruit that escapes the confines of the sheet, while the remaining olives are handpicked by men on tall ladders.

Fresh, unprocessed olives are extremely bitter and inedible, as I discovered one harvest season when my sisters-in-law shook the bottom corners of an immense cloth bag to release a bounty of hard green ovals. Before pickling, each olive must be opened: in the home this is done by mashing between an overturned brass mortar and its pestle, or by using a sewing needle to cut three long slits in each tiny fruit.

After several weeks in a salt-water solution, olives grace the table two or three times a day. In North Africa, they are used to flavor the wonderful *tajeen* stews.

Milder and much more naturally flavored than our popular Spanish manzanilla olives, any variety of green Middle Eastern olives available in your local import food store will lend an authentic and fresh, earthy flavor to this lamb stew. The potatoes are steamed with saffron and served on the side.

1   pound lamb, cubed
6   cups water (divided use)
    salt
1/3 or 1/2 cup green Middle Eastern olives
    pinch saffron
3   potatoes, peeled and cut into medium chunks

Marinade:

- 1 small onion, grated
- 3 tbsp. olive oil
- 3 tbsp. minced cilantro
- 3 tbsp. minced parsley
- 1 clove garlic, minced
- $\frac{1}{2}$ tsp. cumin
- $\frac{1}{2}$ tsp. ground ginger
- salt

Garnish:

minced parsley or cilantro

1. Combine the marinade ingredients and add the meat. In North Africa this would be done in a clay pot, but I prefer to use a sealable plastic container that I can turn upside down at regular intervals. Marinate for at least 2 hours, or refrigerate and marinate overnight.

2. Transfer the meat and its marinade to a saucepan and add 3 cups of water. Add salt and bring to a boil. Cover and simmer for $1\frac{1}{2}$ hours.

3. Add the olives and continue to simmer for 15 minutes more.

4. In another saucepan, bring the remaining 3 cups of water to a boil. Add the saffron, salt, and the potatoes, and simmer until they are tender, about 15–20 minutes. Drain.

5. If there is still a quantity of cooking liquid in the pot when the meat is tender, raise the heat to high to reduce it to a concentrated sauce. Transfer the meat and its sauce to one side of a serving dish. Place the potatoes on the other side and sprinkle with parsley or cilantro.

Fetteh with Lamb and Chickpeas

Fettit Hummos (SYRIA, LEBANON)

Fetteh is yet another tasty meal-in-one-dish, a famous layered creation designed to use God's gifts without waste. Each particular *fetteh* combination built on broken pieces of leftover Arab bread reflects its originator. Custom suggests that a garlicky yoghurt sauce be poured over all as the last step, but this is sometimes omitted.

This particular version is easy but yummy: torn pieces of crisp bread covered by tender, plump chickpeas in a meaty lamb base, with a blush of tomatoes and an ivory yoghurt topping.

1 cup chickpeas, soaked overnight and drained

4 cups water

3/4 pound lamb, diced or coarsely chopped

2 tbsp. olive oil

salt

black pepper

1 rounded tbsp. tomato paste (optional)

4 cups (or more) torn Arabic bread, dried in the oven or microwave until crispy

Yoghurt sauce:

2 cloves garlic, crushed with salt

2 cups low-fat yoghurt

Garnish:

toasted pine nuts

minced parsley

1. Place the chickpeas in a large saucepan and pour on the water. Bring to a boil, then reduce heat and simmer, covered, for 1 hour.

2. Lightly sauté the lamb in the olive oil, sprinkling with salt and pepper. Add to the chickpeas, along with the optional tomato paste. Cover and simmer for another hour, skimming the foam. Add more liquid if necessary, to maintain $1\frac{1}{2}$ to 2 cups in the pot. Taste and adjust seasoning.

3. Mix together the ingredients for the yoghurt sauce.

4. Spread the dried or toasted bread in a flat serving dish with raised sides. An attractive ceramic or glass baking dish is ideal. Then transfer the cooked meat and chickpeas to evenly cover the bread. Drizzle on as much of the broth as you wish: in the Arab world the bread is usually half-soaked. Top with the yoghurt sauce, and garnish attractively with pine nuts and parsley.

Libyan Shakshooka with Sun-Dried Meat

Shakshookah (LIBYA) ◆ *Adja* (TUNISIA)

~~~~~~

Originating in the North African countries of Algeria, Libya, and Tunisia, *Shakshooka* is a light lunch or supper dish now popular even in the remote areas of Yemen and the Gulf. It's hard to beat this classic Mediterranean recipe built on the ubiquitous combination of tomatoes, onions, and garlic.

In typical Arab fashion, the cook is allowed considerable flexibility in its preparation. Small pieces of lamb or ground meat are used when available, but sun-dried meat (*gadeed* or *gargoosh*) adds a luxuriously intense flavor. Or the meat can simply be omitted. Where a hot, spicy flavor is appreciated, whole green chilis, dried red pepper, or *harissa* red pepper paste are tossed into the pot. If ripe tomatoes are not in season, the cook substitutes sun-dried or canned ones. To complete the savory combination, a few whole eggs are gently dropped into the simmering tomato sauce just before serving.

3 ounces natural beef jerky (from a health food store)

1 cup water

1 onion, sliced

2 tbsp. olive oil

2 cloves garlic, minced

3 serrano chilis, whole, or:

1 green pepper, cut into strips

5 ripe tomatoes, coarsley chopped

1/2 cup water

1 rounded tsp. tomato paste

1/4 tsp. cumin

    pinch turmeric

    pinch cinnamon

    pinch allspice

    pinch red pepper

    salt

2 to 4 eggs (optional)

Garnish:

minced parsley or cilantro

1. Gently steam the beef jerky (a substitute for genuine North African *gadeed*) in the water for $1/2$ hour or longer, or until tender. Drain and cut into large bite-sized pieces.

2. Place the onions in a deep frying pan (without oil) over medium-low heat and cook for about 15 minutes. Cover the pan and shake to turn the onions, until they are browned but not burned. (If you prefer, you can sauté the onion in the olive oil until soft and transparent.)

3. Add the olive oil if you have not yet used it, and the garlic and chilis or green pepper. Sauté for 2–3 minutes.

4. Stir in the meat and the remaining ingredients, except for the eggs and garnish. Bring the sauce to a boil slowly, then cover and simmer for about 5 minutes. Taste and adjust seasoning.

5. Break an egg into a small dish and make an indentation in the sauce with a large spoon. Carefully slide the egg into the sauce. Repeat until all the eggs are used. Cover and simmer for about 10 minutes, until the eggs are firm.

6. Divide the meat sauce and eggs evenly among the guests, and sprinkle with parsley or cilantro.

Grilled Kefta Kebab

Kefta (SYRIA. LEBANON. ARAB STATES)

Summer favorites but year-round delicacies, ground-meat kebabs are enjoyed at home as well as in restaurants. Relatively inexpensive because they don't require a prime cut of meat, they're also nearly foolproof and can easily be adjusted to suit different tastes.

The following version is the classic dish served in roadside restaurants across Syria, Lebanon, and Jordan. When the heat and bustle, the smog and noise of city life wear and tear on body and soul, families escape for a day to charming little restaurants in nearby hills or river valleys. As children run cheerfully across the bare concrete floors and through the eclectic collection of tables and chairs filling every nook and cranny, infants explore the inviting dark world under the freshly wiped tables, and tolerant cats groom themselves in anticipation of the treats soon to be tossed their way. Service is often irregular and unsophisticated but the food—Ahhhhhh!—is always impeccably prepared and exquisitely seasoned.

1   pound lean ground beef

3   green onions, minced

1/2 cup minced parsley

    salt

    black pepper

2   loaves Arab bread, cut in half

Garnish:

1   onion, finely slivered

1/2 cup minced parsley

1   tsp. sumac

1. Combine the garnish ingredients and set aside.

2. Combine the meat, onions, parsley, salt, and pepper. Knead together until very smooth. Ideally the mixture should be passed twice through a meat grinder. Some individuals like the smooth texture of *kefta* that has been softened by cautious whirling in a food processor.

3. Shape the meat paste into balls the size of small lemons. With dampened hands, insert a flat barbecue skewer into each ball and squeeze the meat gently around the skewer to form thick cigar shapes. (If round skewers are used, the meat will not cling to the skewer.)

4. Grill over charcoal, turning once or twice.

5. Serve folded inside half loaves of Arabic bread, with a generous portion of garnish. Alternatively, serve on a bed of bread decorated with the garnish. *Kefta* is also delicious with just a sprinkle of sumac or with yoghurt sauce (see **Chicken Kebab with Yoghurt Marinade**, p. 258)

Variations

Armenia: Add dried mint, red pepper, and garlic.

Kuwait: Add 1 egg, 2 cloves minced garlic, and thyme.

Palestine and Syria: Add cinnamon and allspice.

Turkey: Add ⅓ cup cooked rice, season with cinnamon and allspice.

Egypt: Add 2 tbsp. rice flour and season with cumin.

North Africa: Add cumin and mint.

North African Kefta Balls

Kefta (MOROCCO)

The combination of spices in Moroccan ground meat *kefta* is perhaps more complex and tantalizing than in the preceding dish from the Levant. Here the ground meat is seasoned with the North African favorite, cumin, while the broth balances an assortment of extraordinary flavors.

Try it over couscous, rice, or *burghol*, or with the Moroccan version of **Classic Red Lentil Soup** (p. 94).

Kefta:
- 1 pound lean ground beef
- 1 tbsp. minced parsley
- 2 tbsp. minced fresh chervil or mint
- ¼ tsp. cumin
-    salt

Sauce:
- ½ onion, minced
- 2 tbsp. olive oil
- ½ tsp. red pepper
- ¼ tsp. ground ginger or cinnamon
- ¼ tsp. cumin
-    pinch saffron
-    black pepper
-    salt
- 1 cup water

1. Knead together the *kefta* ingredients and shape the mixture into balls the size of small walnuts.

2. Sauté the onion in the olive oil until softened. Add the meatballs to the pan and sauté until sealed and slightly browned.

3. Add the spices and cook over medium-low heat for 1 or 2 minutes, to release the flavors. Pour on the water and bring to a boil. Cover and simmer for about 15 minutes.

4. Serve over couscous, or your favorite *burghol*, pilaf, pasta, or rice.

Variation

Add chunks of zucchini, potatoes, and tomatoes along with the water.

Kefta in a Tray, with Vegetables

Kefta bi Sineeyeh (SYRIA)

One of our favorite family meals, this *kefta* tray features a thin layer of flavorful ground beef baked with a delicious rich topping of tomatoes, sliced potatoes and onions. These vegetables marinate the potatoes and meat with their delicious juices: a basic Mediterranean combination of healthy ingredients that's also an economical way to stretch a small quantity of meat. To round out the meal, serve with Arab bread and a lettuce-based salad like **Fettoosh** (p. 66) or **Shepherd's Vegetable Salad with White Cheese** (p. 71).

The *kefta* layer can be pressed into a pan and frozen, uncooked, ready for the vegetable toppings to be added at some later time.

Kefta layer:
- 1 pound lean ground beef
- 1/4 cup minced parsley
- 1/4 cup seasoned bread crumbs
- 1 egg
- 1 rounded tbsp. dehydrated onion soup mix, or:
- 1/4 small onion, finely minced
- 1/2 tsp. allspice (optional)

¼ tsp. red pepper (optional)

salt

black pepper

Vegetable layer:

2 onions, slivered

2 tbsp. olive oil

4 potatoes, peeled and sliced

salt

2 to 3 ripe tomatoes, cut into wedges

red pepper

black pepper

1. Knead together the ingredients for the meat layer and press them into a thin layer in a 10- or 11-inch round baking dish. (Although the round dish is traditional, you may substitute an 8 x 8-inch square or 9 x 12-inch rectangular pan.)

2. Sauté the onions in the olive oil until soft and transparent. Lift them from the pan with a slotted spoon and arrange over the meat.

3. In the same oil, sauté the sliced potatoes for about 7 minutes. They will only be half-cooked. Transfer to the baking dish and sprinkle with salt.

4. Arrange the tomato wedges over the vegetables, sprinkling lightly with salt and liberally with the two peppers.

5. Cover with foil and bake at 350 degrees for about 45 minutes.

Variations

Lebanon: Top with a thin **Tarator Sauce** (p. 160) before baking.

Saudi Arabia: Top with a thin tomato puree before baking.

Egypt: Omit the red pepper and the onion soup and add 1 tbsp. tomato paste.

Palestine: Substitute 2–3 cups cooked white rice for the potatoes.

Chicken Kebab with Yoghurt Marinade

Sheesh Taook (ARAB STATES)

~~~~~~

If only one choice of chicken entrée is available in an Arab restaurant, whether it be a polished and elegant establishment or a home-style bistro, the dish will be either chicken kebab or grilled chicken. A variety of flavorful marinades for poultry are enjoyed around the southern and eastern Mediterranean. In the following famous version milk or yoghurt tenderizes the chicken and lends it a pristine whiteness.

While you're enjoying this low-fat dish with an accompanying **Saffron Rainbow Rice** (p. 177) or **Pilaf of Rice with Peas** (p. 170), you might like to reflect on a jewel of a proverb: "Live as a rooster for a day and not as a hen for a year."

Yoghurt Marinade:

- 3 cloves garlic, crushed with salt
- 1 tbsp. olive oil
- 1/3 cup low-fat yoghurt
- black pepper
- 1/2 small onion, grated

- 6 boneless half chicken breasts, cubed
- red or black pepper
- 2 loaves Arab bread

1. Combine the marinade ingredients and rub them into the cubes of chicken. Set aside for at least 1 hour.

2. Thread the pieces of chicken onto skewers and broil in the oven or over charcoal. Very little cooking time is required, only around 7 minutes.

3. To serve, cut 2 loaves of Arab bread in half. Grasp each skewer with a half-loaf of bread and slide off the cooked chicken.

Chicken in Light Broth

Fahde (SYRIA)

This is my dear mother-in-law's everyday technique for preparing chicken, steamed in a flavorful broth that is later ladled over dishes of **Vermicelli Rice** (p.168). Once again, the quantity of meat forms a very small portion of the full meal. Each diner helps himself to a bounty of rice and stock but takes only one or perhaps two pieces of chicken.

1 chicken, cut into pieces

2 cloves garlic, crushed with salt

3/4 cup low-fat yoghurt

3 tbsp. olive oil

6 cups water

salt

1 recipe **Vermicelli Rice (p. 168)**

Garnish:

minced parsley

1. Rinse the chicken and dry it thoroughly. Combine the garlic and yoghurt and rub it into the chicken. Set aside for 1 hour to absorb the flavors. (Do not refrigerate).

2. Sauté the chicken in the olive oil until slightly colored on all sides and the juices are sealed in. Pour on the water, add salt, and bring to a boil.

3. Reduce the heat and simmer, skimming the foam. Cover and cook until tender: about 40 minutes. To serve, fill a flat soup bowl with **Vermicelli Rice** and top with one piece of chicken. Pour on enough broth to reach the top of the rice and garnish with parsley.

Variation

Morocco: Steam the chicken by cooking it in a basket or strainer above the level of the water.

Moroccan Roast Chicken

Dejaj Mahammara (MOROCCO)

Along the principal thoroughfares of every Arab city, and in particular in working-class and business neighborhoods, commercial chicken rotisseries tempt the hungry. There, fast food is usually a finger-food snack to pop in the mouth while shopping or during a brief break from work or school. Except in the prosperous Gulf States, take-home fast food is still limited and hard to come by. Most men are seduced homeward for the midday meal by the thought of the special treat prepared by their wives' dedicated hands.

But for picnics, emergencies, and the unlucky man without a spouse, roasted chicken is *the* fast food. Many Arab children know no other way to eat chicken, and I even knew one Syrian mother who used a home rotisserie once a week. It's one of the healthiest cooking techniques because the chicken literally self-bastes to a golden crispness in its own melting fat, which drips away as the chicken turns. Much the same effect is obtained when the marinated chicken is cut into pieces and charcoal or oven-broiled.

1 chicken, whole or cut into pieces

Marinade:

  3 tbsp. olive oil

    1-inch piece leek, minced

  2 tsp. minced fresh chervil or mint

  2 tsp. cumin

  1 tsp. red pepper

    salt

1. Prepare the marinade by whirling all the ingredients in a blender or by pounding them into a paste in a mortar. Rub the mixture into the chicken.

2. Broil, charcoal grill, or roast on a turning spit. During the cooking time (30–40 minutes), brush with additional spice paste. If you prefer to remove the chicken skin, do so after about 25 minutes of cooking, and rub the meat again with marinade before returning to the grill or oven.

Bokhari Chicken and Vegetables

Dejaj Bukhari (SAUDI ARABIA)

~~~~~~

This Saudi Arabian dish originated in Bukhara (now Soviet Uzbekistan). It's a simple but nutritious main dish dating back to the Mongol invasions of Central Asia and Persia.

- 3 cups water
- 1 chicken, cut into pieces
- 2 onions, chopped
- 3 tomatoes, peeled and chopped
- 2 turnips, peeled and quartered
- 4 carrots, scraped and cut into 1-inch long pieces
- 1 serrano chili
- salt
- 3 potatoes, peeled and quartered

Garnish:

- black pepper
- lemon juice
- yoghurt, at room temperature (optional)

1. Bring the water to a boil in a large pot. Add the chicken and steam for 15 minutes, skimming the foam.

2. Add the remaining ingredients, except for the potatoes and garnish, and cover. Simmer for 10 minutes.

3. Add the potatoes and simmer until the chicken and vegetables are tender—about 20 minutes. Taste and adjust seasoning.

4. Remove the chicken and vegetables to a platter, pouring the broth into a large bowl.

5. Sprinkle each serving generously with pepper and lemon juice. Top with optional yoghurt.

Couscous with Chicken and Onions

Cooscoos (MOROCCO)

~~~~~~

Most couscous stews known in the West are comprised of lamb with various vegetables. But I'm intrigued by the following couscous dish built on an unpretentious combination of chicken and onions, exotically perfumed with fresh herbs and spices. Potatoes, carrots, or squash would be delicious additions.

This recipe demonstrates an interesting cooking technique common in Moroccan cuisine. A hefty quantity of onions are added to many meals, often in two steps. One portion is simmered with the other ingredients throughout the total cooking time, enriching it with body and substance, while additional onion is stirred in toward the end of the cooking, to add texture and zip.

1 chicken, cut into pieces

5 cups water

5 onions, sliced (divided use)

1/4 cup minced parsley (divided use)

2 tbsp. minced fresh chervil or mint

1 cinnamon stick, or:

1 preserved lemon

1/2 tsp. saffron

1 tsp. ground ginger

salt

black pepper

1/4 cup raisins

Harissa Red Chili Paste (p. 41), or red pepper, or Tabasco sauce (to taste)

1. In a stewpot, combine the chicken, water, the slices of 1 onion, half of the parsley, and the remaining spices. Bring to a boil, cover, and simmer for 35 minutes.

2. Add the remaining parsley and onions and the raisins. Steam for about 25 more minutes.

3. Mound the cooked chicken in the center of a tray. Arrange the onions on top and surround with couscous.

4. Flavor the broth to taste with *harissa* paste, red pepper, or Tabasco sauce, and pour into small bowls.

Variation

Add 1 tsp. sugar to the broth, or add carrots and zucchini.

Saffron Chicken with Chickpeas and Almonds

Dejaj bil Hummos (ALGERIA)

Here is a delicious Mediterranean way to prepare chicken: steamed with nut-like chickpeas and the understated flavors of cinnamon, saffron, almonds, and fresh herbs.

```
   3  tbsp. olive oil
   1  chicken, cut into pieces
      salt
      black pepper
 ½  tsp. saffron threads
 ½  tsp. cinnamon
   2  onions, chopped (divided use)
   2  cups water
1½  cups cooked chickpeas
   1  rounded tbsp. slivered blanched almonds
   1  cup minced parsley
   3  tbsp. cornstarch
 ¼  cup cold water
      juice of 1 lemon
```

Garnish:

minced parsley

1. In a deep frying pan, heat the oil and add the chicken, sprinkling with salt and pepper, saffron, cinnamon, and 1 chopped onion. Sauté the chicken until golden on all sides.

2. Pour on the water, stir in additional salt and pepper, and bring to a boil. Simmer, covered, for 20 minutes.

3. Add the second chopped onion and simmer for 10 minutes.

4. Add the chickpeas, almonds, and 1 cup minced parsley, and simmer, uncovered, for 10 minutes. If necessary, raise the heat to reduce the sauce.

5. Place the chicken on a platter and top with the chickpeas and almonds. Reserve the broth.

6. Beat the cornstarch into the cold water and add to the reserved broth. Beat in the lemon juice and cook until thickened, stirring constantly. Pour sauce over the chicken and garnish with parsley.

Variation

Substitute raisins for the almonds and ginger, or turmeric for the cinnamon.

Sweets and Pastries

From Morocco to Mesopotamia, in mountain hamlets and desert oases, the preferred choice for dessert is a natural one: fragrant oranges and melons, grapes, and refreshing baby cucumbers picked early that morning are summer favorites, while winter treats include raisins, *amradeen* dried apricot sheets, dates, and nuts. No meal is complete without a cup of tea or coffee and a heaping tray of rosy *Beladi* apricots or canary-green figs glistening from a cool rinse. In season, 4 or 5 tiger-striped watermelons pile up in a corner of every village kitchen, awaiting the moment when they are carved open, tapped to remove the seeds, and cut into bite-sized chunks dripping with sweetness.

Should a guest demur when tiny apples and pears or other fruits are offered, they are pressed upon him or heaped on a small plate that is then placed in his hand. Or, in a ritual of tradition and devotion, the hostess peels an orange and breaks it into sections before gracefully setting it before her visitor.

Although a variety of pastries may grace the elegantly arranged tables of Lebanese and Saudi dinner parties, one immense colorful tray of fruit is fundamental. This is often augmented by a second platter of tiny candied fruits intoxicatingly perfumed, or almond-stuffed dates rolled in sesame seeds or coconut and bursting with energy and nutrition, or perhaps a fabulous crystal bowl filled with vibrant morsels of mixed fruit and tossed with a bit of sugar syrup or honey. Although fruit is not usually baked or stewed, it also flavors homemade ices and puddings and adds natural sweetness and substance to simple cakes.

Other than fruit, the only dessert commonly prepared by most Arab families is a milk-based pudding or custard. These enduring dishes are inexpensive and elegant comfort foods, homey ways to please the extended family or a large group of guests. Nobel Prize laureate Naguib Mahfouz of Egypt reminisces nostalgically that "Home is full of milk pudding and heated rice pudding, milk, honey, molasses and tahini…and fruit!"

Additions may include rice or rice powder, almonds and pistachios, raisins and coconut, and the delicate scent of cinnamon, rosewater, or cardamom. *Crème caramel* is extremely popular with many families in the Levant and the Arabian peninsula. Each of these puddings offers a subtle difference in texture and flavoring. While Westerners concern themselves with eliminating dairy products from their cuisines of overabundance, Middle Easterners appreciate this opportunity to include calcium-rich milk in the diet.

Heavy desserts are so unusual that people in the Middle East consume only 20% of the sugar eaten in the West. After a simple but filling meal of **Kurdish Green Bean Cassoulet**, with a small bowl of garlicky yoghurt and a few slices of juicy ripe tomato, I just don't yearn for a slice of cake or pie. So, as you glance through the multitude of heavenly cookies and sweets in the following pages, keep in mind that there is no dessert course in most Arab homes. In fact, I can recall only two or three occasions when my husband's relatives have served me a sweet pastry after a meal.

Rich confections filled with nuts and steeped in syrup are reserved for rare family festivities and major holidays, or for an occasional visit to a coffee shop, when one can be forgiven a brief indulgence in sweet treats. Precisely because they appear so infrequently, they are enjoyed on these special occasions with enthusiastic gusto.

During the two Muslim Eid feasts, Mother sends one of the men of the family out to a bakery for a few white boxes of *Ghreybeh* **Butter Cookies** rolled in powdered sugar, pistachio-filled shredded wheat *burma*, and magnificent layered *baklava*. Meanwhile, she and her daughters and I, and perhaps a neighbor or two, prepare several hundred pieces of the traditional

Ma'Amool Date Cookies to send to the needy and to serve the horde of friends and relatives who will be dropping by.

Other than for these extraordinary celebrations, or as a rare snack, or perhaps during the Ramadan evenings during the holy month of daytime fasting, desserts other than fruit are a luxury infrequently seen by most families. In fact, the old adage, "One who has pastry in the cupboard will not be able to sleep," suggests that only the rich have sweets. The ordinary man has little to fret about because he owns little that others would covet.

However, for a small wealthy portion of the population in urban centers like Aleppo or Amman, and across the prosperous states of the Arabian Gulf, economic abundance is leading families away from the traditional patterns. Not only can educated young wives afford to purchase trays of the splendid syrupy Middle Eastern pastries from the dazzling displays in pastry shops whenever they choose, but they are also enthusiastically making both simple tarts and fancy pastries at home.

In older neighborhoods of Kuwait City, Mecca, and Cairo, children are sent out to purchase fresh dough from the neighborhood bakery for complex sweets requiring paper-thin layers of *filo* or wispy threads of *knafeh* pastry. In the United States, these specialty doughs are increasingly available in the frozen food section of most supermarkets or in imported food shops, making once-mysterious treats surprisingly easy to prepare.

My Armenian friend Helga Sarkis (her mother thought the name Helga sounded exotically foreign) kept a second refrigerator in her Jeddah kitchen stocked with baking staples and homemade cakes. Yet even though she was one of the best cooks in the city, Helga retained her svelte figure: the sweets were for guests, while she herself rarely touched even a tiny portion. Whenever friends rang the doorbell, a daily occurrence, Helga would pull cheese pastries from the freezer to serve her visitors, along with dishes of mixed nuts and glasses of fresh lemonade. Then, just before the Turkish coffee, dishes piled high with fruit and Arabic sweets or a homemade European pastry would appear. Being with family and friends is an Arab's principal pleasure in life, and not only are the best-laid plans joyfully set aside when guests arrive, but the proper housewife always has something on hand to set before company.

In selecting recipes to include in this chapter, I've focused on the traditional favorites that can easily be reproduced in our kitchens, as well as the humble sweets that have warmed the hearts of countless generations of Arab villagers.

I've taken the unusual step of not listing recipes for baklava and a few other famous syrupy sweets. Yes, these rich delicacies can be made at home, although in the Middle East they are always purchased from specialized bakeries, as Arafa from Sudan reminded me, saying, "I never make desserts, and especially not those! That's a job for men, for bakeries, where they have proper equipment and facilities." Nevertheless, if you'd like to try your hand at them, excellent recipes abound in most Turkish, Greek, Mediterranean, and Middle Eastern cookbooks.

I'd much rather use these pages to introduce the reader to some of the region's other wonderfully delicious desserts, popular treats that are less known in the West: North African **Almond Sesame Cookies** that are easy to prepare, **Kileicha Crescents Stuffed with Walnuts** from Kurdistan, and the irresistible Sudanese **Peanut-Topped Farina Cake**. Many of these, like **Gelatin Mold with Mango or Apricots** and **Kuwaiti Sponge Cake**, are lower in calories and fat than the illustrious *filo* pastries of the baklava family. I've also included many fabulous cakes, cookies, and custards that incorporate the natural sugar of fruit juices and tasty morsels of bananas, dates, or oranges.

When I permit myself an occasional sweet indulgence, a rare extravagant dessert, I want those few bites to be sheer delight. The recipes in this chapter, therefore, include butter, eggs, coconut, nuts, and sugar. It is wise to remember that the peoples of the Mediterranean and across the Arab world prefer fruit as a nutritious everyday dessert and frequent snack. The exquisite sweets of the region are for special occasions and not intended as everyday treats. After all, as the proverb profoundly recommends, "If your beloved is honey, don't eat it all!"

Lebanon's Nights

M'halabeeyah (LEBANON, ARAB STATES)

~~~~~~

One of the classic treats of the Levant, this smooth pudding is now popular all over the Middle East. Rice flour, also labeled "ground rice," is available in imported food stores and natural food shops.

If you're not a fan of the perfumed flower waters that flavor many of these puddings, you may substitute vanilla. Another variation on this basic recipe is to prepare it with fruit juice in place of the milk. Those who cannot afford milk cook it with water.

2 1/2 tbsp. cornstarch

1/3 cup rice flour

6 cups low-fat milk

1 1/4 cups sugar

1 tsp. rosewater or orange-blossom water

Garnish:

blanched slivered almonds or ground pistachios

1. Combine the cornstarch, rice flour, and milk in a saucepan and heat.

2. Stir in the sugar. Whisk continuously as the milk boils and thickens.

3. Remove from the heat and stir in the rosewater or orange-blossom water.

4. Pour into serving bowls, garnish with almonds or pistachios, and refrigerate.

Variations

Palestine: For *Hitaleeyeh*, omit the rice flour and use 1/3 cup cornstarch.

Syria: For *Eishtaleeyeh*, omit the rice flour and use 1/3 cup cornstarch; omit the sugar, glazing the finished pudding with **Sweet Syrup** (p. 305).

Saudi Arabia and the Gulf States: Add cardamom pods.

Libya and Morocco: Sprinkle with cinnamon.

Egypt: Add raisins or top with jam.

Kuwait: Omit the rice flour and add cardamom and 1/2 cup cocoa.

Village Rice Pudding

Ruz ib Haleeb (SYRIA, ARAB STATES)

Once a week, the village milkman Abu Amir climbs up the hill to our home in Syria, laden with several old-fashioned stainless-steel milk bottles filled with the product of his early morning's labor. My mother-in-law Miriam usually purchases just enough milk to be boiled and mixed with powdered Nescafé, in the European style that is fashionable these days. And because she has learned from American television programs that we Americans are a nation of milk lovers, she immediately boils a portion and serves it hot with sugar to me, the foreign wife.

But every 3 or 4 weeks Mother has Abu Amir empty an entire container of milk into her huge 10-gallon cauldron, and we know that it is time for rice pudding.

"Bring the extra bowls," she commands imperiously, and I hurry to comply.

Like a queen guarding her jewels, Mother perches on a high stool above her bottled-gas stove, stirring the milk constantly as it slowly thickens from the starch in the Egyptian rice. A bit of cornstarch and a few drops of flower water, and the pudding is set aside to cool in a gigantic sprawling pyramid of glass bowls.

Once, when I dared to count the stacks of tiny dishes, I discovered 126 servings of rice pudding piled up on Mother's counters. With the armies of relatives and friends that frequented our extended household, they all disappeared within 24 hours.

6 cups low-fat milk

1/2 cup short-grained Egyptian rice, rinsed

1 1/4 cups sugar (more or less, to taste)

2 rounded tbsp. cornstarch

2 tbsp. water

2 tsp. rosewater, orange-blossom water, or vanilla

1/3 cup raisins (optional)

pinch salt

1. Heat the milk with the rice, stirring constantly. Simmer for about 30 minutes, watching carefully that the milk does not scorch.

2. As the milk gradually thickens, continue to stir. When it becomes more custardy, stir in the sugar.

3. Combine the cornstarch with the remaining ingredients and add to the simmering pudding. Continue to stir. When the pudding is the consistency of cream and the rice is very soft, transfer to serving bowls and refrigerate.

Mango or Orange Creme

M'hallabeeyah bil Manga (SAUDI ARABIA) ♦ *M'hallabeeyah bil Portugal* (LEBANON)

The Arabs' love of fruit extends to their prepared desserts, with fruit fillings in tarts and traditional pastries especially popular. In the following elegant presentation, the standard Middle Eastern pudding is layered with a mango-flavored cream enriched with chunks of luscious fresh mango or orange.

2 cups low-fat milk

1/4 cup sugar

2 tsp. rosewater (or more, to taste)

6 tbsp. cornstarch (divided use)

2/3 cup water (divided use)

2 cups mango juice or orange juice

2 mangos or oranges, peeled and coarsely chopped

Garnish:

whipped cream (optional)

ground pistachios

1. Heat the milk in a saucepan over low heat, adding the sugar and the rosewater. Dissolve 3 tbsp. of the cornstarch in 1/3 cup of the water and whisk into the milk. Stir constantly until the milk thickens. Remove from the heat and let stand.

2. In another saucepan, bring the mango juice or orange juice to a boil. Dissolve the remaining 3 tbsp. cornstarch in the remaining 1/3 cup water, and whisk into the juice. Stir constantly until the liquid thickens. Remove from the heat and let stand.

3. Pour half of the thickened milk into attractive stemmed glasses or serving dishes. Carefully cover with a layer of thickened juice and drop in a few pieces of fresh fruit. Pour the remaining milk pudding in a third layer and garnish with the rest of the chopped fruit. For a special occasion, each glass may be garnished with a rosette of whipped cream, surrounded by the chunks of fresh mango or orange. Sprinkle with ground pistachio and refrigerate.

New Mother's Spice Pudding

Meghli (EGYPT) ✦ *Karahweeyah* (SYRIA)

Two months after I arrived in Saudi Arabia, and two days before our son Said was born, my husband astonished me by announcing that he was off to the airport to pick up his mother, whom he had brought as a surprise from Syria to attend me during my confinement. As Mother had spent all of her days in a traditional village without traveling or dealing with foreigners, and as neither of us spoke the other's language, it was a month-long cross-cultural experience for both of us.

Hidden in the mysterious dark recesses of Mother's suitcase were various homemade cloth bags filled with a fragrantly pungent powder: a traditional mixture of spices ground with rice that is the basis for *Meghli*, a zesty pudding served in commemoration of a baby's birth all the way from the Nile valley across the Fertile Crescent. With her usual verve and vitality, Mother mixed up at least 10 bowls of spice pudding every other day, in case visitors should arrive, mounding a colorful wealth of nuts and coconut atop each aromatic serving.

    6   cups water (divided use)
  ³⁄₄   cup rice flour
    1   tsp. cinnamon
    1   tsp. caraway seed
    1   tsp. anise seed
  ¹⁄₄   tsp. ground ginger
    1   cup sugar

Garnish:
    pine nuts
    blanched almond slivers
    chopped walnuts
    shredded coconut

1. Bring 5 cups of water to a boil in a nonstick saucepan.

2. Mix the rice flour with the remaining 1 cup of water, forming a paste.

3. Grind the spices in a spice grinder or with a mortar and pestle and combine with the sugar and the rice paste. Stir into the boiling water and

return it to a boil, stirring constantly. Lower the heat and simmer, stirring occasionally, for about ³/4 hour.

4. Pour into individual serving dishes and decorate lavishly with nuts and coconut. Serve warm or at room temperature.

Gelatin Mold with Mango or Apricots

Almaseeyah bil Manga, Almaseeyah bil Amradeen (GULF STATES)

Now that most villagers own refrigerators, this simple gelatin sweetened with the standard sugar syrup is increasingly popular. Not only is it cooling and inexpensive, but it offers proof of the family's financial position: unlike the preceding rice puddings, it requires refrigeration for the gelatin to set.

The recipe given below is a variation from the Gulf flavored with fruit nectars that is quite similar to Indian recipes calling for milk and food coloring. In the desert sheikdoms the scarcity of fruit until recent years makes it perhaps even more treasured than in the agricultural regions to the north and west. Now that oil has brought prosperity to the desolate dunes, bottled juices are a favorite for nonalcoholic cocktails and for use in cooking.

  ¹/3 cup sugar
   3 envelopes unflavored gelatin
   4 cups cold water
   2 cups mango or apricot nectar

Garnish:
   1 mango, peeled and sliced, or:
   2 fresh apricots, sliced
      ground pistachios

      Sweet Syrup: (p. 305)

1. Stir together the sugar and gelatin in a saucepan. Add the water, stirring until dissolved. Simmer over medium heat, stirring constantly, until the mixture boils.

2. Place the pan in a bowl of ice and water or chill in the refrigerator, stirring occasionally, until the mixture mounds slightly when dropped from a spoon.

3. Stir in the mango or apricot nectar.

4. Pour into serving dishes and chill. (Or use an attractive mold.) Garnish with the mango or apricot slices and pistachios and return to the refrigerator. Serve with chilled **Sweet Syrup**, to be poured over the gelatin as desired.

Variations

Gulf States: Flavor with saffron and ground cardamom, and garnish with slivered or thinly sliced almonds.

Syria: Substitute milk for the juice.

Dried Figs with Milk

Teen bil Haleeb (SYRIA)

〰〰〰〰〰〰〰〰〰〰〰〰〰〰〰〰〰〰〰〰〰〰〰

"The trees of heaven," the Arabs call the orchards of figs that skirt the desert. The honeyed nectar of fresh figs can be savored only for a few weeks in late summer and serves as a harbinger of changing weather. The proverb suggests that "He ate one fig and thought the autumn had come," but dried figs are a staple readily found in the storeroom or the souk.

More a breakfast sweet than a dessert, this no-cook dish is usually popped in the refrigerator late one evening, to be grabbed the next morning on the way to work. But it's delicious at any hour, although all too often it disappears during an evening icebox raid, leaving the unsuspecting one who awaits a morning treat to face disappointment.

Per person:

  3 dried figs, tough stem ends removed
 ⅔ cup low-fat milk (more or less, to taste)

1. Place the figs in a small bowl. Cover with the milk. Refrigerate for 4 hours or overnight.

Cinnamoned Oranges or Peaches

Licheeneh ma Zahr (MOROCCO)

Native to India, the succulent orange was introduced to vast areas of the world as a result of the seventh-century Islamic expansion around the southern Mediterranean and the Arab trade routes. Although abundant for hundreds of years in the Islamic kingdoms of Al Andaluz and across the strait in Morocco, they did not appear in England until 1290, because many Europeans during the medieval period believed that eating raw fruits brought on fevers and diarrhea.

This well-known orange dessert is sometimes made with fresh, juicy peaches.

6 large oranges or peaches
orange-blossom water
powdered sugar
cinnamon

Garnish:
a few strawberries or sliced kiwis

1. Peel the fruit. If using oranges, remove the white pith and the outside membranes. Slice the fruit. (Some cooks break the oranges into sections.)

2. Sprinkle with the remaining ingredients. Set aside for about 1 hour to intensify flavors.

3. Arrange the fruit on serving dishes, dusting with additional powdered sugar and adding a colorful fruit garnish.

Sweet Cardamomed Carrots

Helawat al Jazr (SAUDI ARABIA, GULF STATES, IRAQ)

Juicy sweet carrots, grown in the Saudi highlands around Taif or in desert oases, keep longer in the blistering desert heat than many other agricultural products. Steamed with milk and cardamom, this dessert has a distinct Eastern flavor reminiscent of Indian cuisine.

Like the peoples of the subcontinent, the people of the Arabian peninsula have long chewed cardamom like tobacco. Not only does it refresh the mouth and mask bad breath, but for centuries folk belief suggested that it also helps prevent cavities, a fact recently confirmed by scientists at the University of California at Berkeley.

1	pound carrots, peeled and finely grated
1	cup plus 2 tbsp. sugar
2	cups low-fat milk
1/4	tsp. ground cardamom
2	tsp. grated lemon peel
2	tbsp. butter
2	tbsp. flour

Garnish:

pine nuts, pistachios, almonds, raisins

1. Steam the carrots with the sugar, milk, cardamom, and lemon peel for about 15 minutes, until the carrots are tender. Pour into a sieve, pressing firmly on the carrots to remove all the liquid. Reserve the liquid.

2. Melt the butter in a saucepan and stir in the flour. Add the carrots, stirring to coat with the flour mixture, and toss for 3 or 4 minutes.

3. Pour the cooking liquid over the carrots, mix well, and cook for about 5 minutes, stirring occasionally. Pour into individual serving dishes and garnish with nuts and raisins.

Dates with Sesame Seeds or Coconut

Tamr bil Simsim (GULF STATES)

The poetic, almost reverent language used by Arabs to describe the date conveys its far-reaching cultural significance. The fruit of the date palm, mentioned in the Qu'ran, was until recently the main dietary staple in the Arabian peninsula.

Harvested since 4000 B.C., the date palm provided the "golden fruit of Arabia" that substained the bedouin during long, debilitating journeys across the scorching deserts. Rich in vitamins and calories, the date is virtually non-perishable when dried properly, and often it served as the only solid nourishment for man and his camels while trekking through the desert.

The 13-ounce package of pitted pressed California dates available in ethnic food stores is ideal for cooking purposes and saves on preparation time.

1 package (13 oz.) pitted pressed dates
  pinch ground cardamom
⅓ cup sesame seeds, ground pistachios, or:
½ cup shredded coconut
½ cup almonds, blanched and split in half

1. With oiled hands, knead the dates along with the cardamom until a pasty dough is formed.

2. If using sesame seeds, roast them on a baking sheet in a 300-degree oven until golden, about 10 minutes.

3. Shape the date dough into balls the size of small walnuts. Insert an almond half into each and mold into the shape of a date.

4. Roll in sesame seeds, ground pistachios, or coconut.

Dates with Apricot Pistachio Stuffing

Tamr bil Mush Mush (GULF STATES)

Following the example of the prophet Muhammad, Muslims break their fast with dates every Ramadan evening as the call to prayer echoes across the desert. In Saudi Arabia and the Gulf States, the bedouin heritage lingers in the dates that are offered as a welcome to guests, along with a tiny handleless cup of green cardamom coffee. Varieties known as Red Sugar, Bride's Finger, Mother of Perfume, and Pure Daughter are served whole or stuffed with nuts and other fruits.

Among the multitude of traditional foods prepared from dates are date syrup and preserves, date bread and doughnuts, puddings, breakfast porridges, sweet rice, and meat and fish dishes. The date palm has become a symbol of Arab hospitality and culture and forms part of the national emblem of Saudi Arabia as well as the symbol of the national airline, Saudia.

Stuffing:

- ¹/₂ cup pistachios
- 6 dried apricots, cut into pieces, or a 3 inch by 4 inch piece of **amradeen**
- ¹/₄ cup sugar
- 1 tsp. rosewater

1 ¹/₄ pounds ripe dates, pitted
fine granulated sugar

1. With oiled hands, knead the pistachios with the apricots, sugar, and rosewater, until a pasty dough is formed.

2. Stuff each date with a spoonful of the apricot pistachio mixture. Roll in sugar.

Orange Ice

Boozit Portugal (SAUDI ARABIA)

In the days before commercial ice cream was available in the Gulf countries, homemade ices were a special treat during the sweltering months of summer. This is a basic recipe calling for oranges and lemons, which withstand the blistering climate moderately well. You can easily substitute crushed melon or strawberries or your favorite fruit.

> 1 cup sugar (more or less, depending on the sweetness of the fruit)
> 2 1/2 cups water
> 1 1/3 cups fresh orange juice
> 1/2 cup fresh lemon juice
> the rind of 1 orange, finely grated
> the rind of 1 lemon, finely grated

1. Bring the sugar and the water to a boil. Boil 5–10 minutes, until the sugar is completely dissolved. Cool slightly and strain.

2. Add the juices and rinds, stirring to mix well, or whirl in a food processor.

3. Transfer the liquid to a glass bowl and freeze to a mush.

4. Use an electric mixer or a food processor to beat the frozen mixture until smooth. Pour into a container of your choice, and return to the freezer. Freeze until firm.

Triangles with Sweet Almond Filling

Samboosak Hilwah (SAUDI ARABIA)

This is a sweet version of the meaty triangles popular in the Gulf States during the holy month of Ramadan.

½ package (16 oz.) frozen **filo** dough, completely defrosted

½ cup unsalted butter, melted

Filling:

    pinch saffron, soaked in:

 2 tbsp. rosewater

½ cup almonds, pulverized in food processor with:

⅓ cup sugar

½ to 1½ tbsp. ground cardamom (to taste)

Glaze:

1 egg, beaten

    sugar

1. Combine the filling ingredients.

2. Preheat the oven to 375 degrees. Grease 1 or 2 baking sheets.

3. Cut the *filo* into strips 2½–3 inches wide, stacking and covering with a slightly dampened towel to prevent drying. Lay 3 or 4 strips on your work surface and brush lightly with melted butter. Layer a second strip on top of each.

4. Place a tbsp. of the filling toward the bottom right-hand corner of each strip. Fold that corner diagonally over to the top left-hand corner, forming a triangle. As you fold, be certain that the side of the strip lines up perfectly with the folded portion. Then fold straight up. Continue as if folding a flag, alternately folding the bottom corners in a diagonal pattern and up. Place on the baking sheet. Repeat with remaining dough.

5. Brush the tops of the pastries lightly with a bit of egg and sprinkle with sugar. Bake for 15–20 minutes, until golden brown.

Variations

Tunisia: Substitute grated orange peel for the saffron and cardamom, and drizzle with **Sweet Syrup** (p. 305) after baking.

Lebanon: Substitute walnuts for the almonds, cinnamon and nutmeg for the saffron and cardamom.

Bride's Fingers

Asabia el Aroos (ARAB STATES)

These lovely slender crisps of *filo* filled with sweetened nuts are as heavenly as baklava, much easier to prepare and to eat, and lower in calories and fat. Nuts provide protein and healthy quantities of fiber, as well as containing traces of many important elements necessary to good health.

Sweet Syrup: (p. 305)

½ package (16 oz.) frozen **filo** dough, completely defrosted
¼ cup unsalted butter, melted (optional)

Filling:

½ cup almonds or pistachios, pulverized in food processor with:
⅓ cup sugar

Glaze:

1 egg, beaten
sugar

1. Prepare the syrup in advance and chill in the refrigerator.

2. Combine the filling ingredients.

3. Preheat the oven to 375 degrees. Grease 1 or 2 baking sheets.

4. Cut the *filo* in half crosswise and again in half, stacking and covering with a slightly dampened towel to prevent drying. Lay 2 rectangles on your work surface with the shorter sides facing you, and brush lightly with melted butter.

5. Place a rounded tbsp. of the filling in a line across the shorter side of *filo* that faces you. Fold the longer edges of the pastry inward, sealing in the sides of the filling, and roll the pastry up from the short side, forming a fat cigar shape. Place on the baking sheet with the cut edge down. Repeat with remaining dough.

6. Brush the tops of the pastries lightly with a bit of beaten egg and sprinkle with sugar.

7. Bake for 15–20 minutes, until golden brown.

8. Dip the warm fingers into cool **Sweet Syrup** and arrange on a serving tray. Serve at room temperature.

Butter Cookies

Ghreybeh (SYRIA, ANDALUSIA, ARAB STATES)

~~~~~~

I simply cannot resist these wickedly delicious morsels that melt in your mouth.

   2 cups unsalted butter, softened
   1 cup powdered sugar, sifted
   1 egg yolk
   1 tbsp. milk (low-fat)
   1 tsp. vanilla extract
4 1/2 cups flour, sifted
   1 tsp. baking powder
      powdered sugar

1. Preheat the oven to 350 degrees.

2. Cream the butter until lemon colored. Gradually beat in the sugar and blend well. Add the egg yolk, milk, and vanilla, beating until the mixture is fluffy.

3. On low speed, gradually mix in the flour and baking powder.

4. Form the dough into balls the size of limes. Gently roll each ball back and forth to shape a short, fat sausage about 3 inches long. Join the two ends together to form a ring, pressing one end slightly over the other.

5. Bake on an ungreased baking sheet for about 15 minutes, until just beginning to turn color. Do not brown.

6. Roll the warm cookies in powdered sugar to coat completely.

Variations

Syria: Substitute semolina for the flour.

Kuwait: Substitute split-pea flour for half of the flour.

Gulf States: Sprinkle the cookies with sesame seeds before baking

Andalusia: Use only 1/4 cup sugar but when the cookies are cool, roll them a second time in sugar.

Kileicha Crescents Stuffed with Walnuts

Kileicha (KURDISTAN, IRAQ)

When I visit my Kurdish refugee friends during the Eid holidays, I am greeted at the door of each apartment with an exuberant warmth of spirit and a generosity parallel only to the kindness with which I am received in my husband's humble village. As I make the required salutatory calls to each family, immense trays of **Kileicha Crescents** filled with nuts, coconut, and dates are set before me, along with an ample tumbler of Pepsi-Cola and the traditional sweet tea in its tiny gilded glass. In each home a huge bag of pastries is pressed upon me with a big smile as I leave, until I am carrying nearly enough to entertain an army.

Dough:

1/2 tsp. yeast

3/4 cup warm milk (about 105 degrees)

2 cups flour

    pinch salt

1/4 cup butter, melted

Filling:

1 cup ground walnuts or almonds, ground coarsely

1/4 cup sugar

    pinch salt

1/2 tsp. rosewater (optional)

Glaze:

 1 egg yolk, beaten (optional)

1. Add the yeast to the warm milk and stir to dissolve. Add the remaining ingredients for the dough and combine. Knead on a floured board until smooth. Set aside in a warm place, covered, for about 1 hour.

2. Preheat the oven to 375 degrees.

3. Mix together all the filling ingredients.

4. Roll out the dough about as thick as pie crust, and cut into circles 3 or 4 inches in diameter. Fill each round with a tsp. of the filling and fold in half to form a crescent. Press edges to seal. Place on an ungreased baking sheet. Brush with beaten egg yolk if desired, to delicately tint the cookie.

5. Bake for about 15 minutes at 375 degrees, until golden.

Easter Crown of Thorns with Date Filling

Kaak bi Ajweh (PALESTINE)

Flaky little ringlets of pastry filled with creamy dates, these cookies are prepared in huge quantities by Palestinian Orthodox Christians to mark the passion of Christ. Armenians, Maronites, and Greek Orthodox all claim similar specialties, but I'm captivated by the charming shape of the Palestinian version. It's surprisingly easy to pinch into shape without rolling and cutting the dough.

Dough:

 3 cups farina

 1 cup clarified butter (sold in jars or cans labeled "ghee")

 1 tsp. yeast

 1/2 cup warm water

Filling:

1/2 of a 13-oz. package of pitted, pressed dates

2 tbsp. corn oil

pinch cinnamon

pinch nutmeg

1. Combine the farina with the clarified butter and set aside to rest for 6 hours or overnight.

2. Stir the yeast into the water until dissolved. Add 1/3 cup of the water to the farina mixture, or more if necessary, to make a soft dough. Set aside for 5 minutes.

3. With oiled hands, knead into the dates the remaining filling ingredients until a pasty dough is formed. Tear off pieces of filling the size of a walnut and shape each into a long cord about 1/2 inch in diameter.

4. Tear off a piece of dough the size of a lime and shape it on your work surface with your fingers to form a small flat rectangle 2 1/2 inches long and slightly narrower. Break off a piece of date filling 2 1/2 inches long and place it over the dough. Roll up the dough over the filling to create a fat, short cigar. To shape the crown, bring the ends of the cigar together and join. Pinch the top surface of the crown with your fingers all the way around to form a row of bumpy protrusions. These are very similar to the crimped finish on American pies. Repeat the process until all of the dough and filling are used.

5. Preheat the oven to 350 degrees. Bake on an ungreased baking sheet for about 20–25 minutes, until golden brown.

Ma'Amool Date Cookies

Ma'Amool (SYRIA, ARAB STATES)

The Muslims claim the following cookie, which differs only in shape from the preceding Christian treat. *Ma'Amool* is the traditional pastry served to family and friends during the obligatory visits made during the two lengthy Muslim Eid feasts. The following recipe produces a crumbly pastry that melts in your mouth with a velvety-rich date filling. A flat wooden mold with floral cutout pattern is used for the date cookies, and a deeper rounded mold with geometric cutout pattern shapes the alternate nut-filled *ma'amool*.

Dough:

- 3 cups farina
- 1 cup clarified butter (sold in jars or cans labeled "ghee")
- 1 tsp. yeast
- ½ cup warm water

Date filling:

- ½ of a 13-oz. package of pitted, pressed dates
- 2 tbsp. corn oil
- 2 tbsp. water
- ½ tsp. cinnamon
- ¼ cup coarsely chopped walnuts (optional)

Nut filling:

- ¾ cup walnuts
- ¼ cup sugar
- ½ tsp. rosewater or cinnamon
- 1 ½ tsp. corn oil

1. Combine the farina with the clarified butter and set aside to rest for 6 hours or overnight.

2. Stir the yeast into the water until dissolved. Add ⅓ cup of the water to the farina mixture, or more if necessary, to make a soft dough. Set aside for 5 minutes.

3. For the date filling, place the dates in a saucepan with the corn oil and water. Cook over low heat until thickened, stirring constantly. Remove from the heat and stir in the cinnamon and optional walnuts.

4. For the nut filling, grind ½ cup of the nuts and finely chop the remainder. Combine with the remaining ingredients.

5. To shape the cookies, take one walnut-sized ball of dough and make an opening in the middle using the thumb or index finger. Slip in a teaspoonful of the desired filling and close carefully. Press the stuffed dough into the

wooden *ma'amool* mold. Tap the mold firmly on the edge of a table to release the cookie. If you don't have access to a mold, slightly flatten the stuffed cookie between the palms of your hands. Repeat process until all the dough is used.

6. Preheat the oven to 350 degrees. Bake on an ungreased baking sheet for about 20–25 minutes, until golden brown.

Variation

Saudi Arabia and the Gulf States: Flavor the fillings with cardamom.

Almond Sesame Cookies

Selloo (MOROCCO)

As with many other dishes, immeasurable versions of this recipe exist. Except for the educated few who want to explore other cuisines, Arab women do not use cookbooks. Recipes are carried in the memories of the older and middle generations, and there is no Middle Eastern *Joy of Cooking* or *Betty Crocker Cookbook* to standardize classic dishes across the region. Some cooks, for example, toast the sesame seeds and almonds that flavor these cookies, others omit the baking powder or eggs. Many prefer to use corn oil in pastries, maintaining that it produces a fluffier texture, although they acknowledge the richer flavor imparted by butter or ghee.

- 1/2 cup sesame seeds
- 1/2 cup almonds
- 1 1/4 tbsp. anise seeds
- 1 cup butter or corn oil
- 2 medium eggs
- 3/4 cup sugar
- 1/2 tsp. cinnamon, vanilla extract, or rosewater
- 2 cups flour, sifted
- 1 tsp. baking powder

1. Preheat the oven to 375 degrees. Grease 2 baking sheets.

2. In a food processor or blender, grind the sesame seeds with the almonds and anise seeds.

3. Cream together the butter or corn oil, eggs, sugar, and your choice of flavoring.

4. Gradually incorporate the dry ingredients and the ground sesame mixture.

5. Drop by spoonfuls onto the baking sheets and bake for about 15 minutes, or until the cookies just begin to turn color.

Variation

Andalusia: Substitute 1 cup almonds for the sesame seeds and flavor with cinnamon.

Sesame Seed Cookies

Barazeh (SYRIA, ARAB STATES)

Famous throughout the Middle East, these thin, dry cookies with a topping of golden sesame seeds are among my favorites.

- ½ cup sesame seeds
- 1 tbsp. honey
- 1 tbsp. water
- 2 ½ cups flour, sifted
- ½ tsp. baking powder
- ¾ cup sugar
- ¾ cup unsalted butter, softened
- ⅔ cup water
- 2 tbsp. coarsely chopped pistachios (optional)

1. Scatter the sesame seeds on a baking sheet and toast in a 350-degree oven until a light golden brown.

2. Combine the honey with the water and use to moisten the sesame seeds. Spread in a saucer.

3. Stir together the flour, baking powder, and sugar.

4. Cut in the butter, as if you were making pie crust dough. Gradually add the water until the dough is smooth.

5. Form balls of dough the size of walnuts and dip one side of each ball into the sesame seed mixture to coat. The bottom side may be very lightly touched to the pistachios. Place on greased baking sheets, sesame side up.

6. Bake at 350 degrees for 15–20 minutes, until golden brown.

Date Crescents

Acras Tamar (GULF STATES)

These flaky pastries from the Gulf are filled with a creamy combination of cinnamoned almonds and dates.

Dough:

> 1 cup butter, softened
> 2 eggs
> 1/2 cup low-fat milk
> 1/2 tsp. salt
> 1 1/2 tsp. vanilla extract
> 3 cups flour
> 2 tsp. baking powder

Filling:

> 3/4 of a 13-oz. package of pitted pressed dates
> 3/4 cups ground blanched almonds
> 1/4 cup sugar
> 1/4 cup butter, melted
> 1/2 tsp. cinnamon
> 1/8 tsp. nutmeg
> 1/8 tsp. ground cloves
>
> powdered sugar

1. Beat together 1 cup butter with the eggs, milk, salt, and vanilla until smooth.

2. Sift together the flour and baking powder and beat into the milk mixture.

3. Turn the dough out onto a floured board and knead until smooth, about 3 minutes. Shape into small balls the size of walnuts, cover, and set aside to rest for about 1 hour.

4. Meanwhile, prepare the filling by combining the ingredients and kneading them with oiled hands into a smooth paste.

5. Preheat the oven to 350 degrees. Grease 2 baking sheets.

6. Roll out the balls into circles about 3–4 inches in diameter. Place 1 rounded tsp. of filling on each circle and fold over to form a crescent shape, pinching the edges together.

7. Bake on greased baking sheets for 20 minutes, or until golden brown.

8. Remove from the oven and cool. Then sprinkle generously with powdered sugar.

Kuwaiti Sponge Cake with Iraqi Pomegranate Sauce

Gato bi Rummaan (KUWAIT, IRAQ)

The original recipe for this Kuwaiti dessert produced a cake that was somewhat heavy for American tastes. By whipping the egg whites and folding them into the batter, I've improved the texture while retaining the integrity of the traditional dish.

The flavorful topping is made from the juice of sweet red pomegranate seeds. This romantic fruit is a favorite from the eastern Mediterranean through Mesopotamia and Iran. A hadith (traditional saying) of the prophet Muhammad suggests that eating pomegranates will clear the body of impurities.

For the sauce, be sure to use a sweet juice, which can be found in import stores, usually bearing an Iranian label. Sweet pomegranate molasses and the sour-sweet *hamod er rummaan* syrup are not suitable for this recipe. (*Hamod* is Arabic for "sour.")

Cake:

    4 eggs, separated
    1 tsp. vanilla extract
1 1/2 cups powdered sugar
1 1/2 cups flour, sifted with:
    1 tbsp. baking powder
  1/4 cup butter, softened, or corn oil

Pomegranate sauce:

    2 tbsp. sugar
    1 tsp. cornstarch
  1/2 cup sweet pomegranate juice
  1/4 tsp. rosewater

Garnish:

pomegranate seeds

1. Preheat the oven to 350 degrees. Grease and flour a large loaf pan.

2. Cream the egg yolks until thick and lemon colored.

3. Gradually add the vanilla and the powdered sugar.

4. Add the dry ingredients and the butter, beating with an electric mixer 3 minutes on high speed, scraping the bowl occasionally.

5. Whip the egg whites until stiff and fold them lightly into the cake batter. Spread the mixture into the prepared pan.

6. Bake for 20 minutes.

7. To prepare the sauce, combine the sugar and cornstarch in a saucepan. Whisk in the sweet pomegranate juice. Bring to a boil, whisking continuously. Boil for about 2 minutes, until smooth and thick. Remove from the heat and stir in the rosewater. Chill.

8. To serve, brush a plate with pomegranate sauce and arrange 2 or 3 overlapping thin slices of cake over the sauce. Drizzle additional sauce over the cake and garnish with pomegranate seeds.

Peanut-Topped Farina Cake

Basba (SUDAN)

~~~~~~

Simple peasant desserts made with wheat flour known as farina, or its yellow larger-grained cousin semolina, are popular in every country and in every subculture of the Middle East. The following Sudanese recipe is my favorite because it is lighter and moister than most and requires the addition of far less syrup. With or without its crunchy peanut topping, it's absolutely irresistible when served hot from the oven. The variations from Saudi Arabia and the Gulf States, layered with nuts or dates, are equally scrumptious.

Sweet Syrup: (p. 305)

1	cup unsalted butter, softened
1/2	cup sugar
2	eggs
1	tsp. vanilla extract
2	cups farina
1	tsp. baking powder
1/4	tsp. salt
1/4	cup shredded coconut
1	cup low-fat milk
2/3	cup unsalted peanuts, chopped (optional)

1. Prepare the syrup in advance, and chill in the refrigerator.

2. Cream the butter with the sugar and beat in the eggs and vanilla.

3. Combine the farina, baking powder, salt, and shredded coconut. Add these dry ingredients to the creamed mixture alternately with the milk. Beat until smooth, and let rest for 1 hour or longer.

4. Preheat the oven to 350 degrees and grease and flour a 9 x 9-inch baking pan. Pour in the batter and sprinkle with the peanuts.

5. Bake until golden, about 25 minutes. Transfer to the highest shelf of the oven for about 5 minutes, to attractively brown the top.

6. Immediately pour chilled **Sweet Syrup** over the hot cake.

Gulf States: Spread half the batter in the pan and top with the filling from **Triangles with Sweet Almond Filling** (p. 297), then cover with the remaining batter; omit the peanut topping.

Saudi Arabia: Spread half the batter in the pan and top with the date filling from **Easter Crown of Thorns** cookies (p. 284), then cover with the remaining batter; omit the peanut topping.

Egypt: For *Basboosah*, omit the coconut.

Palestine: For *Namoorah*, omit the coconut and peanut topping; substitute ²/3 cup low-fat yoghurt and 1¹/2 teaspoons baking soda for the eggs and milk.

Orange Cake with Lemon Orange Glaze

Gato Bortukal (SYRIA)

The following recipe is the only cake my sisters-in-law regularly prepare. Its texture is smooth and the suggestion of orange is especially inviting to peoples of the region. When oranges are not in season, Tang, which has been smuggled in from across the Lebanese mountains, is substituted.

The lemon orange glaze is my own addition. Cakes are such unusual delicacies in traditional hamlets that each morsel is usually consumed before the cook has time to think about preparing an icing.

Cake:

6 eggs

2 cups sugar

1 tsp. vanilla extract

1 cup orange juice

1 tbsp. grated orange peel

2 cups flour, sifted with:

1 tbsp. baking powder

pinch salt

Glaze:

- 1 cup powdered sugar, sifted
- 2 tbsp. orange juice
- 1 tbsp. lemon juice

1. Preheat the oven to 325 degrees. Grease and flour a tube or bundt pan.

2. Cream the eggs with the sugar. Beat in the vanilla and the orange juice.

3. Add the remaining cake ingredients and mix until smooth. Pour into the prepared pan.

4. Bake about 35 minutes. Remove from the oven and let rest for about 10 minutes before unmolding.

5. Combine the glaze ingredients and pour them over the warm cake immediately after unmolding.

Variations

Saudi Arabia and the Gulf States: Add cardamom.

Iraq: Add ¹/₂ cup shredded coconut.

Basna's Kurdish Coconut Nut Cake

Kalkookeh Kurdistani (KURDISTAN)

~~~~~~

Cakes are uncommon in traditional village fare because the only domestic ovens are conical clay structures set into the ground. These lack baking racks and are used only for flat bread, which a sweating, red-faced housewife sticks to the inner walls of the tannour.

So I was in for a surprise when I visited Basna, an outspoken Kurdish matron whose silvery braids swayed captivatingly over her long, full-skirted robe. A recent arrival in Dallas from a squalid Turkish refugee camp, Basna is known as one of the best cooks among the local Kurdish community, and I supposed that her cake's feathery texture was due to a special talent not shared by her Iraqi countrymen.

"Come tomorrow morning," Basna suggested with the customary Middle Eastern kindness. "We'll prepare the cake together and I'll show you how to do it." But when I continued to press for details, she sent her 15-year-old daughter-in-law to bring a plastic bag from the kitchen. "This much walnuts and an equal amount of almonds," Basna explained, measuring the ingredients in the cup of her hand. "Or pistachios if you prefer. And some coconut. And water and 3 eggs."

And what about the flour, I wondered?

Another bag emerged from the kitchen. Farina? Semolina? How did my hostess produce such a fine cake that was flaky and deliciously fruity, neither as solid as the other Middle Eastern pastries I had tasted nor as fluffy and tasteless as many American prepared cakes?

Basna reached into the plastic supermarket bag and pulled out a box of yellow cake mix. "We used to make it from scratch back in Kurdistan, but this is much better," she said, watching as incredulity spread across my face.

Her charmingly flirtatious husband Ismael slapped his leg and joined me in a round of laughter. "My wife Basna veeeerrrry good wooman!" he exclaimed proudly in English, planting a kiss on her weathered brown cheek.

I needed no translation to understand her mumbled protests at Ismael's improper show of intimacy.

And that is why a yellow cake mix appears in a cookbook of traditional Middle Eastern foods.

1   package yellow cake mix

1/4 cup walnuts, pulverized in food processor with:

1/4 cup almonds

1/4 cup shredded coconut
     powdered sugar

1. Preheat the oven to 350 degrees. Grease and flour a bundt pan.

2. Prepare the cake mix according to package instructions. Add the walnuts, almonds, and coconut. Pour into the bundt pan.

3. Bake for about 45–50 minutes. Remove from oven and let rest about 10 minutes before unmolding.

4. Unmold and sprinkle with powdered sugar.

Raisin Cake with Almonds

Cake lil Afraah (IRAQ)

~~~~~~

Dried fruit and nuts play an important role in Iraqi cuisine. Extremely nutritious and protein-rich, they are healthy natural snacks and essential ingredients in the region's sweets.

    4 eggs
  ½ cup butter, softened
    1 tsp. vanilla extract or ground cardamom
    1 cup milk
    3 cups flour, sifted
    1 cup sugar
    2 tsp. baking powder
  ¼ tsp. salt
    1 tsp. cinnamon (optional)
    1 cup raisins or minced pitted dates
  ⅓ cup chopped blanched almonds or walnuts

1. Preheat the oven to 325 degrees. Grease and flour a loaf-shaped pan.

2. Cream the eggs with the butter and vanilla. Add the milk. Gradually add the flour, sugar, baking powder, salt, and optional cinnamon. Blend until smooth, then stir in the raisins or dates and the nuts. Spread the batter in the pan.

3. Bake for about 35 minutes, or until firm.

Date Molasses Nut Cake

Kaakit i Tamr (GULF STATES)

This lovely dark cake is rich with the exotic spices and flavors of the Arabian Gulf: moist, ripe dates, precious cardamom, and the fragrant Eastern perfumes of cinnamon, cloves, and nutmeg. Rather than looking for a bottle of date molasses (date syrup), you can make your own by dissolving pitted dates in water.

       1   package (13 oz.) pitted, pressed dates
       2   cups boiling water
       2   eggs
       2   cups sugar
       1   tsp. vanilla extract
     1/2   cup softened butter or corn oil
       3   cups sifted flour
  1 1/2   tbsp. baking powder
       1   tsp. baking soda
       2   tsp. ground cardamom
     1/2   tsp. cinnamon
     1/4   tsp. ground cloves
     1/4   tsp. nutmeg
           pinch salt
       2   cups walnuts, coarsely chopped

1. Place the dates in a large bowl and cover with the boiling water. Set aside.

2. Preheat the oven to 300 degrees. Grease and flour a bundt pan.

3. Cream the eggs with the sugar, vanilla, and butter until smooth.

4. In a food processor or blender, briefly whirl the dates and the water in which they have been soaking. Process only long enough to break the dates into smaller pieces, but do not puree them. Add to the egg and sugar mixture.

5. On low speed, beat in the flour, baking powder, baking soda, and spices. Stir in the walnuts. Spread the batter in the prepared pan.

6. Bake for 1 to 1¼ hours, or until firm.

Variation

Soak and process only half of the package of pressed dates; chop the remainder and add to the batter.

Fruit Tart

Tart il Fawaaky (LEBANON)

In 1979 the Swiss Bakery opened in Saudi Arabia's international port of Jeddah, the door through which millions of pilgrims to Mecca have entered the Kingdom, and these European-style glazed fruit tarts soon became the rage. Long enjoyed by Gulf residents during vacations to Lebanon and Egypt, and a standard feature of stylish Lebanese dinner parties, tarts permit the Arabs to combine their sweet tooth with their profound respect for fruit.

The recipe for this lovely pastry, the embodiment of artistic presentation, was shared with me by a Lebanese friend who learned it from her mother.

Crust:

½ cup powdered sugar

½ cup butter

1 cup flour

1 egg

Custard:

1 cup low-fat milk

1 egg

¼ cup sugar

3 tbsp. cornstarch

½ tsp. vanilla extract

Glaze:

2 tbsp. strawberry or apricot jam

2 tbsp. water

Fruit layer:

1 quart or more strawberries (halved or whole), or sliced apricots or kiwis

1. Preheat the oven to 350 degrees.

2. For the crust, cream together the sugar and the butter until fluffy. Add the remaining ingredients. Roll out on a floured surface to ¼ inch thickness. Place in a greased pie or tart tin and prick the pastry evenly with a fork. Bake for about 25 minutes, or until golden. Cool until ready to fill.

3. While the crust is baking, prepare the custard. Whisk together the ingredients in a saucepan. Over medium heat continue to stir until the milk comes to a boil and thickens. Simmer for 1 minute and remove from the heat. The mixture should be smooth. Refrigerate or set aside to cool, covering the surface of the custard with plastic wrap to prevent a skin from forming on top.

4. Spread the custard evenly over the cooked tart shell.

5. Combine the glaze ingredients in a saucepan and heat until smooth. Or, heat in a microwave, stirring until blended. Remove from the source of heat and cool.

6. Artistically arrange seasonal fruit in a colorful design over the custard. Slices may overlap in artistic circles.

7. Use a pastry brush to glaze the surface of the fruit with the jam mixture. Refrigerate.

Shredded Wheat Pastry with Banana or Honeydew Filling

Knafeh bil Moz (SAUDI ARABIA)

My favorite place is the wonderland of the Syrian bazaar, the astonishing and alluring Souk El Hamideeyah, a rabbit warren of fascinating alleyways and dimly lit narrow, winding streets, of centuries-old adobe buildings, *khans*, caravansaries, and Roman columns. The memory of its flashes of color and pungent odors makes my heart race.

But even more thrilling than the walls of glittery gold and silver shoes and the impossible loads of fragrant, freshly baked bread being transported on the head of a young boy is the casual welcoming glance that turns into a kinsman's warmth.

On my first approach to the labyrinth last year, I tried futilely to control my excitement and avert my eyes with proper modesty from the scene at my left, where famished male merchants and vendors were noisily enjoying their lunches in a series of coffee shops.

But at the spotless white-tiled *knafeh* workshop my knees weakened with excitement as I came upon a timeless scene: a wrinkled pastry chef was guiding a suspended perforated cylinder in a semicircular arc, releasing a thin stream of batter onto the revolving heated plate below. Opening the cylinder's valve for a brief second, he allowed the delicate threads of dough one counterclockwise turn on the metal griddle before scooping them off into a basket.

Noticing the excitement in my eyes, he smiled in welcome and gestured broadly for me to enter the small establishment and approach the *knafeh* machine for a closer examination. "Please take a photo, if you like," he proudly offered, calling to his small assistant to bring a tea tray.

It's a long distance from the bewitching East back to suburbia, a trip through centuries of time to a less personal but more organized and comfortable place.

Threads of semicooked dough for this crisp, fruit-filled disk are available frozen here in most supermarkets or import food stores, labeled in Greek *konafa*, *kunafa*, or *kadaifa* dough.

Sweet Syrup: (p. 305)

Pastry:

   1 package (16 oz.) frozen **konafa** pastry, defrosted

  1/2 cup unsalted butter, melted

Filling:

   3 ripe bananas, or:

  3/4 honeydew melon

  1/4 tsp. ground cardamom

   2 tbsp. sugar

1. Prepare the syrup in advance, and chill in the refrigerator.

2. Preheat the oven to 350 degrees. Butter a round 12- or 13-inch baking dish.

3. Spread the pastry on your working surface, separating threads and discarding any coarse strands. (Old dough will be dry and should be freshened by sprinkling it with 2 or 3 tbsp. of cold milk.) Moisten with the butter, rubbing gently to coat all threads.

4. Line the dish with half the pastry, gently pressing the dough into the pan.

5. For the banana filling, mash the bananas with the cardamom and the sugar. The mixture will be lumpy. Spread over the dough in the pan. (Some cooks just slice the bananas, arrange them over the dough, and sprinkle with sugar and cardamom.)

6. For the less common honeydew filling, peel and very thinly slice the honeydew. Arrange the melon over the dough, and sprinkle with sugar and cardamom.

7. Cover with the remaining pastry, patting down firmly.

8. Bake for about 45–50 minutes, until the pastry is a light golden brown. Invert onto a round serving platter and immediately pour on some of the chilled **Sweet Syrup.** Serve warm, with additional syrup.

Shredded Wheat Pastry with Cheese Filling

Knafeh bil Jibneh (LEBANON)

~~~~~~

This *knafeh* filling is a more common one: ricotta cheese for creaminess, along with a smaller portion of another cheese for elasticity. It can be used with threads of pastry, as in the previous recipe, but more commonly is layered between dough that has been broken up in a food processor. The texture of this second variation is light and soft, yet uniquely crumbly.

Sweet Syrup: (p. 305)

Pastry:

1 package (16 oz.) frozen **konafa** pastry, defrosted

½ cup unsalted butter, melted

Filling:

¾ pound ricotta cheese

½ cup grated mozzarella, Monterey Jack, or Muenster cheese

2 tbsp. sugar

1 tsp. rosewater (optional)

1. Prepare the syrup in advance, and chill in the refrigerator.

2. Preheat the oven to 350 degrees. Butter a round 12- or 13-inch baking dish or spray it with nonstick cooking spray.

3. Spread the pastry on your working surface, separating threads and discarding any coarse strands. (Old dough will be dry and should be freshened by sprinkling it with 2 or 3 tbsp. of cold milk.) Moisten with the butter, rubbing gently to coat all threads.

4. Process half the dough briefly in a food processor, breaking up the threads of dough into small crumbly pieces. Line the baking dish with the crushed pastry, gently pressing the dough into the pan.

5. Break up the remaining portion of dough in the same way.

6. Combine the cheeses with the sugar and optional rosewater. Spread over the dough in the pan.

7. Cover with the remaining crumbled pastry, patting down firmly.

8. Bake for about 45–50 minutes, until the pastry is a light golden brown. Invert onto a round serving platter and immediately pour on some of the chilled **Sweet Syrup**. Serve warm, with additional syrup.

Variation

Gulf States: Flavor the cheese filling with ground cardamom.

Ataif Wedding Pancakes with Ricotta Cheese

Ataif (ARAB STATES)

One of my favorite Egyptian wedding ballads has choruses of guests at an extravagant feast intoning the praises of these heavenly pancakes. *"Ataif Ataif!"* chant the lilting voices of the ladies, while the gentlemen spiral a firm demand: *"HALA!* NOW!"

These spongy little sweets were traditionally distributed to well-wishers all along the processional route that led the bride, her furniture, and the wedding gifts to the house of the groom.

In Egypt, *Ataif* is also the special pastry of the first Eid, which takes place after the holy month of Ramadan.

Batter:

- 1 tsp. yeast
- 1 tsp. sugar
- 1¼ cups lukewarm water
- ½ cup milk (low-fat)
- 2 cups flour, sifted

    oil for frying

Filling:

- 1 pound low-fat ricotta cheese
- 1 cup sugar

Sweet Syrup: (p. 305)

Garnish:

ground pistachios

1. In a mixer bowl or a food processor, dissolve the yeast and the sugar in ½ cup of the lukewarm water.

2. Add the remaining batter ingredients, mixing until smooth. Cover with a towel and let it rest in a warm place for 10 minutes. (If the batter seems too thick, additional water may be added.)

3. Very lightly oil a griddle or heavy frying pan. Pour 2 tbsp. of the batter into the pan, tilting it to form a round shape. When the cake starts to bubble like a pancake, flip it over and cook on the other side. Set aside to cool. Continue with the remaining batter.

4. Combine the filling ingredients.

5. When the pancakes are cool, place 1 tbsp. of filling on each, folding in half and slightly squeezing the sides so the cheese emerges attractively from the middle. Arrange folded pancakes in a tray, leaning on each other, and drizzle with **Sweet Syrup**. Sprinkle with ground pistachios.

Sesame Seed Brittle

Simsimeeyah (ARAB STATES)

The simplest of sweets, **Sesame Seed Brittle** is a favorite inexpensive high-energy snack consumed during breaks between classes. Vendors of this popular candy crowd the paths leading to schools, the intoxicating alleyways of the souks, the entrances to movie theaters, and any other places children might frequent.

In tiny workshops across the region, *Simsimeeyah* is pulled manually, like taffy, to incorporate air and create a chewy sweet. In the home kitchen, the secret ingredient is the squeeze of lemon juice that keeps it slightly moist.

1 cup plus 2 tbsp. sugar

2 tsp. water

1/2 tsp. lemon juice

1/2 tsp. rosewater or banana extract (optional)

1 cup sesame seeds

1. Carmelize the sugar with the water by heating it slowly in a saucepan over medium heat. Stir frequently and take care that it does not burn. Beat in the lemon juice and optional flavoring.

2. Reduce the heat to the lowest level and add the sesame seeds. Beat until thick.

3. Immediately spread as thinly as possible onto a greased baking sheet, or roll it flat with an oiled rolling pin. Use a pizza cutter or knife to cut it into pieces quickly before it hardens.

Variations

Gulf States: Substitute honey for all or half of the sugar.

Sudan: For *fooleeyah*, substitute peanuts for the sesame seeds.

Egypt: Substitute presoaked chickpeas (for *hummosseyah*) or presoaked *foul* beans (for *fooleeyah*) for the sesame seeds.

Iraq: Substitute pistachios (for *fistokeeyah*) or coarsely crushed hazelnuts (for *bindookeeyah*) for the sesame seeds

Sweet Syrup for Middle Eastern Pastries

Atar (SYRIA, LEBANON, EGYPT) ✦ *Sheerah* (IRAQ, SAUDI ARABIA, GULF STATES)

The general rule for syrup is to pour hot syrup over cold (or room temperature) pastries and to serve cold syrup over hot pastries.

In some areas, eating syrup and honey is superstitiously believed to ward off the *djinn* (evil spirits) and to make life sweeter.

    3 cups sugar
 1 ½ cups water
    1 lemon
    1 tbsp. orange-blossom water or rosewater

1. Boil the sugar with the water until dissolved and viscous, about 10 minutes.

2. Stir in the remaining ingredients and remove from the heat.

Bibliography

Abdennour, Samia. *Egyptian Cooking: A Practical Guide*. Cairo: The American University in Cairo Press, 1984.

Abeed, Hala, and Kauthar Abeed. *Suaanee Khaleejee*. Beirut: Al Maktab al Watanee.

Adib, Naziha, Ferdous Al-Mukhtar, and Ban Ismail. *Arabian Cuisine Fron the Gulf to the Mediterranean*. London: LAAM, Ltd., 1993.

Al Sheikh, Zahra. *Min el Tabah al Khaleejee*. Beirut: Al Musa al Matheeda al Kitab.

Algar, Ayla Esen. *The Complete Book of Turkish Cooking*. Kegan Paul International, 1985.

Anthony, Dawn, and Elaine Anthony and Selwa Anthony. *Lebanese Cookbook*. Australia: Ure Smith, 1978.

Antreassian, Alice. *Armenian Cooking Today*. St. Vartan Press, 1975.

Antreassian, Alice. *Classic Armenian Recipes: Cooking Without Meat*. Ashod Press, 1981.

Arab Women's Union. *Sahtein*. 1976

Atiyeh, Wadeeha. *Scheherazade Cooks!* Gramercy Publishing, 1960.

Bazjian, Alice. *The Complete Armenian Cookbook*. Rosekeer Press, 1983.

Cadora, Nameh. *Nameh's Cookbook*.

Corey, Helen. *The Art of Syrian Cooking*. Doubleday, 1962.

Dammam International Women's Group. *Cookbook 1984*. Saudi Arabia: 1984.

Day, Irene. *The Moroccan Cookbook*. Quick Fox, 1976.

Debasque, Roger. *Eastern Mediterranean Cooking*. Galahad Books, 1973.

Edmonds, Brian. *The Doctor's Book of Bible Healing Foods*. Globe Communications, 1992.

FAO. *Food Composition Tables for the Near East*. United Nations, 1982.

FAO. *Traditional Foods in the Near East*. United Nations, 1991.

Farah, Madelain. *Lebanese Cuisine*. 1972.

Gabbori, Mona. *Recipe Memories of Desert Storm*. Jubail: Support Industry Printing Center.

Ganor, Avi and Ron Maiberg. *Taste of Israel*. Canada: McClelland & Stewart Inc., 1990.

Hamady, Mary Laird. *Lebanese Mountain Cooking*. David R. Godine, 1987.

Haroutunian, Arto der. *Complete Arab Cooking*. London: Granada Press, 1982.

Haroutunian, Arto der. *Patisserie of the Eastern Mediterranean*. McGraw-Hill, 1988.

International Women's Club of Riyadh. *International Cooking*. Riyadh: Saudi Arabian Printing Company, 1885.

John, Fourth Marquess of Bute, K.T. *Moorish Recipes*. London: Oliver and Boyd, 1954.

Karaoglan, Aida. *Food for the Vegetarian: Traditional Lebanese Recipes*. Interlink Books, 1988.

Khayat, Marie Karam. *Food from the Arab World*. Beirut: Eastern Art, 1959.

Mallos, Tess. *The Complete Middle East Cookbook*. Summit Books, 1979.

Mallos, Tess. *Filo Pastry Cookbook*. London: A.H. and A.W. Reed, 1983.

Man, Rosamond. *The Complete Meze Table*. London: Ebury Press, 1986.

McConnell, Malcom and Carol McConnell. *The Mediterranean Diet*. W. W. Norton & Co., 1987.

Mousily, Zobaida, Safiya Suleiman, and Samia Al Harkan. *The Art of Saudi Cooking*. Riyadh: Al Nahda Women's Charity Society, 1987.

Muslim Students' Association of the United States and Canada. *Muslim World Cookbook*. Islamic Book Service, 1973.

Mutawwa, Fatimah Hussain. *Dishes from Kuwait*.

Nabor, Julia. *Babylonian Cuisine*. Vantage Press, 1981.

Nader, Rose B., and Nathra Nader. *It Happened in the Kitchen: Recipes for Food and Thought*. Center for Study of Responsive Law, 1991.

Nathan, Joan and Judy Stacey Goldman. *The Flavor of Jerusalem*. Little, Brown and Co., 1974.

Nickles, Harry G. *Middle Eastern Cooking*. Time-Life Books, 1969.

Osborne, Christine. *Middle Eastern Food and Drink*. The Bookwright Press, 1988.

Ozel. *The Turkish Cookbook*. Nash Publishing, 1977.

Ramazanoglu, Gulseren. *Turkish Cookery*. Turkey: Ramazanoglu Publications, 1989.

Rayess, George N. *Rayess' Art of Lebanese Cooking*. Beirut: Librarie du Liban, 1966.

Roden, Claudia. *A Book of Middle Eastern Food*. Alfred A. Knopf, 1972.

Roden, Claudia. *Mediterranean Cookery*. Alfred A. Knopf, 1987.

St. George's Guild. *Gourmet Cooking from Syria & Lebanon*. 1992.

Salah, Nahda. *Arab World Cook Book*.

Scott, David. *Recipes for an Arabian Night*. Pantheon Books, 1983.

Shihab, Aziz. *A Taste of Palestine*. Corona Publishing, 1993.

Sidom, S.A. *5,000 Years of Good Eating*. 1968.

Skipwith, Ashkhain. *Saudi Cooking of Today*. London: Stacey International, 1986.

Soovneer Book Haws. *Al Matbah al Khaleejee*.

Soovneer Book Haws. *Al Matbah al Maghrabee*.

Stillman, Norman A. *The Jews of Arab Lands*. The Jewish Publication Society of America, 1979.

Taamuna. Beirut: Dar al Shura, 1975

Tzabar, Bainu and Shimon Tzabar. *Yemenite & Sabra Cookery*. Tel-Aviv: Sadan Publishing, 1963.

Uvezian, Sonia. *The Cuisine of Armenia*. Harper & Row, 1974.

Waines, David. *In a Caliph's Kitchen*. London: Raid el-Rayyes Books, 1989.

Ward, Susan. *Lebanese Cooking*. Chartwell Books, London, 1992.

Wells, Suzi. *Arabian Gulf Cookbook*. Kuwait: The Kuwait Bookshops Co., Ltd., 1985.

Wolfert, Paula. *Couscous and Other Food from Morocco*. Harper & Row, 1973.

Yassine, Sima Osman and Sadouf Kamal. *Middle Eastern Cuisine*. Beirut: Dar el-Ilm lil-Malayin, 1984.

Zane, Eva. *Middle Eastern Cookery*. 101 Productions, 1974.

Index